The Fitzalans

The Fitzalans
Earls of Arundel and Surrey, Lords of the Welsh Marches
(1267-1415)

by
Michael Burtscher

Logaston Press

LOGASTON PRESS
Little Logaston Woonton Almeley
Herefordshire HR3 6QH
logastonpress.co.uk

First published by Logaston Press 2008
Copyright © Michael Burtscher 2008

ISBN 978 1904396 949

Typeset by Logaston Press
and printed in Great Britain by
Bell & Bain Ltd., Glasgow

*Front cover: Victorian stained glass window from the Fitzalan Chapel,
Arundel. By kind permission of his Grace the Duke of Norfolk and the
Trustees of Arundel Castle. Cover design thanks to Anna FitzGerald*

Contents

For Charles

Acknowledgements

During the preparation of this book I have incurred a number of debts which I am grateful to be able to acknowledge here. Much of the inspiration for this work came from Professor Sir Rees Davies, my academic supervisor at Oxford for four years until his sudden death in May 2005. I am also indebted to Dr Rowena Archer who took over from him and has provided much advice and encouragement since then. Andy Johnson and Karen Stout of Logaston Press have significantly eased the process of publication.

This work has been enriched by the manuscript material at Arundel Castle, some of which has been used for the first time. I am, therefore, thankful to His Grace The Duke of Norfolk and the Trustees of Arundel Castle who granted me access, and to Sara Rodger and Heather Warne of the Arundel Castle Archives for their support.

As is the case with all books, personal debts are always outstanding. First, I would like to thank my family: my parents Monika and Josef Burtscher, and my sister Sarah Burtscher. Second, Vally Suter-Marmillod and the late Ernst J. Suter, *Commandeur de l'Ordre du Mérite Agricole* and *Chevalier de l'Ordre de Léopold II*. Finally, my partner Charles S. Heppleston who, while others may read or consult this volume, had to live with the author and the earls of Arundel through the long years of its gestation. *Grazie*!

Michael Burtscher
April 2008

The pedigree of the Fitzalan, earls of Arundel and Surrey

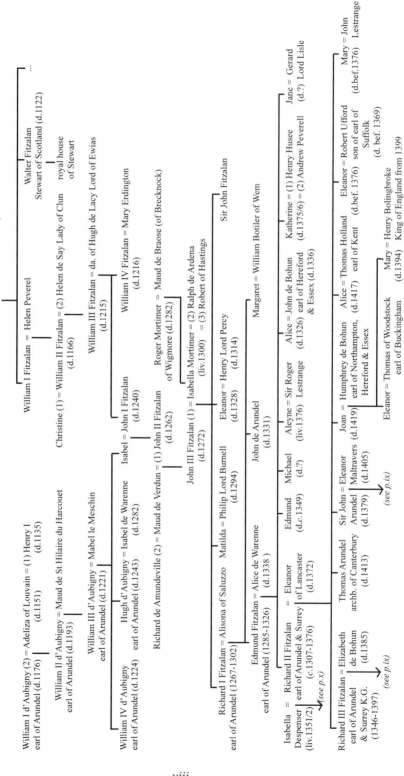

The Pedigree of Richard III Fitzalan, earl of Arundel and Surrey (d.1397)

The Pedigree of Sir John Arundel (d.1379)

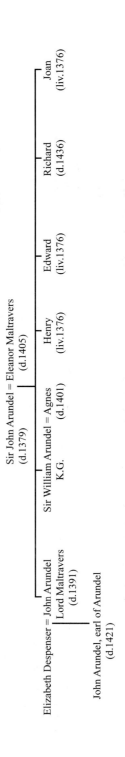

The Pedigree of Sir Edmund Arundel

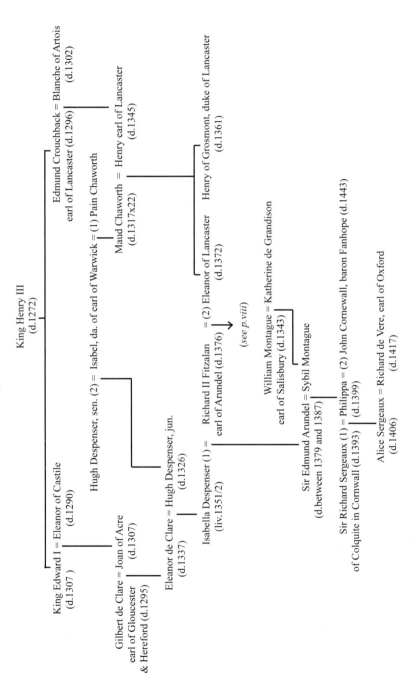

(see p.viii)

Introduction

This book is concerned with the lives of the five Fitzalan earls of Arundel, who flourished during the later middle ages. Originally from Brittany, where they were hereditary stewards of Dol, the Fitzalans settled in England after 1066. Alan FitzFleald (or Fitzalan) came to England during the Conquest and became a powerful lord in the Marches of Wales. King William I rewarded him with the lordship of Oswestry which was strategically placed on the border between Wales and England, and was to be an important military location until the late thirteenth century when much of the Edwardian conquest of Wales was conducted from there. The town remained an important centre and was know in the fourteenth century as the 'London of Wales'. Alan's eldest son and heir, William I Fitzalan, married locally while his brother, Walter Fitzalan (d.1177), entered the service of King David of Scotland as steward of his household and thus became the ancestor of the Scottish royal house of Stewart.

During the three centuries following their arrival in England the Fitzalans were able to increase their powerbase considerably by acquiring further Marcher lordships, mostly through marriage. This expansion enabled them to become powerful lords both territorially and politically. By the late twelfth century they gained control over the lordship of Clun and by the mid fourteenth century they secured the lordships of Chirk and the lordship of Bromfield and Yale. However, the Fitzalans rose to the top of the pecking order principally through the acquisitions, again by marriage, of the earldom of Arundel (1287/8) and the earldom of Surrey (1347). The Fitzalans' Marcher heritage remained, nonetheless, a central component of their power and indeed of their wealth. Though the title to two earldoms enabled them to join the body formed by the higher nobility, most of their revenue came from their Marcher estates. By the mid fourteenth century they could count on about £3,000 in landed revenue, of which £2,000 came from the Marches, which placed them among the top five earners of the realm. The elevation to the earldom allowed the Fitzalans to become the natural companions and councillors of their respective kings.

Richard I Fitzalan (1267-1302) was the first member of his family to be styled earl of Arundel when he came of age in 1287/8. Although a well-known soldier in his time he was unable to reach any position of significance under Edward I, who generally did not rely on him and it was only from 1296 that Arundel began witnessing royal charters. Earl Richard's chronic lack of money also frustrated his career, especially during the 1290s, in that he could ill afford the military campaigns launched by Edward I. These financial difficulties also meant that for most of his tenure he was forced to alienate considerable portions of his estates to raise money, while other parts of his estates were confiscated by the Crown as surety for his debts.

His son Earl Edmund (1285-1326) dramatically changed the family's fortunes by securing a position among Edward II's favourites which resulted in the cancellation of all debts owed by the Fitzalans to the Crown. He remained a loyal supporter of Edward II during the entire reign which enabled him to become influential and wealthy. His proximity to the king also earned him enemies and in 1326, when Edward II was deposed by his queen and her lover Roger Mortimer, Arundel was captured and summarily executed. Earl Edmund was considered a martyr to Edward II's cause and there is evidence suggesting that a cult existed. Following his father's downfall, Richard II Fitzalan (c.1307-1376) was disinherited and his estates and properties were declared forfeit. For a time Richard remained in England with his mother; but, when in 1330 it was discovered that he was organising a plot to overthrow Queen Isabella and Mortimer he was forced to escape abroad.

Later that year, Edward III assumed direct control of government and called Richard back from exile, and in 1331 re-granted him his titles and estates. There followed a remarkable career. In the early years of the reign he regularly fought on the Scottish border and later also in France. His political and diplomatic abilities made of him one of the king's most important advisors, and there was hardly an event in which he was not involved. Earl Richard's brilliant career and his niggardliness enabled him to become incredibly wealthy. Because his wealth was largely in cash, a luxury which other magnates did not necessarily have, Earl Richard also became, especially in the 1370s, one of the major lenders to the Crown. By the time of his death he had accumulated a hoard of £72,123 of which £60,180 were readily available in hard cash in his treasuries. Another remarkable episode in Earl Richard's personal life was his divorce, in 1344, from Isabella Despenser, to re-marry the following year Eleanor of Lancaster, the sister of Henry of Grosmont, earl of Derby (later earl and then duke of Lancaster). This was undoubtedly quite a scandal but enabled Arundel to advance his political career by marrying into the most powerful family of the time.

Thus it was their son, Earl Richard III (1346-1397) and not Sir Edmund Arundel, Earl Richard II's son from his first marriage, who inherited his father's considerable wealth. Earl Richard III is particularly well known for his role, with his brother Archbishop Thomas Arundel, as one of the Lords Appellant.

In 1387-88 the Lords Appellant launched an Appeal of Treason against some of the king's favourites and raised the necessary military and political support to take their actions to their natural conclusions. In many ways the appeal was a reminder of the Ordinances issued by the Lords Ordainer in 1310-11 which similarly had attempted to restrain the king's ability to advance specific royal favourites. King Richard II resented these restraints as much as his grandfather had the Ordinances. When, in 1389, the king came of age he resumed power and dismissed Arundel from the council. The king never forgave the Appellants, though a formal pardon was granted and Arundel was readmitted to the council. Eventually, though, the king took his revenge and had Arundel executed for treason in 1397. Arundel's poise at his trial and execution won him the people's admiration so that he was immediately hailed a martyr and pilgrimages were organised to his tomb in London.

Once more the Fitzalan estates were declared forfeit and the heir disinherited. Following his father's execution, Thomas Fitzalan (1381-1415) managed to escape from his custodians and joined his uncle Archbishop Thomas in exile in Cologne. Both eventually joined Henry Bolingbroke, earl of Derby, in Paris who was to usurp the English throne in 1399 as Henry IV. The connection is particularly significant because Henry had been married to Mary de Bohun (d.1394) the granddaughter of Earl Richard II Fitzalan, therefore linking the Fitzalan lineage even more closely with the (now royal) house of Lancaster. Thomas Fitzalan was thus able in 1399 to secure the restoration to his titles and estates. His early years were then spent fighting in the Welsh borderland which had been destabilised by the revolt of one of the most famous heroes of the Welsh fight for independence, Owain Glyn Dŵr.

Earl Thomas's military service brought him into close contact with his cousin, Prince Henry, with whom he fought for many years. After 1405, Earl Thomas fell out with his uncle Archbishop Arundel and thus progressively dissociated himself from Henry IV at whose court his uncle's influence prevailed. Earl Thomas's association with Prince Henry enabled him to be appointed Chancellor in 1410 for a brief time when the prince took control over government. Once Henry V ascended the throne in 1413 Arundel prospered as a military and political leader especially being charged with the preparations for the relaunch of the war with France. But his death during the campaign on 13 October 1415 prevented him from sharing the glory of the English victory at the battle of Agincourt.

The Fitzalans are a remarkable paradigm of how the relationship between a magnate and his king could shape the politics of the reign as well as the territorial and financial success of his family. In this respect hardly any family remained static; they evolved as their priorities changed. The funeral, in 1376, of Earl Richard II was particularly notable in this respect because it was the first time that a Fitzalan had been buried at Lewes Priory in Sussex, the traditional burial place of the Warennes, earls of Surrey. Traditionally the Fitzalans were interred at their family foundation of Haughmond Abbey in Shropshire. Far from merely being a breach in tradition Arundel's funeral symbolised the moment which redefined the family's heritage as English rather than Marcher, and thus sealed the ascendancy of the Fitzalans from their origins as Marcher lords to the higher echelons of the English nobility. The inheritance of the earldoms of Arundel and Surrey significantly shifted the Fitzalans' focus from the Marches to their role at the English court and the glories and profits that could be gained there.

One must, nonetheless, not be fooled by this symbolism since much of the Fitzalans' income still came from their Marcher estates. The Warenne inheritance acquired in 1347 also comprised the lordship of Bromfield and Yale and, in 1354, Earl Richard II successfully asserted his claim to the Mortimer lordship of Chirk. In the 1380s and 1390s the Fitzalans' influence in the Marches was further strengthened through Earl Richard III's control of a third of the lordship of Abergavenny after the death of its lord in 1389; from 1384-93 Arundel chaired the consortium that administered the Mortimer inheritance; and in 1391 he married Philippa Mortimer, dowager countess of Pembroke thus extending his lordship over her dower lands in Ireland, Herefordshire, Pembrokeshire, and the March of Wales. Later, Earl Thomas was forced to impose his lordship by suppressing Owain Glyn Dŵr's revolt. Ironically, the rising only strengthened the control and oppression which it was intended to remove in the first place.

The death of Earl Thomas in 1415 without legitimate heirs of his body marked the end of the Fitzalans, earls of Arundel and Surrey. The earldom of Arundel passed, through the cadet line of Sir John Arundel (d.1379), to John Arundel, lord Maltravers (d.1421) and then to his son, another John (1408-1435). The earldom of Surrey reverted to the Crown. The rest of the estates were partitioned between Earl Thomas' three sisters and became attached to the inheritance of their respective families, thus leaving a much smaller and less profitable estate to Earl John, whose title to the earldom of Surrey was hotly contested by the Mowbrays, dukes of Norfolk. The loss of these territories after 1415 and the pursuit of the Mowbrays' claim until 1433, when parliament confirmed John (d.1435) as earl of Arundel, considerably damaged the Fitzalan lordship for the remainder of the fifteenth century. Thus came to an end the golden age of the Fitzalans.

1 The Penniless Earl
Richard I Fitzalan, earl of Arundel (1267-1302)

In 1267 was born Richard I Fitzalan. His family were prominent lords in the Marches of Wales, but it was Richard who was to become the first Fitzalan to be styled earl of Arundel, becoming earl when he came of age and entered into his inheritance in February 1288.[1] The Fitzalans, originally from Brittany, had come to England in the train of William, duke of Normandy during the Conquest of England, in 1066. The following year William held his Christmas celebrations at Gloucester, and on that occasion he rewarded his most important supporters and loyal lieges. Alan FitzFleald (or Fitzalan) was given the lordship of Oswestry, strategically significant to the security of the Anglo-Welsh frontier. This also made Alan the immediate neighbour of Roger de Montgomery, whose granddaughter he subsequently married. Roger was kinsman to King William and had stayed in Normandy during the Battle of Hastings to protect William's interests, and for so doing he was rewarded with large estates in the Marches of Wales as well as a third of Sussex. There Roger erected Arundel Castle as part of William's new coastal defence system to prevent anyone else invading England as he had done. Thus the castleries of Arundel, Bramber, Lewes, Pevensey and Hastings, with the royal castles of Dover in Kent and Carisbrooke on the Isle of Wight, were built to secure the Conqueror's new kingdom.[2]

Roger de Montgomery died in 1094 and was succeeded at Arundel by his eldest son Robert de Bellême. Robert's rebellion against Henry I and the subsequent siege of Arundel Castle resulted in his defeat and exile, while his lands and castles passed to the Crown. Between 1102 and the 1130s Henry I was in possession of Arundel and at his death, it was granted to his second wife, Adeliza of Louvain, as part of her dower. In 1138 she remarried, her new husband being William II d'Aubigny, and the following year they entertained Empress Matilda, daughter of Henry I, who had come to England to press her claim to the throne against that of Stephen.

Little is known of the Fitzalans' early tenure and rule in the Marches. The lordship of Clun was added to the Fitzalan inheritance through Alan FitzFleald's grandson, William II Fitzalan (d.1166), who had taken as his second wife Helen de Say, lady of Clun. By the end of the twelfth century the Fitzalans were ruling over the lordships of both Oswestry and Clun. Then, before 1240, the Fitzalans acquired the rights to the earldom of Arundel by the marriage of John I Fitzalan to Isabel d'Aubigny, one of the sisters and ultimately co-heiresses of Hugh d'Aubigny, earl of Arundel, who died without direct issue in 1243. At his death, the estates were divided among the husbands of his four co-heiresses: John I Fitzalan, Robert Tateshale, Roger Maude, and Roger Somery. John I Fitzalan's widow obtained the castle and honour of Arundel, with its forests, chases, and liberties.[3]

After John I Fitzalan's death in 1240, the Shropshire lordships of Oswestry and Clun were granted to John Lestrange, sheriff of Shropshire, until 1244 when John II Fitzalan (1223-1267) came of age. In May of that year he offered a relief of £1,000, the payment due from the heir to his lord, to take possession of Arundel and the family's Shropshire lands, including the castles at Clun, Oswestry, and Shrawardine.

Internal border skirmishes were reduced considerably by King Henry III, by virtue of his ability as a negotiator rather than his prowess as a soldier. In 1237 he concluded the Treaty of York, which established an alliance with Scotland and defined the boundary between England and Scotland. Then, in 1247, he concluded a similar agreement in the Treaty of Woodstock with the Welsh Princes. One consequence of this was that the Northern and Marcher barons, released from the need for constant warfare, had time to turn their attention to matters of state, and this became a problem for Henry.

Early in his reign Henry had populated his council with a clique of favourites. One of these, Peter des Roches, bishop of Winchester, was from Poitou and had progressively filled the offices of states with fellow Poitevins, to the dismay of the barons who felt that England was coming under foreign control if not rule. In 1234 a delegation of barons, led by the archbishop of Canterbury, Edmund Rich, and Richard Marshall (the son of William Marshall, the late regent), secured Henry's capitulation; the king expelled the Poitevins and dismissed des Roches. From that moment Henry took government into his own hands, having realised the power his barons could wield. Although Henry had asserted himself in this way, he was not a good soldier and lost most of his lands in France. In 1259, in the Treaty of Paris, he renounced his rights in Normandy, Maine and Anjou, but retained Gascony as a fiefdom subject to Louis IX of France, Henry's brother-in-law. This treaty and the deposition of Edmund Crouchback, Henry's youngest son, from the Sicilian throne, in 1266, were the last straw for the barons. Henry had only been able to secure Sicily for Edmund, in 1254, by diverting the money he had raised for a crusade, using it instead to support the pope in his battle against Manfred, king of Sicily. In 1266, however, the pope deprived Edmund of the Crown and bestowed it on Charles of Anjou.[4]

Opposition to Henry III was first voiced in 1258, when Henry was forced to accept the Provisions of Oxford, under which he agreed that the barons were allowed to select half of the king's council. Among the barons was Simon de Montfort, Henry's brother-in-law. In 1260, when Henry returned from concluding the Treaty of Paris, he denounced Simon, who had caused an uprising in Gascony during his governorship there, and overturned the Provisions of Oxford, obtaining papal support for his actions. England slid into the abyss of civil war again. John II Fitzalan, who in 1253 had accompanied Henry III to Gascony, was in August 1257 appointed captain for the custody of the March north of Montgomery, and in March 1258 was ordered to lead his men to Chester to participate in an expedition against Llywelyn ap Gruffudd who had been able successfully to unite the Welsh princes against the English. But the conflict in Wales continued unabated until 1265, since Llywelyn also appeared as a supporter of the Montfortist cause. Henry III secured a short-lived success by capturing Simon de Montfort's son in April 1264 at Northampton, but de Montfort fought back and defeated and captured Henry at the battle of Lewes on 14 May. However, in July 1265, Henry's son, Edward, escaped from custody and raised an army against de Montfort, who was defeated and killed, on 4 August at the battle of Evesham, which enabled Henry to return to power.[5]

Nothing more is known of the career of John II Fitzalan, who died shortly afterwards in 1267, to be followed only five years later by his son John III Fitzalan.[6] For the ensuing decade the Fitzalans were eclipsed, since Richard I Fitzalan was still only a minor. Part of the Fitzalan estates was held in dower by Maud de Verdun (d.1283),[7] while another part was in the hands of Isabel de Warenne, widow of Earl Hugh d'Aubigny and hence dowager countess of Arundel. This meant that none of the three John Fitzalans was ever styled earl of Arundel. At the death of the long-lived Isabel de Warenne in 1282, the young Richard I Fitzalan, heir to the Arundel estates, was still a minor, and seizin (full possession) of the estates could not yet be granted to him. About 1284, Richard married Alisona (d.1292), daughter of Tommaso, marquis of Saluzzo, in Piedmont, and of Luisa, daughter of the marquis of Ceva, an alliance which is thought to point to a sojourn in Italy. Alisona was also a kinswoman of Eleanor of Provence, Edward I's mother, which may explain why their son, Edmund, was born at the royal residence of Marlborough Castle, in Wiltshire, on 1 May 1285.[8] On 8 December 1287 Earl Richard paid homage for his lands, which were then granted on 3 February 1288. It is unclear why there had been such a delay, but it may have had to do with ongoing troubles on the Welsh border, for in 1287, Arundel was summoned to fight the revolt led by Rhys ap Maredudd, lord of Ystrad Tywi, who, having been a supporter of Edward I during the wars of 1277 and 1282, became embittered by the financial extortions and administrative harassment to which he was subjected.[9]

Earl Richard was fortunate that the dowagers Maud de Verdun and Isabel de Warenne had died almost simultaneously, thus preserving most of his estates as a single unit.[10] One portion of his estates which remained outside his control was held by yet another widow, his mother, Isabel Mortimer, who had been granted dower on 1 August 1272.[11] She was already a woman of influence and wealth and had held the wardship of the children of John de Warenne, earl of Surrey, and the castle of Farnham since 1267; in 1268 she was also granted Portchester Castle, but this she had to give up in 1272. As well as the grants, farms, and other properties Isabel also had a claim to her dower. Little is known of the manors and rents that composed it but in 1273 she requested an inquisition involving a certain number of manors to which she had expressed a claim. In Shropshire this included a third part of the manors of Halston and Rodington, and in Sussex a third of the rents in West Dean and Singleton. In the county of Southampton she had claimed a third of the manor of Borhunte. Isabel also claimed part of four watermills in Arundel and nearby Swanbourne, which had been granted to her father and Robert Aguyllon, the king's bailiff there.[12]

In 1276 Isabel obtained lands in West Dean and Cherleton, in the hundred of Singleton, and half the hundred of Stockbridge, valued at £28 8s 2d yearly. By that stage she had taken a second husband, Ralph de Ardena, whom she had probably married in 1273. By July 1281 she was also keeper of the honour of Arundel; and the following year, on 7 November 1282, a royal mandate ordered her accounts for the castle of Oswestry to be audited and thereafter she was ordered to take upon herself the costs of the works undertaken there. That audit also clarified that she would have to pay £668 for the farm of the castle and hundred of Oswestry and Arundel Castle,[13] which shows that she did not in fact hold these castles as part of her dower. In acquiring the farm of these lordships she asserted her own influence over large and profitable estates, and by so doing, as a Mortimer, she considerably expanded her family's influence in the northern March during the 1280s, a crucial phase in the conquest of Wales and its consolidation as an English colony.

On 27 May 1285, it was assessed that Isabel would have to

Norman entrance to the undercroft at Arundel Castle (Arundel Castle Trustees Ltd)

*The original Norman shell keep at Arundel Castle, together with the later
Bevis Tower on the left (Arundel Castle Trustees Ltd)*

pay £439 for the farm of the castle and honour of Arundel, payable at a rate
of £100 yearly; and £500 for the farm of the castle and hundred of Oswestry,
payable at £200 yearly. The sharp increase in the value of these farms in
just three years may have been due either to an initial underestimate or to
an increase in the expected revenue under Isabel's management. Despite the
cost, however, Isabel had already paid most of the farms and only owed £21
to the Crown, which suggests that she had considerable wealth at her disposal.
Her income had been further increased by the death of her second husband in
1283, and the grant of her dower in the 'Welshery'. On 2 September 1285 she
married her third husband, Robert of Hastings, but not having obtained royal
licence she was fined £1,000. This sum was remitted on 6 June 1287 when
it was established that Isabel had had the authorisation of her late husband's
executors to remarry.[14]

Although Isabel Mortimer appears to have been a wealthy lady, her son Earl
Richard found himself in financial difficulties for most, if not all, of his life.
In 1292, seemingly short of cash and beleaguered by his creditors, he granted
a sizeable number of manors, probably located in the Marches, to his fellow
Salopian Robert Burnell (d.1292), bishop of Bath and Wells and chancellor
of England, for a period of 12 years for the sum of £1,819.[15] Bishop Burnell
already had extensive properties totalling 82 manors in the Marches alone, and
in 1283, possibly because Richard's mother had remarried, he had purchased

9

from the abbot of Vale Royal the custody of the honour of Whitchurch, near Oswestry, and the castle and honour of Arundel, which until then had been in Isabel Mortimer's hands. Arundel's additional grant clearly allowed the bishop

The thirteenth-century barbican at Arundel Castle
(Arundel Castle Trustees Ltd)

to increase his influence in the region still further, and thus empowered, that same year he arranged for his nephew and heir, Philip Burnell (d.1294) to marry Arundel's sister, Matilda.[16]

If Matilda's marriage strengthened the Fitzalan lordship in the Marches, the marriage of her sister Eleanor (d.1328) to Henry, lord Percy (d.1314) strengthened the newly-acquired lordship in Sussex, since Henry was the heir to the honour of Petworth in the rape of Arundel and, therefore, the scion of one of the most important families of the Fitzalans' Sussex affinity.[17] The Percies were also an influential family in the north, with vast interests in Scotland, including a claim to the earldom of Carrick and the baronies of Urr in Galloway and Red Castle in Angus. The Fitzalans also had strong northern links through a claim to the stewardship of Scotland through Walter Fitzalan (c.1110-1177), the second son of Alan FitzFleald, who became hereditary steward around 1136 when he entered the service of David I of Scotland (see chapter 3).[18]

The Percies remained within the sphere of the Fitzalan influence in the fourteenth century. Henry Percy (d.1368) was in Arundel's retinue at Crécy in 1346, although the following year he had migrated to that of Lancaster. At his death Percy bequeathed to Arundel some objects that had been given to the Percies by Edward Balliol, king of Scotland, and a salt cellar Percy bequeathed to his son bore the arms of Percy and Arundel, a family heirloom that perhaps commemorated the marriage of Eleanor Fitzalan to Henry Percy earlier in the century. Furthermore there is evidence, from at least the late thirteenth century, of a room in Arundel Castle known as Percy's Hall containing stained-glass windows bearing the Percy arms.[19]

Since in 1283 Richard I Fitzalan was only aged 16, it is likely that the marriage between Matilda and Philip was the idea of Bishop Burnell and the Mortimers of Wigmore. There can be little doubt about the significance of this alliance in securing and stabilising the Marcher frontier in the light of the English conquest of Wales. Indeed, in the 1280s and early 1290s royal control over the Welsh borderlands was considerably extended by an increasing number of disputes among Marcher lords being settled in royal courts rather than in the traditional Marcher way of negotiation and private war. Oswestry was extremely important in this period and in 1294-95 it had become the base for the operations of the English army. In 1294, Arundel was appointed to command the forces sent to relieve Bere Castle, in Meirionydd, which was threatened by a new insurgence under the leadership of Madog ap Llywelyn, who had assumed the title of Prince of Wales. Edward I, taken by surprise, reacted vigorously by assembling an army of 35,000 men. In the spring of 1295 the revolt collapsed, and on 5 March, Madog was finally defeated by the earl of Warwick at Maes Moydog, near Welshpool. Although the revolt had been short-lived and was, significantly, to be the last of its kind until the revolt of Owain Glyn Dŵr over a century later, it also proved an embarrassment to

Edward, who had thought that the Welsh dragon had been tamed once and for all. The huge cost of the campaign, estimated at £55,000, as well as his extensive building work at Beaumaris Castle and Caernarfon, which had cost at least £16,000 by 1300, were to be factors which contributed to the financial crisis of the late 1290s.

Finance was an acute problem. The seizure in 1294 of Gascony by King Philip IV of France ushered in a period of warfare that lasted until the autumn of 1297. In 1294-95 there was also a revolt in Wales, and from 1296, war with the Scots. The total military expenditure in 1294-98 was at least £750,000 and in 1297 the strain led to a major political and constitutional crisis. Early in 1297 the clergy refused to grant a tax. Royal officials acted harshly by taking the horses of the archbishop of Canterbury and by sealing Canterbury priory's granary until the grain was rotten. By July 1297 an agreement was reached with the archbishop.

Edward I also encountered increasing resistance from his magnates. In 1295 he had been able to persuade the earl of Arundel and others to serve in Gascony only by means of financial blackmail. But at the Salisbury Parliament in February 1297, when he made the same request, Roger Bigod, earl of Norfolk and Marshal of England, refused to go. Eventually the king was forced to yield to pressure, and he offered wages to all those who were prepared to sail. [20]

The government's taxation and wars had a considerable impact on Arundel. Unfortunately, the estates Bishop Burnell had received from him proved far from sufficient to cover the initial investment. Furthermore, Robert Burnell had died in the year of the transaction, 1292, and the manors must thus have descended to Philip Burnell, the bishop's heir. Upon the latter's early death in 1294, the manors reverted to the Crown, and it was only on 24 April 1297 that Arundel obtained relief from his debts due at the Exchequer; while the lands were eventually granted back to him on 4 November, a clear illustration of the manner in which Edward I sought to rally and reward earls who had opposed him during the crisis earlier that year.[21]

Because of his debts, Arundel virtually lost control over a good portion of the estates he held from the Crown for most of the 1290s. In 1297 he was granted permission to farm out £100 worth of his land for a period of ten years, but he was unable to find any buyers. Furthermore, his campaigns in Wales, Scotland and Gascony had forced him to demise lands worth £500. On 27 August 1294 he had been authorised to grant for life lands and rents worth £100 in West Dean, Singleton, Cherleton, East Dean and North Stoke in Sussex to Henry Guldeford, a king's clerk; and that same year, Edward I had also confiscated Arundel's hundred of Purslow, part of the lordship of Clun, for the repayment of monies he owed the Crown.[22] Wars are often thought of as a financially lucrative affair for aristocrats, but it certainly did not prove so for Arundel. He was one of a group of magnates who were blackmailed into fighting for the king by means of threats to collect all debts due to the Crown. As early as 1292, he was undoubtedly short of cash, a predicament which he must have hoped might be resolved by joining the king's forces.

An additional factor which could have decided Earl Richard to campaign may have been his humiliating submission to Gilbert de St Leofard, bishop of Chichester, after a quarrel about his right to hunt in Houghton Forest. The conflict had its origins in the fact that the forest of Arundel was not all the earl's demesne but contained lands which had been granted to other lords such as the archbishops of Canterbury, the bishops of Chichester, and the families of St John and de Haia, successive owners of the manor of Halnaker in the middle of the forest. In the late 1250s it was agreed between the lords of Arundel and the current archbishop that the latter was not to hunt outside his own wood of Slindon except for one deer once a year, and in return, John Fitzalan and his heirs were not to hunt in the archbishop's wood. Both parties agreed to secure confirmation of this from the pope and the king. By the 1290s the conflict had shifted to the north-eastern edge of the forest and park of Houghton. Arundel had intended to assert his rights by hunting throughout his forest, notwithstanding the rights of the bishop, but St Leofard would have none of it and in 1292 excommunicated Arundel, threatening to extend the interdict to his chapel and lands in the diocese of Chichester. The dispute was eventually resolved when on Christmas Eve Arundel and his brother Sir John sought absolution and agreed to a penance and pilgrimage to a local shrine. Far from being exceptional, Arundel's case reflected the general fact that magnates saw the shared ownership of parks as a nuisance. Indeed, at about the same time the earls of Warwick, Cornwall, and Gloucester found themselves embroiled in similar disputes.[25]

If in 1295 Edward I had been able to blackmail Arundel into fighting, by 1296/97 this was no longer possible. His poverty literally prevented him from fighting overseas in Edward I's campaign in 1297. It is probably because of this that the Crown returned his lands to him in the November of that year. Unfortunately for Arundel, Bishop Burnell's death in 1292 had cost him his closest ally in royal circles. Michael Prestwich has remarked that Arundel 'was never a man on whom Edward relied to any great extent', and it was only in 1296, after the Gascon campaign, that he began witnessing charters.[23] In this decade Earl Richard was, however, granted at least some relief from his financial difficulties. In 1275 some of his debts had been granted by the king to the queen mother, Eleanor of Provence. At Queen Eleanor's intervention, in 1291, Richard was allowed to pay off his debts at the Exchequer at a rate of £50 per annum instead of £100, as had been arranged by Henry III with Richard's grandfather.[24]

Arundel's refusal to serve in Gascony in 1295 was met by the Crown's demand for £5,232, largely the result of an unpaid relief from the time of King

John. Under such circumstances Arundel could do little but serve his king, albeit grudgingly.[26] In this difficult situation, and with a king who showed few scruples, Arundel fulfilled his role as a knight of the realm rather well, fighting in the Welsh wars in 1288, in Gascony in 1295 and 1297, and in the Scottish Wars in 1298-1300, when he was present at the siege of Caerlaverock and was described as being 'a fair, beloved, and richly armoured knight'.[27] But although Earl Richard I served in these wars and was a prominent Marcher lord he was unable, possibly because of lack of royal patronage, and certainly because of his financial misery, to extend his family's interests significantly. He did, nonetheless, renovate and extend Arundel Castle. His military campaigns were certainly expensive, but his penury may have been exacerbated by the extensive building work he carried out at Arundel. He completed the curtain wall, reconstructed the north bailey postern gate to form Bevis Tower, and built the Well Tower and the barbican with two square towers in front of the Norman gateway. The work was inspired by the king's building work in Wales, and may have been as expensive. At his death, in 1302, Earl Richard I still owed the Crown £1,000, for the repayment of which the Fitzalans' goods and chattels in Clun and Oswestry were confiscated.[28] (This was on top of the monies the family owed and which the Crown demanded in 1295.) Arundel and his wife Alisona were buried in their family foundation of Haughmond Abbey.[29]

2 The Martyr Earl
Edmund Fitzalan, earl of Arundel (1285-1326)

At his father's death in 1302 Edmund Fitzalan was aged 17. The wardship of his lands was granted to Amadeus, count of Savoy, to whom the king owed large amounts of money; while the boy's wardship was granted to John de Warenne, earl of Surrey, who also received Edmund's marriage (the right to choose his bride). Upon Warenne's death in 1304 the marriage was granted to his daughter, Alice de Warenne, who was to marry Edmund in 1306, although, when John de Warenne had previously offered Alice to Edmund, he had simply refused her. Later that year, on 15 April 1306, Arundel was granted seizin of his lands.[1] The match was territorially significant, for the Warennes were also influential Marcher lords in their own right as lords of Bromfield and Yale (the lordship was integrated with the Fitzalan inheritance in 1347, at the death of the last Warenne earl of Surrey). As had been the case with Earl Edmund's aunts, Matilda and Eleanor, the family's position in the Marches was further strengthened when his sister, Margaret, was married to an influential Marcher lord, William, lord Botiler of Wem. Earl Edmund's younger brother, John, was destined for a career in the Church, being advanced for preferment in 1319-20. He studied at the University of Oxford and obtained his MA in 1323, but died, probably before 1331; at the time of his death he was papal chaplain.[2]

On 22 May 1306 Edmund Fitzalan was knighted at the same time as Prince Edward and 267 other young men who were to embark on a military campaign on the Scottish border. In a rather surprisingly generous gesture, Edward I pardoned £4,234 of Earl Edmund's debts on 24 April 1307[3], possibly as a reward for his good service in the campaign. On 10 March 1308, Arundel was granted restoration of the hundred of Purslow which Edward I had seized from his father. The grant may have been made in recognition of his service at Edward II's coronation on 25 February, at which Arundel officiated as hereditary chief butler, carrying the king's robes during the procession. This particular office was attached to the earldom of Arundel and may originally simply have entitled the holder to serve the king at table on special occasions. A first reference appears in 1186 when William, earl of Arundel was called upon to discharge this duty at King Henry II's Christmas celebrations in Guildford, and later earls of Arundel, with the exception of Earl Richard II Fitzalan (d.1376), also served in that capacity. In this office they were assisted by the mayor of London, traditionally accompanied by 25 aldermen, 2 sheriffs and 11 commoners. At the coronation of Edward III, however, by which time the earldom of Arundel had been forfeited, the mayor of London officiated, with 360 valets all clad in the same livery.[4] Unlike other offices of state, such as that of chamberlain or marshal, the office of chief butler does not appear to have been vested with any particular political relevance but seems to have been purely honorific.

Edward II's coronation was marred by the press of people which caused a wall to collapse, bringing down with it the high altar and the royal staging and crushing to death one of the knights. The coronation was hastily concluded. The banquet that followed was similarly mismanaged. Most of the attention at the coronation, however, was directed towards the king's favourite Piers Gaveston who, controversially, having been granted the earldom of Cornwall the previous year, carried the crown during the coronation and then, to add insult to injury, appeared at the banquet in purple garments embroidered with pearls, thus outshining the king. The diplomatic incident was complete when the queen's uncles, perceiving that the king preferred Gaveston's couch to that of his 12-year-old bride, returned to France in great indignation. The fury Gaveston's undue prominence aroused among the English nobility was expressed at the Lent parliament which assembled two days after the coronation. Three articles were brought, accusing Gaveston of treason for encroaching on royal power and making himself the king's equal. On 18 May Edward II reluctantly sanctioned the measures and exiled his favourite.

In August 1309, however, Gaveston was recalled from exile and restored to the earldom of Cornwall. His behaviour went from bad to worse, especially his nicknaming of the earls. According to the chroniclers he called Gloucester 'whoreson', Lincoln 'burst belly', Warwick 'black hound of Arden', Pembroke 'Joseph the Jew', and Lancaster 'ceorl'.[5] Subsequently the earls and barons repeatedly refused to attend parliament while Gaveston remained at court. Eventually, assured of their safety, the earls accepted an invitation to attend the Westminster Parliament of February 1310, where they presented a petition that deplored evil counsel and the waste of resources it caused. Gaveston was the unnamed target. On 19 March, three days after the appointment of a body that came to be known as the Lords Ordainer, a set of ordinances was issued. Along with the usual general calls to protect the franchises of the Church and the maintaining of Magna Carta, they also called for the king to be banned from making gifts without the counsel and assent of the Ordainers. The final version of the ordinances was issued in September 1311 and included the perpetual exile of Gaveston as of 1 November. But by Christmas Gaveston had returned, and was staying with the king. In January 1312 the magnates set out to capture Gaveston, and this was achieved on 19 May when Gaveston surrendered at Knaresborough, and was taken into custody by Pembroke. On 10 June, Warwick removed Gaveston from Pembroke's custody, and took him to Warwick Castle, where he was judged and condemned to death. On 19 June he was run through by a Welsh foot soldier, and his head was cut off by another.

Though Arundel had been one of the Ordainers, it is unlikely that he was one of the main ringleaders behind Gaveston's execution. Earl Edmund provides, in fact, a rare example of Edward II's ability to win to his side and retain the allegiance of a magnate who had earlier opposed him. The royal pardon of Arundel's debts, on 2 November 1313, marked the beginning of a new era for Arundel, who from that moment was to enjoy the king's patronage and friend-ship until the end of the reign.[6] Now that the issue of debt had been settled the Fitzalans were in the premier league of English noblemen in terms of wealth, though still less wealthy than Clare and Lancaster, who commanded £6,000 and £8,000 yearly respectively. It is possible that since Arundel had become a prominent magnate, the king aimed to secure his allegiance by cancelling his debts; and it may not be completely fortuitous that in the same year the debts of the king's new favourite, the younger Hugh Despenser, were also pardoned. The alliance between the Fitzalans and the Despensers, now powerful Marcher lords in their own right, was cemented in 1314-15 by the betrothal of Richard II Fitzalan to Isabella Despenser.

In Isabella, Earl Edmund secured for his son a bride of royal descent. She was the daughter of the younger Hugh and Eleanor de Clare, who had been married in 1306. Eleanor, one of the queen's ladies-in-waiting, was the daughter of Gilbert de Clare, earl of Gloucester (d.1295) and Joan of Acre, daughter of Edward I and Eleanor of Castile. Isabella's royal descent conferred prestige, and her mother was one of the three sisters who received a share in their father's inheritance at the death of their brother, Gilbert, at the battle of Bannockburn on 24 June 1314. Gilbert's death made of his three sisters wealthy heiresses in their own right and, given their royal connections, prized political weapons. The significance of securing some additional influence in the Marches and Wales was certainly not lost on Arundel.

The union was also of great advantage to the younger Hugh Despenser. Although he had replaced Piers Gaveston as the king's new favourite he was still a *parvenu*, and it is likely that he relied on Arundel's lobbying power and influence to support his claim to the more delectable parts of the Clare inherit-ance, since Arundel now appeared to enjoy particular favour at court. The fact that the king and Arundel were about the same age, and may have grown up together in the royal household, may have strengthened their relationship. The division of the Clare estates took a while, and was not to be completed until 1317. That same year Arundel's political position was further reinforced by his appointment to the wardenship of the Marches of Scotland.[7] Although the three Clare sisters should legally have received equal shares in their inheritance, the lion's share went to the younger Despenser. At the Northampton Parliament in July of that year, the barons made an attempt to oust him, but instead Hugh was appointed king's chamberlain. On 20 October, his appointment was renewed in parliament at York, and he was to remain in that capacity until the end of the reign, apart for the time of his exile in 1321.

Earl Edmund's position was also, on occasion, compromised by the changing political winds. Despite his rise in favour and his appointment to offices of considerable importance he was among those named, with the earls of Hereford and Surrey, as planning confederacies and disturbances against the king. On 10 April 1320, Arundel was forbidden from bringing armed supporters to Southwark to attend a court case brought against him.[8] Possibly to secure Arundel's absolute allegiance, the marriage ceremony between Richard II Fitzalan and Isabella Despenser was arranged to take place, on 9 February 1321, in the king's presence at the chapel of the royal manor of Havering-atte-Bower near London. Edward II disbursed 40 shillings of his own money to the attending crowd, the coins being thrown from the chapel's door.[9]

The union between Richard and Isabella united two of the most politically powerful families. King Edward's presence at the wedding ceremony further underscores the importance of this union to him. The precarious political climate meant that Edward had to ensure that he cemented the alliances on which he could rely most, and by endorsing the marriage he secured Arundel's indefatigable allegiance.

In March 1321 England was on the brink of a civil war. In May, confederates started pillaging the Despensers' goods and properties in Wales and the March, while Arundel suffered at the hands of Roger Mortimer, who captured his castle of Clun. With a change of fortunes for the king and the Despensers, those closely associated with them could do little beyond siding with the victors of the civil and baronial insurgence.

Earl Edmund remained loyal to Edward II. On 1 August formal complaints were submitted to the king in London, and Edward II had to accept, albeit reluctantly, the exile of the Despensers, who were to leave England by 29 August. Even Arundel was forced to accept their exile.[10] Early in December the earl of Lancaster gathered the opposing factions at Doncaster and reiterated his grievances to the king, but that same month Edward had the Despensers' exile declared illegal by an assembly of prelates. Following this, new revolts broke out.

After Edward II managed to suppress the insurgence of Sir Bartholomew Badlesmere in Essex, the royal army converged at Shrewsbury to confront the Mortimers and the earl of Hereford, but the Mortimers were already too weak, and lacking Lancaster's assistance. On 13 January 1322, safe-conducts in the names of the king's two half-brothers, and the earls of Arundel, Pembroke, Richmond, and Surrey were issued at Newport to enable them to attend peace negotiations. The lords surrendered on 23 January at Ross in expectation of the king's grace but instead, the Mortimers were attacked and imprisoned in the Tower of London. On 18 March the earl of Lancaster was arrested and brought to his castle of Pontefract, where the comital judges (Arundel, Surrey, Kent, Richmond, Pembroke, Atholl, and Angus) condemned him. He was beheaded on 22 March.

To profit from this success the king determined to recall the Despensers from their exile. Archbishop Reynolds was ordered to summon a provincial council to that purpose, at which the earls of Arundel and Richmond, with the Lord of the Privy Seal, Robert Baldock, were to present the Despensers' protest against their sentence. As early as 4 January, however, Arundel, Richmond and Pembroke asserted that they had only given their consent to the Despensers' exile because they feared 'the undue power that the said magnates suddenly caused to be brought without their knowledge'. In May 1322, then, Arundel sought pardon for the offence of the Despensers' exile to which he had agreed the previous year.[11] This, however, was only a formal apology, for Arundel and the Despensers had sealed their alliance soon after Lancaster's execution in the marriage between Arundel's son, Richard II, and the younger Despenser's daughter, Isabella.

After Lancaster's insurgence, those whom the king considered his enemies were condemned and became known as the Contrariants. Many of them lost their lands and incomes and were reduced to brigandage. The period following the political turmoil of 1321-22 also saw the formation of a new group of powerful courtiers composed of the Despensers, Arundel, Robert Baldock (Chancellor from 1323 and bishop of Norwich from 1325), and the Treasurer Walter Stapeldon, bishop of Exeter, who were later blamed for the oppressive regime of 1322-26. Arundel's fortune was made and his position in government was also reinforced. He was granted important governmental offices such as the justiciarship of north Wales (granted in 1322), which had previously been held by Roger Mortimer. On 10 May 1326, he was appointed captain and principal surveyor of array — that is to say, he was responsible for the recruitment of troops for the royal host in Wales, Shropshire, Stafford and Hereford, and in July of that year also of Lincolnshire.[12] Arundel, naturally, also profited considerably, financially as well as territorially, from the Contrariants' demise. The lion's share was, however, once again reserved for the Despensers.

Clues as to Arundel's fortunes and financial dealings in the 1320s are given in a document now preserved in The National Archives and dating probably from 1327.[13] This records debts due to him followed by a list of briefs rendered, presumably to the sheriff in charge of the investigation, by the earl's receivers of Oswestry and Chirk, and the bailiffs of Shrawardine and Lydley.[14] A small schedule attached thereto records two cases from the sheriffs of Dorset and Norfolk for the recovery of debts totalling £200 and 225 marks respectively. The sums thus recorded total £6,025 as well as six tuns of wine. It would be simplistic, however, to consider these sums merely as debts resulting from Earl Edmund's financial activities for many of them were sums extorted from the losers of the 1322 civil war. Indeed most sums included were contracted between 1323 and 1325. These records do show, however, that Arundel's financial fortunes were considerably changed in the 1320s.

The list was presumably compiled after the dramatic disorders of the winter of 1326-27, when Queen Isabella and Roger Mortimer invaded England and deposed Edward II, and most sums are recognisances. These were bonds pledged as surety to observe loyalty to Edward II and his allies and were extorted from former Contrariants, such as a fine for 400 marks contracted at Clun, on 1 May 1323, by 59 people from the Marches headed by Sir Roger de Cheigny, an important Marcher lord, and also including, perhaps surprisingly, John de Warenne. Another sum of 300 marks, but unfortunately undated, was contracted by several members of the Cheigny family, including Sir Roger's son. A further sum of 100 marks, contracted on 28 May 1323 at Ludlow, comprises nine Marcher men, possibly former supporters of Mortimer, such as John le Rous of Cleobury. Sir Hugh Mortimer, Henry lord Bradelegh and his son, John, were held for 40 marks contracted on 11 October 1323 at Clun.[15] Other sums on the list, however, may be genuine debts: a sum of £20, owed by Thomas de Wynnesbury, dated 1320; £484 from John le Walsh a merchant of Shrewsbury, and £50 from Thomas atte Brugge, a citizen of Winchester.

Another person to profit considerably from the Contrariants' downfall was the elder Hugh Despenser who, created earl of Winchester on 10 May 1322, received substantial grants of lands of deceased Contrariants. The properties included those formerly belonging to the earl of Hereford, Sir Roger Damory, Lord Giffard of Brimsfield and Sir Bartholomew Badlesmere, thereby extending the Despenser holdings from Wiltshire and the Midlands to Surrey and Sussex, where his lands were based on the manor of Kennington near London. His son, the younger Hugh, saw an extension of his lordship in South Wales and the Marches. In 1326 his estates were estimated at £7,150 yearly, while those of his father provided £3,800 yearly. In 1324 the younger Hugh also had almost £6,000 deposited with the Italian bankers Bardi and Peruzzi, and a further £1,000 was discovered in Caerphilly Castle in 1327.[16] The spoils reserved to Arundel were Badlesmere's London properties by Aldgate, William de Wauton's Somerset and Dorset estates, and Sir Roger Cheigny's properties, probably in Wales.[17] He also received the Mowbray honour of Axholme and the Mortimer lordship of Chirk worth £400 per annum in tail male, that is to say, only male heirs in the direct line could inherit it.[18]

Another source of revenue was probably Arundel's intervention on behalf of some of the rebels for the remission of fines. In 1322 the Crown issued 158 fines amounting to £15,000 to secure the good behaviour of the rebellious barons by enacting what Natalie Fryde called genuine 'long-term political blackmail'.[19] Earl Edmund asked for a fine remission for Sir Hugh Mortimer, who was indebted to the earl for 40 marks. The remission may have been done through the payment of a smaller sum directly to the earl, but it mainly guaranteed Sir Hugh's allegiance, thereby enhancing Arundel's prominence within the Marches. In 1326 Arundel requested additional pardons for former rebels such as Henry de Salesbury and Warin de Rugge.[20] Arundel had also profited in 1322 by receiving as a gift from the king the plundered goods of Roger Mortimer.

Having already secured a union with the Despensers through his son Richard in 1321, Earl Edmund planned marital alliances with the earls of Hereford and Warwick. This could have contributed to a more pacific relationship between the feuding aristocratic families following Lancaster's insurgence and subsequent execution in 1322. Natalie Fryde once commented that 'personal connections and family feuds rather than principles guided most magnates through the dangerous maze of the court. Their alliances and enmities were characterized by great fluidity and opportunism rather than adherence to anything like "parties".'[21] When, in 1325, the king's court came under attack again, Earl Edmund secured a union between his daughter Alice and John de Bohun, the son and heir of Humphrey de Bohun, earl of Hereford, and that of another daughter to the son and heir of Guy de Beauchamp, earl of Warwick, who had been one of Lancaster's staunchest friends and allies.[22]

Earl Edmund secured John de Bohun's marriage from the king on 6 May 1325.[23] The alliance was, however, only short-lived. John entered into his inheritance, as earl of Hereford and Essex, in November 1326, the same month his father-in-law was executed, while Alice died in childbirth that same year, and was buried with her infant son at Walden Abbey in Essex.[24] John then married Margaret, daughter of Ralph, lord Basset of Drayton. At his death in 1336, without issue, his inheritance passed to his brother, Humphrey. That the Bohun alliance was of great importance to the Fitzalans is clearly shown by the fact that it was renewed in 1359 with the marriage of Richard III Fitzalan to Elizabeth de Bohun, and of his sister, Joan Fitzalan, to Humphrey de Bohun, both children of William de Bohun, earl of Northampton (d.1361). As two of the most powerful Marcher families the alliance made perfect sense, for together they could control the whole region, both politically and judicially, particularly since in 1335 William de Bohun had married the wealthy Elizabeth de Badlesmere, dowager countess of March and co-heiress of Giles de Badlesmere.

The second alliance which Earl Edmund had planned was with the Beauchamps, earls of Warwick. At Warwick's death in 1315 his heir, Thomas, was still a minor and in 1317 his estates were granted to the elder Hugh Despenser. In 1319 a dispensation was granted for the marriage between Thomas and Catherine, the daughter of Roger Mortimer. These plans were eventually put aside for several years, partly because of Mortimer's capture in 1322. In 1325, however, Arundel managed to secure the papal dispensation necessary for one of his own daughters to marry Thomas Beauchamp.[25] This marriage, however, never took place, possibly because of the political turmoil that erupted the following year.

When, in 1325, the French king seized Edward II's French possessions, Queen Isabella was sent as a delegate to her brother in France to negotiate a peace treaty. During her time in France she became amorously involved with Roger Mortimer and became a focal point for the lords disenchanted with Edward II's government. Edward demanded her return, but she and Mortimer were now determined to open hostilities. In the summer of 1326 they travelled to Holland where they received the support of William, count of Hainault, to whose daughter, Philippa, Prince Edward was betrothed. On 21 September

The keep at the Fitzalans' castle at Clun. Built, unusually, on the side of the original motte, controversy has raged about its actual building date, with some favouring c.1272 and others the early fourteenth century, meaning it could have been built on the orders of any of John (III) Fitzalan, Earl Richard I or Earl Edmund

Isabella and Mortimer landed in Suffolk with an army. The invasion was a success and Edward II's allies soon began to desert him.

The relentless plundering of the Contrariants' goods, as well as of those of supporters and neutral members of the gentry, had created a basis for much of the resentment that erupted in 1326. In April Arundel's men in Chichester had been assaulted and his goods stolen.[26] On 2 October, the king left London for Wales, where he intended to levy troops, but his departure left the city in a critical position. Many Londoners started taking up arms and bound themselves to put to death any who opposed the queen or encroached on their liberties. As the city erupted, the Tower was taken, and Arundel's treasure in the priory of Holy Trinity was pillaged, as was Robert Baldock's manor of Finsbury and his treasure in St Paul's. Walter Stapeldon, beheaded by the mob, had his property outside Temple Bar ransacked along with the house of the Bardi, where the younger Despenser had left large deposits. The elder Hugh, unlike his son, held relatively little there in 1326, and most of his cash reserves were deposited in various places in Leicestershire and Wiltshire. It is possible, therefore, that Arundel may have kept little money with the Florentines in 1326, a year in which he held assets of £1,044 in cash at his castle in Clun and £581 in the treasury of Chichester Cathedral. In Shrewsbury it was recorded that £303 of Arundel's money was looted.[27]

Some of Arundel's money, which had escaped the rapacity of the mob in London and elsewhere, was confiscated by the Crown. In late 1326, £1,748 was delivered into the king's wardrobe, as well as £868 that had belonged to the younger Despenser. On 21 November 1326, a sum of £524, seized at Chichester Cathedral, was delivered into the queen's treasury. Part of the treasure Arundel kept there included 17 silver cups and an enamelled silver salter worth a total of £57.[28]

As a prominent magnate it was natural that Arundel would undertake business, notably in London. There is evidence that highlights his dealings with London merchants such as Sir Richard Peres, Henry Nasard, Oliver de Ingham, Hugh Matefray, Simon Swanland and others.[29] These men still owed money to Arundel after his death and these sums were later reclaimed by his son Earl Richard II in the 1330s.[30] Earl Edmund was obviously used to lending money to leading London merchants.

Henry Nasard, a Frenchman from Arras, was a prominent draper and became a citizen of London in 1309, but it would seem that it was only from the moment he became an alderman, in 1318, that he began borrowing money from Arundel. The loans taken by him and his associates ranged from 500 marks to over £560.[31] Nasard made his fortune through the royal market, specialising as a wardrobe merchant, particularly during the Scottish wars. As a king's merchant between 1312 and 1317, he regularly received assignments on customs and subsidies to pay his advances to the Crown of up to

£600-£700 at a time, and his purveyance in cloth for, among other things, the queen's Christmas liveries and the Scottish garrisons. By 1315 he was rich enough to acquire a house in London.[32] Another draper, Simon Swanland, also borrowed from Arundel. On 7 February 1321 he took out a loan with his brother, John, of 500 marks.[33] In the tax of a twelfth of 1319 Swanland had been assessed at £20, the third highest on the roll in London. He was kinsman of William Melton, archbishop of York from 1317 to 1340, and was on one occasion stated to have been a member of the company of Antonio Pessagno, the king's Genoese banker and royal favourite.[34] In 1323-24, with £110 worth of cloth, Simon was the leading supplier of worsted to the royal wardrobe, and from September 1326 until January 1327 he supplied a third of the total worsted. His fortunes continued under Edward III, in which reign he supplied the cloth for the Christmas liveries.

Arundel was lending large sums of money, but only to the most prominent and well connected of London merchants. As might be expected, many of the merchants who fell victim to the Despensers' greed also figure in Arundel's list of creditors: Nasard, Abyngdon, Swanland and the fishmonger Hugh Matefray. All were prominently removed from their London offices and deprived of their trading privileges in the 1320s. Unsurprisingly, in 1326, they emerged as supporters of Mortimer, and Swanland became mayor of London in 1329.

The strife between Mortimer and Arundel ran deep, and the earl's capture and execution in 1326 had the hallmarks of a private vendetta. To escape the queen's invading force Arundel had allegedly sailed to Glamorgan in the company of the king and the younger Despenser.[35] But as their attempts at levying troops failed, the king and the younger Hugh embarked for the Isle of Lundy, in the Severn Channel, while Arundel went to Shropshire to raise more troops on his estates. Near Shrewsbury, Arundel met John Charlton of Powys, who captured him and subsequently led him to the queen at Hereford, where he was executed on 17 November.[36] The animosity and rivalry between Arundel, Charlton and Mortimer is certainly an important aspect of those years, and goes far beyond the simple antagonism between Marcher lords. In a sense Arundel's swift and ruthless execution reflected the dramatic change in the way traitors were dealt with that had begun in 1322, under Edward II. Arundel was sentenced in the same swift and ruthless manner in which the Contrariants had been judged. At least he was spared the farce of a trial which, fortuitously, enabled his son in 1354 to recover full possession of his inheritance.[37] By the 1320s the offence of treason was considered 'so atrocious that the traitor should suffer the last punishment of bodily pain, the loss of all his goods and the perpetual disinheritance of his heirs so that they be admitted neither to the paternal nor the maternal inheritance'.[38] The 22 strokes it took the executioner to sever Arundel's head is an indication that it was not a clean and swift execu-

*Roger Mortimer greeting Isabella, wife of Edward II, in front of Hereford in
1326 with the younger Despenser being led off for execution by the gateway
into the city after his and Edward II's capture at Neath
(British Library MS Roy 15 E IV f.316v)*

tion, and it is possible that, as the chronicler's account suggests, the use of a
blunt blade was ordered.[39]

A similarly cruel ending befell the Despensers. The elder Hugh, earl of
Winchester, taken prisoner the previous month at Bristol, was drawn by
horses, beheaded, and then his mutilated body suspended from the gallows
in his armour with his quartered coat and arms reversed and destroyed for the
dishonour he had brought to chivalry. The younger Hugh Despenser, captured
with the king near Neath, was also taken to Hereford. Outside the city he was
stripped and then reclothed with his arms reversed, and was crowned with
stinging nettles. His execution was rather more violent than that of Arundel,
for on 24 November he was drawn on a hurdle to the gallows, and then hanged
from a height of 50 feet. Still alive, he was cut down and eviscerated before
finally being beheaded. The fact that the executions took place at Hereford
reinforced the idea that they were to avenge the executions of 1322, of which
the earl of Hereford had been a victim. They also purged England of that clique
of councillors which had dominated Edward II's court.

Immediately following his execution Earl Edmund was interred in the
Franciscan church of Hereford, but he was not destined to rest there.[40] It seems

Haughmond Abbey, the traditional burial place of the Fitzalans
until supplanted by Lewes Priory with the burial of Earl Richard II in 1376
Above: The chapter house with its 12th-century entrance
Above right: Norman doorway leading from the nave of the church into the
cloister with figures of St Peter and St Paul
Lower right: the west end of the hall

that he may have bequeathed his body to Haughmond Abbey, and that is where he was eventually buried. The abbot of Haughmond, Nicholas of Longnor, resisted the burial in Hereford and after several appeals to Queen Isabella managed to secure a reburial in the abbey. In 1343 provision was made for a chantry in the abbey for the repose of Earl Edmund's soul and those of his ancestors.[41] Incidentally, but not completely surprisingly, this happened the year after the commonalty of Shrewsbury, not far from Haughmond, alienated four marks yearly of land to a chaplain to celebrate mass in the hospital of St John the Baptist to pray for Earl Edmund's soul, as well as the souls of his ancestors and heirs,[42] as an expiatory gesture for the role the Salopians had played in the earl's capture in 1326. In 1343, this gesture was matched by John Charlton of Powys, who had captured Earl Edmund; he granted the advowson of the church of Lydham to Haughmond Abbey to fund three chaplains who were to celebrate mass for the earl's soul.[43] Though symbolically important this was also, ironically, the last time the abbey was to serve as burial ground to the Fitzalans.

At his death, Arundel held movable assets worth £10,000, of which Queen
Isabella and her lover Roger Mortimer were among the main beneficiaries.
Isabella also received much of the property of the younger Despenser in
Glamorgan and Gloucestershire, as well as more mundane goods such as one
of Arundel's barrels of venison, which was delivered to Westminster on 8
January.[44] Another who benefited from the spoils was Edward II's half-brother,
Edmund, earl of Kent, who received all goods, chattels, and arrears of farms
and rents that had belonged to the Despensers and Arundel. He also received
Arundel's lands in Sussex and Norfolk.

Another person to profit from Arundel's fall was Roger Mortimer,
who had his eye on Wales and the Marches. On 20 February 1327 he was
appointed justiciar of North and South Wales, an appointment which then was
granted for life on 27 August 1328, and was followed by his elevation, at the
Salisbury Parliament, to the earldom of March. He obtained Arundel's castles
of Oswestry, Shrawardine, and Clun, and the manor of Chipping Norton in
Oxfordshire, as well as all Edmund's other castles and lands in Shropshire,
Wales and the Marches. These grants were increased, after the execution of
the earl of Kent in March 1330 (accused by Queen Isabella and Mortimer of
treason for conspiring to put Edward II back on the throne), with the goods and
chattels that had been granted to the latter. In conjunction with the forfeitures
of land, in February and July 1327, all fines, ransoms, recognisances, sales
of lands, made under duress by the Despensers, Arundel and the others were
revoked.[45]

These proceedings also brought to light one of Arundel's more unsavoury
sides. On 13 March, the widow of Henry Nasard, Isabella, and Stephen de
Abyngdon, alderman and royal butler, petitioned the king for redress. Henry
Nasard owed 1,000 marks to Arundel for which he had made a recognisance;
as an additional security Stephen had also made a recognisance of 1,000 marks
for the same sum, totalling 2,000 marks for a loan of 1,000 marks. This was not
an uncommon practice, and was known as double bonds. On payment of 1,000
marks both recognisances were to be cancelled. However, when Henry paid
his debt, Arundel refused to withdraw Stephen's recognisance, and upheld it
in court where Stephen, eventually, accepted to pay a recognisance which had
been discounted to 600 marks. The king duly cancelled the latter recognisance
after Adam Orleton, bishop of Hereford, who had taken Arundel's confession, had come forward to testify 'before the king and his council that the earl
acknowledged before him, when he was about to die, that the recognisance for
600 marks was made to him by Stephen to have acquittance for the aforesaid
1,000 marks, and that he had been fully satisfied for all debts due to him from
Henry and Stephen by any recognisances, and requested the bishop to testify
this to the king and his council in exoneration of his soul'.[46] This case had an
important political significance, reinforcing not only the idea that Arundel and

The marginalia depict the wake and funeral of Earl Edmund Fitzalan. The scene is associated with the resurrection of Jesus, here represented by the visit to the tomb by Mary Magdalen, Mary and Salome to embalm Christ's body. Having found the tomb empty they leave, and then return with Peter and John who witness the disappearance of the body. In the final scene an angel announces the news of the resurrection (British Library MS Egerton 3277, f.142)

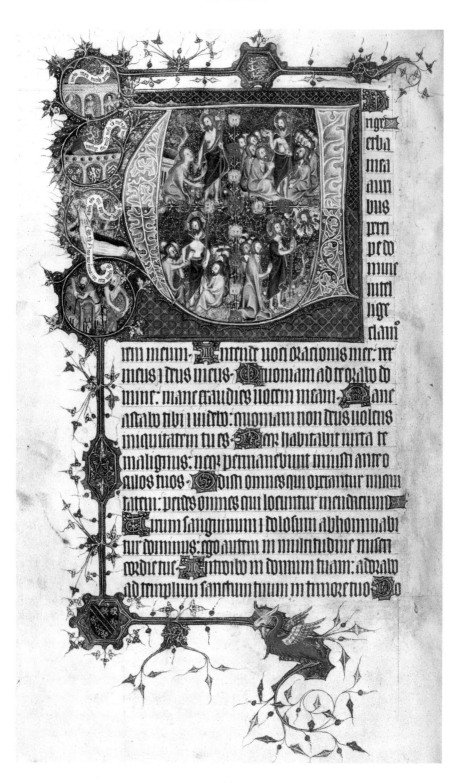

his associates had abused their position to enrich themselves, but also that their ruthless removal was justified.

Earl Edmund's violent death gave rise to a cult around his person. Although there is no evidence that he was considered a martyr soon after his death, in the 1390s the Fitzalans promoted him as such, particularly associating him with St Edmund of East Anglia, a martyr king who had been brutally executed in 870 by Danish invaders.[47] It is likely that this piece of propaganda was commissioned by the family to support the rising cult around Earl Richard III Fitzalan after his death in 1397 (see chapter 4).

The royal treasury continued to be depleted by Isabella and Mortimer so that, by December 1329, orders were given, contrary to the 1327 annulments, that all the monies made by recognisances to Arundel, Despenser, and Baldock should, notwithstanding, be levied.[48] The queen's and Mortimer's task to keep their allies close and their enemies at bay was facilitated, at first, by the enormous treasure that they were able to take over from Edward II. Through the king's and the Despensers' efficiency and greed, they had filled the royal coffers to unprecedented levels. In November 1326 the treasure in the Tower and at Westminster was valued at £62,000 in hard cash, and this sum did not include the king's hoard of plate, jewellery, and relics. To Isabella and Mortimer's spoils of war were further added the treasures of the proscribed earl of Arundel and the Despensers. A total amount of some £78,000 has been calculated to have fallen into the queen's hands. Isabella and Mortimer were prompt in paying their army, compensating their allies, and rewarding themselves, so that by March 1327 only about £12,000 remained in their coffers.[49]

The earl of Kent's condemnation to death at the Winchester parliament, on 11 March 1330, now precipitated the end of Isabella and Mortimer's regime. As early as June 1330 Richard II Fitzalan, the disinherited heir to the earldom of Arundel, conspired to end Mortimer's rule through a rising of men in Shropshire and Staffordshire. He was found out, and an order to arrest him and his associates was issued on 4 June. The proximity of the Fitzalan estates in the Marches to those of Mortimer may well have been among the main causes that precipitated the discovery of the plot. In following up the abortive plot, Roger Mortimer came to realise that many of Arundel's goods in the Marches had actually not been confiscated, with some being concealed among

Left: The resurrection of Earl Edmund Fitzalan; note the juxtaposition with the tomb of St Edmund of East Anglia above Arundel's. This continues the story from f.142 reproduced on the previous page: one of the women who went to the tomb to embalm Jesus finds him risen; later a number of disciples meet Jesus before he addresses the five hundred brethren; and then immediately before his ascension, he appears again to the eleven disciples.
(British Library MS Egerton 3277, f.145ᵛ)

his still faithful supporters, and it is possible that his former local officials may also have been able to hide some of the Marcher revenues. In August 1330 Mortimer ordered that all those goods that had been concealed should be recovered.[50]

In the meantime Richard II Fitzalan managed to avoid arrest and escaped to the Continent, from where he was to return in December 1330. In July of that year, all the counties and towns were ordered by Mortimer to array troops for the defence of the realm; meanwhile, Wales was purged of its potential rebels under Mortimer's justiciarship, and the court took up position at Gloucester, in proximity to the earl of March's estates. When, in 1331, the disinherited earl of Arundel recovered his earldom he was not penniless, so part of his father's treasure must have still remained outside the clutches of the Mortimer regime.

Earl Edmund had been an influential figure of Edward II's reign. The personal rapport he built with the king and maintained until his death enabled him to advance his family's position considerably in terms of wealth. His prominent political position also allowed him to secure important dynastic ties to some of the most powerful families of the reign. Although his role during the civil unrest of 1322 may be considered controversial, his achievement was to survive the political upheavals of the reign unscathed, until his staunch support of the king cost him his life. Certainly to his family he was a martyr to Edward II's cause.

3 The Rich Earl
Richard II Fitzalan, earl of Arundel and Surrey
(*c*.1307-1376)

The execution for treason of his uncle, the earl of Kent, in March 1330 moved Edward III to assume direct control over government. Having found a number of supporters, including William Montague (earl of Salisbury from 1337), he seized the queen and Mortimer on 19 October. The queen was exiled to Castle Rising in Norfolk, while Mortimer was executed for treason in November.

Edward III now called many of the exiles back to England. On 8 December 1330, the disinherited earl of Arundel Richard Fitzalan was invited to the king's court under the family's most ancient title of 'lord of Oswestry'.[1] Four days later, Richard presented to parliament his petition to be reinstated in his inheritance. This petition was refused, however, because he asked to be restored in blood with an annulment of his father's death sentence. Although Edward III wanted to show favour to Richard he also had to ensure that his trust was not misplaced. Richard was therefore allowed to resubmit the petition asking to have his property reinstated as a royal act of grace. The restoration was facilitated by the fact that both earls of Kent and March had been executed that year, and the Arundel estates that had been granted to them could be restored to Richard without having to go through any further legal wranglings. Parliament eventually granted Richard's request and the charter reinstating him as the rightful heir to the earldom of Arundel was issued on 8 February 1331.[2]

The king's favour towards Earl Richard after 1330 was shown through various grants and gifts.[3] Arundel, nonetheless, remained in the king's mercy and this is plainly shown by the fact that on 30 January 1331 he betrothed his firstborn, Edmund, to Sybil, the daughter of William Montague who had been instrumental in the capture and overthrow of Queen Isabella and Mortimer.[4] This marriage was undoubtedly of greater import to Montague than to Arundel, who had certainly hoped to marry his only son and heir to a lady wealthier and more influential than the daughter of a mere knight. It is uncertain whether Montague and Arundel already knew each other before the coup of 1330. For the Montagues the marriage was a significant dynastic prize as it enabled

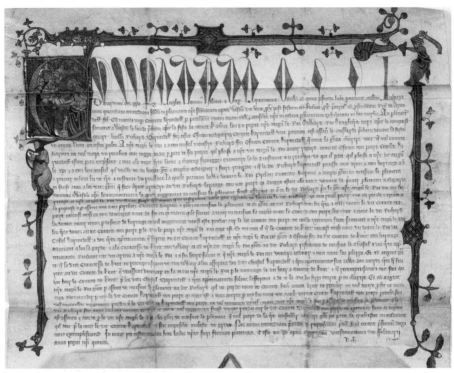

Above: Grant of the Fitzalan inheritance to Richard II Fitzalan, 1331, with a detail (left) of the marginalia showing Edward III making the grant (British Library, Harleian Charter 83 C 13)

them to become part of the ruling aristocracy, a position which was sealed by William Montague's own elevation to the earldom of Salisbury in 1337. The union between Fitzalan and Montague therefore proved advantageous to Arundel after all, especially since Montague remained one of the king's most trusted companions, as part of that coterie which later constituted the core of the so-called newly-created earls of 1337.[5]

Arundel's early military career was spent on the troubled Scottish border, where he took part in the king's campaigns in 1333-35. In January 1333, Arundel was at York attending the king as a member of his council, and later, in July, he was one of the guarantors of the peace of Berwick-upon-Tweed. Edward Balliol had recognized Edward III as his overlord but a Scottish uprising, on 12 June 1334, forced him to flee to England and ended the peace. A military campaign was organised in England to restore Balliol to the throne and Arundel, as leader of one of the largest retinues of 160 men, was among the magnates engaged in these campaigns in the winter of 1334-35. He was involved again, with 130 men, in June-September 1335.[6] Even though the campaigns seemed to have restored Balliol's authority, soon after the departure of the English troops, new revolts spread across the region.

In 1336 there were also concerns that the English coast could become an easy target for French attacks because of Edward's reception of the French king's enemy, Robert d'Artois. On 4 June, Earl Richard was ordered to secure his castle of Arundel and to provide it with a sufficient number of armed men. That same month he was also appointed keeper of Portchester Castle in Hampshire, and required to make the necessary repairs and garrison it with 50 men. In May 1341 Arundel complained that the farm he was paying for Portchester was too high and that whatever revenue he could extract from it was insufficient. Possibly as part of this complaint, on 5 June, Edward III granted the keepership to Arundel for life.[7] Portchester was of particular significance as it gave control over Portsmouth, one of the major southern harbours. In September Arundel was empowered by the king, who had travelled to the Low Countries, to receive his envoys and to do what he thought best for the safety of the realm.[8]

The Norman keep to Portchester Castle, the main defence for Portsmouth harbour. Earl Richard was appointed keeper of the castle in 1336 and ordered to repair it

Arundel's involvement in the Scottish campaigns remained important. He served there again from 14 October to

35

11 December 1336.[9] Interestingly, during that period, on 28 November, he sold his hereditary stewardship of Scotland to Edward III for 1,000 marks.[1] Arundel had a claim to the title through his ancestor Walter Fitzalan (d.1177) who, in 1136, had entered the service of King David of Scotland as steward of his household, which title then became hereditary.[10] Walter had also been granted the lordship of Renfrew and the northern parts of Kyle in Ayrshire. However, while the English steward presided over the Court of the Household, in Scotland this honour was the preserve of the constable while the steward was a councillor to the chamberlain. It is possible that Edward III was interested in the purchase of the stewardship for the right it gave him to interfere in Scottish affairs. By that time, however, the title had lost much of its original significance and it had also acquired a different meaning from the equivalent English office. Only later did the title regain some importance, with the birth of Robert II, crowned king of Scotland in 1370. He was the son of Walter the sixth High Steward and Marjory Bruce, daughter of Robert I; hence the title of steward received a new significance and became the name of the Scottish royal house of Stewart.[11]

Edward III seems to have paid dearly for a title of little practical value. Since Edward I's reign the heir to the English throne had been styled as Prince of Wales. In this same tradition, an appanage had been created for the Scottish heir, the Principality of Scotland; thus the heir to the Scottish throne was styled as Prince and Steward of Scotland. This conferred on him a claim over the lands of the stewartry which, at least in the early fifteenth century, became the hereditary lands of the Stewarts, with the earldom of Carrick and the Lordship of the Isles (Western Isles, the Sundreys, and Man).[12] It is possible that Edward III considered using the custom regulating English appanages for those in Scotland. Furthermore this Scottish appanage was without the Scottish king's authority and could have constituted an English dominion if Edward III had been able, or wanted, to defend his newly acquired title successfully.

The acquisition of the title could also have made Edward III a rallying figure for a number of barons, and in particular those known as the Disinherited, the Anglo-Scottish nobles who, following the Battle of Bannockburn in 1314, had lost their Scottish properties. Indeed, later in 1348, the settlement with Scotland included the restoration of these men and families to their Scottish estates.[13] After years of campaigning in the north, Edward III may have considered settling the Scottish conflict by claiming Scotland's throne for himself. Simultaneously, the tension with France had been escalating and thus the attention was focused more clearly on this pressing issue. In 1336, Robert d'Artois had escaped to the English court and in May 1337, Philip VI of France seized Gascony, thus precipitating the Anglo-French conflict. An open conflict with France supported by an English claim to the French throne may at that moment have seemed a very alluring prize for the young King Edward. Furthermore, the *auld alliance* between France and Scotland had been one of his problems since the beginning of his reign. Audacious as it may have seemed at the time, Edward III certainly must have mused on uniting the three kingdoms under one crown.

Whilst reasons may be found for Edward III's interest in the purchase of the stewardship of Scotland, one may wonder what induced Arundel to sell it. Like his fellow magnates, Arundel was a man driven by financial need and it is possible that his sole reason for this transaction was money. There could, however, also have been a political reason behind the sale. Later, in 1352, Arundel similarly sold his life-justiciarship of Wales to the Black Prince. Payment came, on 11 November 1352, in the form of the fee farm of Chester which the prince granted to Arundel. The exchange and Arundel's goodwill allowed the prince to augment his authority considerably within Wales while at the same time removing the direct judicial influence of one of the most powerful English magnates.[14] This move may also have helped Arundel secure, in 1353, the lordship of Chirk at the expense of Roger Mortimer. This grant to Earl Richard may be surmised as a token of royal favour in recognition of Arundel's support for the king's policies and possibly also for his willingness to sell his justiciarship to the Prince of Wales.

If Edward III was willing to collaborate and tolerate an 'overmighty' magnate in the Marches, the Black Prince may have felt differently about Wales. However, those years were full of political manoeuvring, especially because Edward III needed the support of his most powerful magnates. As one of the key members of the king's council, Arundel certainly played no small role in the establishment of the 1351 Statute of Provisors and the 1353 Statute of Praemunire which established the supremacy of the English royal courts over the ecclesiastical courts.

In the meantime, Edward III was in conflict with both Scotland and its ally France. In October 1336 and from February to April 1337, the Scots carried out raids into English territory. Early in November 1337, Arundel and Salisbury were appointed again to lead an army to Scotland. On 15 November, they were advanced 1,000 marks to cover some of their costs and, on 20 November, orders were issued to prepare the ship *La Seint Edward* and other vessels to be sent from Sandwich to Scotland for the earls' service.[15] The campaign was of great importance, for it was vital to secure the Scottish border now that Edward was in open conflict with France. Thus the earls of Warwick, Derby and Huntingdon were also dispatched to the north to fight alongside Arundel.[16] For Earl Richard, 1337 was an important year. In March, at the moment of the creation of six new earls, he received the life grant of the justiciarship of north Wales, which he then granted to the Prince of Wales in 1352.[17] The following year, also in March, he was granted the sheriff's turn and liberties so extensive in his rapes of Arundel and Chichester that he set up a new court at Arundel, called the shire-court. This provoked great resentment and remonstrances were eventually presented to the Good Parliament of 1376, after Arundel's death.[18] These grants of hereditary offices with extensive jurisdictional rights came at a time when Edward III felt the need to reward the closest men of his entourage for their loyal support. The grants were made, as T.F. Tout remarked, 'in a way hardly compatible either with the interests of the crown, or with sound finance'.[19]

In January 1338, Arundel and Salisbury besieged Dunbar but failed to capture it. The chronicler Henry Knighton commented that 'after spending a long time there they raised the siege and withdrew, to their no small discredit'.[20] In some mitigation the castle was defended by no less than the fearsome Agnes Randolph, countess of Dunbar, better known as Black Agnes. The siege proved a costly failure at £6,000 and the king's expedition overseas was used as an excuse for the besiegers to withdraw gracefully.[21] The king nevertheless rewarded Arundel, 'for his good service', with the sheriff's turn in Sussex, a clear sign that he did not blame him for the failed siege.[22] On 25 April, Arundel was elevated to the sole command of the armies, with full powers to treat with the Scots. He was also granted sole command, as well as financial independence and extensive authority, over all northern counties. In practice, this meant that Arundel's position was that of a viceroy, thus limiting the regency council's sphere of influence to the regions south of Trent.[23] Thus empowered, Arundel concluded a truce under the mediation of the pope's envoy, who had been trying to reach a settlement since Christmas 1337. This peace came to a swift end when, in the spring of 1338, French ships attacked Portsmouth and the Isle of Wight. The borough of Arundel was devastated by a fire in August, but it is uncertain if this was caused by the French.[24]

On 13 July 1338, the king appointed Arundel, Huntingdon, and Ralph, lord Neville to attend the duke of Cornwall's council while he was in the Low Countries to secure alliances.[25] Meanwhile, French troops were able to ransack the Welsh coast, and in October, Arundel was ordered to secure the castles of Caernarvon, Beaumaris, Conwy, Criccieth and Harlech, which, because of the negligence of the chamberlain of North Wales and 'the lightness of the head of the Welsh', had been attacked.[26] Later that year, Arundel personally accompanied the king to Antwerp, where they landed on 13 December; and in January Arundel was granted the sheriffdom of Caernarvon for life.[27]

In January 1340 parliament appointed Arundel admiral of those ships at Portsmouth and the West that were to assemble at Mid Lent and on 24 June, Earl Richard took part at the victorious battle of Sluys, although nothing is known about the nature of his involvement. However, Edward's subsequent expedition was cut short by his allies' refusal to move without pay. Thus in

Loading ships at the quayside (Bodleian Library, MS Douce 208, f.120ᵛ)

July, Edward sent Arundel, Gloucester, and Sir William Trussell with letters to the parliament assembled at Westminster. They were to describe the glories of the victory of Sluys, and to argue for the king's financial demands, but parliament was unable to meet these demands as the tax collection of the ninth had been unsuccessful.[28]

When, in July 1338, Edward left for the Continent to start what were to be the first campaigns of the Hundred Years war, he appointed a regency council headed by Arundel, Huntingdon and Ralph, lord Neville.[29] At Walton, a set of ordinances was compiled to coordinate the working of the royal administration, but these proved to be ineffective and contributed to the crisis that was to ensue in 1340-41. By September 1339 Edward had to send Archbishop Stratford back to England to take over the administration, over which the regency council was losing control, but even the levy of the parliamentary grant of a ninth secured in March-April 1340 proved a failure. This personal bankruptcy and the failure of the siege of Tournai forced Edward into accepting a truce at Espléchin in September. The regency council that had been re-appointed in 1340 was this time led by Archbishop Stratford and the earl of Huntingdon. It was staffed by the earls of Lancaster and Surrey and the lords of the northern marches: Percy, Wake, and Neville. Only later were they joined by Arundel and Gloucester, although Arundel had certainly been attending on the king since April. On 29 August Arundel was summoned to appear before the king on 8 September to discuss with the council matters concerning his expedition overseas.[30]

Most of the English earls were therefore busy at home, although the earls of Warwick, Derby and Northampton had given themselves up as hostages to guarantee the repayment of Edward's debts in the Low Countries. By November 1340, when Edward returned to England, leaving the initiative for the war with Salisbury, he was in such a fury about the ways in which government had been conducted in his absence that he dismissed the chancellor and the treasurer, and ordered the arrest of four judges and of two merchants involved in the wool monopoly, William de la Pole and Reginald Conduit. On 6 July 1341, Arundel was appointed, with Derby and Huntingdon, to audit de la Pole's wool accounts.[31]

It was on 26 January 1340, at Ghent, that Edward had formally assumed the title of King of France, although he had been using it in his correspondence since 7 October 1337. However, by the end of 1340 very little had been achieved on a military level; the Scottish campaigns had proved, on the whole, to be a costly failure, and the recruitment of allies in the Low Countries was putting an enormous financial strain on royal resources. Although the early years of the Anglo-French conflict are often now remembered by the 1340 naval victory of Sluys, this had little impact on English political opinion, for it was the impending financial crisis that was of concern. When Edward had returned from the Low Countries, Archbishop Stratford, having retired to Canterbury, refused his summonses to court during the winter of 1340-41. When parliament met in April 1341, Edward put guards at the door to forbid entrance to Stratford, whom he had decided to ostracize. But Edward failed to gain the support of his earls. Arundel, Surrey and Huntingdon, probably with the support of Salisbury, asserted that it was the right of the magnates to advise and support the king in the great affairs of the realm, and that the charges of corruption he had made against the archbishop's brother, the bishop of Chichester (chancellor from June to December 1340), should be heard by his peers.[32] Arundel was among those nominated to the subsequent committee called to investigate the charges against Stratford, but nothing more was heard of this case until Edward dropped all charges against the archbishop in 1343.

An official reconciliation between the king and Stratford took place in late October 1341, through the mediation of the earl of Derby, who is also credited with reconciling the king with the other magnates. The relations between the king and certain magnates had been cooled by the alleged refusal of seven earls, including Arundel, to serve him during his expedition to Scotland in the winter of 1341-42. On his return from Scotland, Edward organised a tournament at Dunstable, most probably to revive the collaboration and the fraternity among his magnates, but Arundel, Gloucester, Devon and Surrey excused themselves on grounds of age and infirmity. Huntingdon was also absent. Of the five earls, Arundel and Huntingdon were not old enough for age to be an excuse, and whatever infirmity they may have had, both still served on subsequent military expeditions.

In June 1341, Arundel, Surrey, and Michael, the abbot of St Albans, acted as godfathers to the king's newborn son, Edmund of Langley.[33] Symbolically, that ceremony marked their reconciliation with the king. The following month Arundel was charged with important royal business, being excused from his office as chief justice in Shropshire and Stafford, where he had been appointed in January to examine a series of trespasses.[34] It could be argued that this appointment had been a sort of exile from central administration, and may explain Arundel's initial absence from the new regency council. Certainly for an earl of his stature to examine simple trespasses personally, when the affairs of the realm were undoubtedly more pressing, must have been regarded as time ill-employed. Arundel's new job, however, appears to have been of some importance. The clerks at the Chancery were informed not to expect the earl's presence during the examination of the papers he had sent there 'because the earl is occupied upon divers other affairs with which the king has specially charged him in divers parts'.[35] As late as October 1341, Arundel was in the king's service in Shropshire. This would explain his absence from the winter expedition to Scotland, and invalidates Anthony Tuck's supposition that he refused to serve the king during that period.[36]

The death of John III of Brittany, in April 1341, ignited a new region as a place of conflict between England and France. Of the duchy's two possible heirs, John de Montfort was the candidate preferred by Edward III, while the French preferred Charles of Blois, who had a claim through his wife Joan, the niece of Duke John III. On 24 September, Edward granted the duchy to John de Montfort, while Philip VI, hoping at last to annex Brittany to the French kingdom, had already recognised Charles of Blois as the rightful heir, on 7 September. Brittany was an important territorial ally for the English, for military and commercial routes led through it to Gascony. The dukes of Brittany were furthermore also earls of Richmond, and therefore subjects of the English kings. In November, Charles of Blois, at the head of an armed force trying to recover the duchy, managed to capture John de Montfort. The strategic importance of Brittany persuaded Edward to send an expedition led by Walter Mauny in March 1342, and to follow personally in the autumn with a further military force, which enabled the recovery of large portions and numerous strongholds of the duchy.[37]

It has been argued that Arundel, with Huntingdon and Surrey, had refused to serve the king on the Continent in the same manner as during the previous winter. However, Arundel and Huntingdon had agreed, in May, to serve on the Scottish border, from 15 July until mid-October 1342.[38] If they did not fight with the king on the Continent, it was surely because Edward did not want Arundel to abandon the volatile Scottish border, especially since the Scots were allies of the French. Only once Arundel had agreed with the Scots on a truce to last for a year did he, according to the chronicler Jean Froissart, join Walter Mauny at the siege of Vannes, which lasted from October 1342 until January 1343 when, eventually, the English had to admit defeat.[39] At what stage Arundel returned to England is unclear, but he returned to organise a new expedition, for on 31 January, Arundel and Huntingdon were making preparations to sail back to the Continent. On 1 March they were in Portsmouth ready to sail to Gascony with a fleet of 44 ships.[40] Meanwhile, in Brittany, the victory of Morlaix, on 30 September 1342, which saw the joint use of men-at-arms and foot-archers, later used again at the battle of Crécy in 1346, forced the French to seek a truce. This was concluded at Malestroit and intended to last for three years, but in the event it lasted only until the summer of 1345, when Edward found a new ally in Godfrey d'Harcourt, a Norman noble who had defected from the French cause in 1343 after Philip IV executed several Breton nobles, including some of his relatives.[41]

Nevertheless, the peace agreement reached at Malestroit gave Edward and his magnates some time to concentrate on other matters. For Arundel this included his remarriage. On 12 March 1345, in the presence of Edward III and Queen Philippa, Arundel and Eleanor, the daughter of Earl Henry of Lancaster, contracted marriage clandestinely, that is to say, without a public reading of the banns, in the royal chapel at Ditton, Surrey. The condition upon which the dispensation for Arundel's union rested, was that three chaplaincies, worth ten marks, were to be founded in the parish church of his main residence. This foundation was to materialise after Arundel's death in the form of the College of the Holy Trinity in Arundel, also known as the Fitzalan Chapel.[42]

This union is of particular interest because in order for it to happen, Arundel had to seek an annulment of his first marriage. This had taken place in February 1321, though the betrothal had been contracted sometime in 1314-15, when he and Isabella Despenser were aged seven and eight respectively. When in 1344, Arundel petitioned for this union to be annulled he stated that it had been arranged without his consent (which was certainly the case in 1314-15 since he was still a minor) and that he had been forced into the marriage in 1321.[43]

Although the union between the Fitzalans and the Despensers remained crucial until the end of Edward II's reign, the political eclipse of the Despensers thereafter meant that from the Fitzalans' point of view, the union between Richard and Isabella had lost its initial political appeal. It is not surprising, therefore, that Arundel was tempted by the prospect of cementing a new union with England's most powerful and prestigious family, the house of Lancaster. Annulments were certainly not unheard of, but canon law limited the circumstances in which they could be granted; and the circumstances under which this particular annulment came about are quite extraordinary indeed.

Eleanor of Lancaster's first husband, Lord John Beaumont, had died in May 1343. In December of that year, as his executrix, Eleanor seems to have had rather a hard time, for when the news of Beaumont's death had spread she was robbed of eight horses worth £40, together with various goods from the manor of Towcester in Northamptonshire, where her men and servants were also assaulted and injured, and some possibly killed. The following year she had fulfilled her duty as Beaumont's executrix and was authorised, in March 1344, to go on pilgrimage to Santiago. This pilgrimage had originally been planned in 1332, when Eleanor arranged to travel with Margery de Chaumpaigne, but for some reason it was delayed.[44]

Arundel profited from the timely and almost simultaneous deaths of John Beaumont and the earl of Salisbury, without which this marriage could not have been envisaged. Salisbury would have strongly opposed Arundel's rejection of Isabella, for such an annulment would mean that their son Edmund would be bastardised and his wife, Sybil Montague, would never attain the high rank her father had intended for her.[45] On 30 January 1344, however, Montague had succumbed to injuries sustained in a tournament at Windsor, and his heir, another William, was still a minor and in the king's ward.

On a political level, Arundel's second marriage allowed Edward III to tie him even more closely to the Crown's cause. The conflict with France was now dominating politics, for a successful outcome to the war must have seemed far from certain. Further alliances were being sought and Derby and Salisbury had been to Spain in 1343, where on 2 September they had been empowered to treat with Alphonso XI of Castille as Edward III needed to secure Aquitaine, and by 14 March 1344 an alliance seems to have been reached. Then, on 24 March 1344, Derby and Arundel were appointed lieutenants of Aquitaine.[46]

Since Eleanor had planned her pilgrimage to Santiago, it is possible that her brother the earl of Derby's appointment to Aquitaine may have been the factor that enabled her to undertake this spiritual journey under safe conditions before being remarried, in rather dubious circumstances, to Arundel. Although we do not know if they were travelling together, it is known that Arundel halted at the Augustinian priory of Roncesvalles, near the French border of north-eastern Navarre. There he made a grant of 40 shillings yearly to the hospital because of the great charity he had seen shown to the pilgrims. The priory may already have been known to him, as it had a cell called St Mary of Roncesvalles by Charing Cross, London. It is certain, therefore, that Arundel had accompanied Derby on his mission to join Alphonso at the siege of Algeciras. When they arrived at Logroño, on the frontier between Navarre and Castile, they were informed that Algeciras had already surrendered. Since Logroño was on the official route from Bordeaux to Santiago it is possible that they accompanied Eleanor and her household for protection.[47] Derby then returned to Bayonne but it is not certain whether Arundel returned with him or stayed with Eleanor, possibly to meet Alphonso.

The annulment of Arundel's marriage to Isabella Despenser was granted on 4 December but a further dispensation to marry Eleanor was only granted after the marriage in July 1345.[48] This latter dispensation may have been needed for matters had been complicated by Arundel's excommunication, which the pope revoked, early in 1345, before the wedding took place.[49] It is not clear who excommunicated Arundel. Crucially, only the pope and the bishops had the authority to do this. Clement VI had clearly not done it, since it was he who granted the annulment and, later, revoked the excommunication. Someone who certainly had a valid motive to excommunicate Arundel was Bishop Simon Montague of Ely, brother of the earl of Salisbury and therefore uncle to Sybil. The death of Simon Montague on 20 June 1345 could explain why, since the excommunication had been revoked early that year, the case was not pursued.

But to return to the matter of the annulment of Arundel's marriage, in order to obtain it, he argued that he was still below the age of consent when he fathered his son, and that he was forced to that act under duress.[50] He further stated that after the act he had refused to live with Isabella. Further reasons for the invalidity of a marriage were consanguinity between the two parties, or the existence of a pre-contract. Marriages validly entered into were theoretically indissoluble for any cause which arose after they had been contracted. So far as his second marriage was concerned, Arundel also had to deal with the fact that he was prohibited by canon law from marrying Eleanor of Lancaster because she was related to Isabella Despenser in the second degree on her mother's side, and in the third and fourth degree on her father's side.[51] This affinity would be an impediment for Arundel unless he obtained a dispensation from the pope.

The person with most reason to challenge the validity of the annulment and remarriage was Arundel's son, Edmund, who was made a bastard by this change in circumstances, and thus lost all claim to his inheritance. Edmund, now aged about 20, sought to have the annulment reversed by appealing directly to the papal curia. In July 1347 he petitioned the pope, possibly to clarify certain matters that, in his opinion, had misled the curia in granting the annulment, and thereafter his father's licence to remarry. An added incentive for Edmund to regain the right to his inheritance was that it had been considerably increased by the Warenne inheritance, the earl of Surrey having died on 30 June. Unfortunately, the original petition has not survived. Reference to it is made in a papal mandate, dated 31 July 1347, citing all parties involved to the curia to clarify the matter regarding the annulment and dispensation to remarry. The mandate refers to a number of petitions and events which raise more questions than can be answered. It is, nonetheless, evident from the text that attempts had been made to disguise Eleanor of Lancaster's true identity, to eliminate the impediment of consanguinity. The use of the term 'surreptitiously' in the 1347 petition probably indicates that an attempt had been made to disguise Eleanor's identity by giving her name as Joan de Bellomonte, possibly because she was John Beaumont's widow.[52]

Edmund Arundel had requested that he be allowed to take an oath, presumably, to testify to the truth and thus show that the annulment of his parents' marriage should never have been granted. This was the only hope Edmund had of ensuring his claim to his inheritance, and it is thus a crucial piece of evidence that highlights what at the time must have been regarded as a highly controversial papal decision, and one which could have set a dangerous precedent.

Edmund lost his appeal. Despite this, he considered himself the son of an earl and certainly he was married to the daughter of another earl. Though legally he was hugely disadvantaged, his lineage still conferred a certain importance on him. In 1352 he was knighted; in 1359-60 he fought with his own retinue in France; and in 1363 he was appointed to a commission of oyer and terminer in Devon. In 1364-67 he was among the envoys sent to Flanders on a royal mission and in 1368 he was sent by the pope on a diplomatic mission to Edward III to discuss matters concerning the state of the Roman church in Italy. Certainly his standing by the late 1360s was significant.[53]

That Edmund remained a thorn in his father's side is clearly shown by the way in which Arundel referred to him in his testament, in 1375. Earl Richard talks about 'that certain Edmund who claims himself to be my son', evidently fearing that he might challenge the validity of his will or the right of his children by Eleanor.[54] Arundel had clearly rejected any familiarity between himself and Edmund, but knew that his death might move Edmund to try once more to recover what he considered was his. Thus, Arundel devised 5,000 marks to fight any of Edmund's attempts at challenging his will. The money could also be used as a settlement if Edmund agreed to behave. The settlement was certainly generous, but nothing compared to the £72,000 in cash which his father possessed. If both of these plans of action were to fail, certain wise men, probably lawyers, were to be sent to Avignon to discuss the situation before Edmund might attempt anything in the curia. It seems that in case an agreement between the executors and Edmund could not be reached, the 5,000 marks could also, eventually, be distributed in the papal and English courts as tokens of patronage – essentially bribes.

But if Earl Richard had thought he could buy Edmund's good behaviour with 5,000 marks, he was mistaken. Edmund had clear views on his lineage and right. In the armorial he used on his seal, of which only one example survives from 24 March 1368, his arms are represented as quarterly, first and fourth, *Gules a lion rampant or* (Fitzalan); second and third, *Chequy or and azure* (Warenne), over all a file with three labels (the sign of primogeniture).[55] His use of the arms of Arundel quartered with Warenne stressed his claim to the earldom of Surrey as part of his inheritance. His father had adopted the title to the earldom only in 1361, after Joan of Bar's death, when he also quartered his arms with those of Warenne. As by that stage Edmund had already been bastardised, there was no reason why he should have augmented his armorial and, indeed, on a copy of the Salisbury Roll dating from 1483-85 he is represented bearing only the Fitzalan arms over all a file with three labels, although his Warenne connection is highlighted by the Warenne arms represented in an escutcheon pending from a chain linking Edmund and Sybil, presumably an allusion to the bond of marriage.[56] Furthermore, one of Sybil's seals, dating from 1350, bears in the central shield only the Fitzalan arms over all a file with three labels, flanked on either side by her paternal and maternal arms.[57]

There is further evidence to indicate that the armorial used in 1368 by Edmund was in fact that of his half-brother, Richard III Fitzalan. In the chapel Earl Richard II built at Oriel College, Oxford, in the early 1370s the arms of his legitimate offspring were represented, including those of Richard III Fitzalan, described in the 1660s by the antiquarian Antony Wood.[58] It is

Seal of Sir Edmund Arundel, 1368 (British Library, Harleian Charter 53.E.II)

evident that Edmund's intention was to assert his claim to the Fitzalan inheritance in this manner and, although no evidence has survived regarding a possible dispute over this matter, it is clear, from other cases in the Court of Chivalry, that the use of another man's arms was certainly neither permitted nor condoned.[59] When, in 1325, Henry of Lancaster, earl of Leicester was accused of treason, one of the charges brought against him was that he had adopted his brother's arms after his execution in 1322. Although this case was not pursued, Henry claimed that he had adopted his father's arms which were his by hereditary right, since his brother had died without heirs.[60]

Arundel's worries regarding Edmund were not unfounded, and the measures he took in his will proved necessary. On 10 December 1376, the king wrote to Edmund and his proctor and cousin Henry Despenser, bishop of Norwich, forbidding him to leave the kingdom, under pain of forfeiture, unless it was to come to the king or the council to discuss and prosecute his dispute with his half-brother, the new earl of Arundel. Apparently the two parties had made an arrangement in the king's presence regarding 'the cause, quarrel, dissensions, strife and controversy between them',

Sir Edmund Arundel and Sybil Montague united by the chains of marriage, which also highlight his Warenne ancestry. After a 1483-85 copy of the Salisbury Roll of Arms (c.1460) (British Library, Add. MS 45133, f.55)

and because the agreement had been accepted upon oath by both parties before him, Edward could not accept that this matter be brought before any other court than his own. On 28 January 1377 Edward III thus called Edmund to order and summoned him to appear at Westminster on 16 February to lay out these matters, ordering him to cease all excuses and pretexts.[61]

Edmund did not hesitate to take revenge on his half-brother. On 20 March and 27 November that year, two commissions were issued on complaint by Earl Richard III against Edmund, nine of his servants, one London tailor and three other individuals, who had broken into his closes and houses in Essex, had fished in his free fishery at High Rothing, had stolen fish, various goods, and £100 in cash, and had assaulted and imprisoned his men and servants. On these charges Edmund was arrested and imprisoned in the Tower of London. On 5 June, his two brothers-in-law, Sir Guy Brian and John Montague, together with Robert Rous, received custody over Edmund. Under the guarantee that he would not leave the realm, Edmund was freed.[62] Sir Guy Brian was in the awkward position of being one of the late earl of Arundel's executors; he was obviously a close member of the family and must have felt torn between his friendship to Arundel and his family ties to Edmund.

After this last episode all trace of Edmund Arundel disappears, but we know that he died sometime between 1379 and 1387. On 16 July 1387, a mandate was issued concerning a court case against Edmund and Richard Sergeaux, his son-in-law, who on 27 July 1379 had made, before William Walworth, then mayor of the staple of Westminster, several recognizances of debt worth £500 to Sir Matthew Gournay. These monies had never been reimbursed, and an inquisition was issued. The sheriff of Oxford found that Edmund was already dead, and that there was no trace of Richard, so Edmund's manor of Chipping Norton in Oxfordshire was confiscated. But after all the quarrelling, Edmund came to a kind of peace with his half-brother for ironically both were buried in the Austin Friars' Church in Broad Street, London.[63]

This whole affair had one further outcome in that it prevented Earl Richard II from becoming a companion of the Order of Garter. This omission has always been regarded with great puzzlement by historians, especially since Arundel had been included in the king's new project, dating from 1344, to refound the Arthurian Round Table which did indeed culminate, in 1348-49, with the foundation of the Garter. The Garter had the practical political role of galvanising the relationship between the king and the nobility with special regard to the war in France, and the victory of Crécy in particular. It was, however, also to be the expression of the highest aspirations of chivalric ideals. The main requirements for members-to-be was to prove their valour in the traditional chivalric virtues such as martial diligence, honour, and service, with a particular focus on gentleness of birth and an unblemished reputation. Hence, it was arguably unacceptable to include among its members a man who had rejected his wife to remarry for his own political advancement, even if this had been done with the king's blessing. Arundel's inclusion in the Garter could have quickly curtailed the reputation of an order which put so much emphasis on honour.

This brings us back to the progress of the war in France. Until 1340 Edward III had personally directed the military campaigns in Scotland, the Low Countries and Brittany. When he assumed the title of king of France that year the way in which war was directed changed. The assumption of this title gave a figurehead to a common cause to which all parties discontented with the Valois regime could rally. In order to support all these new local parties, Edward needed two or three armies ready to intervene simultaneously on the Continent. The troops which, therefore, could not be led by the king, had to be placed under the command of a powerful leader invested with large, almost vice-regal authority, as captain-general or lieutenant. It is in this context that the earls of Derby and Arundel were appointed, on 24 March 1344, joint-lieutenants of Aquitaine and Languedoc. The earl of Northampton received command of the troops leaving for Brittany, and Hugh Hastings command of those for Flanders. On 12 July 1346, Edward III landed at Saint-Vaast-La-Hogue, in the Cotentin, where he was to assemble with Godfrey d'Harcourt's troops. That month they captured Caen, and from there they continued their march towards Paris. A few miles before the capital they turned north to return towards the Channel. On 26 August, the English troops met the French army at Crécy to fight the battle that became a symbol of English military supremacy.

At Crécy, the English army was divided into three. The vanguard was led by the Prince of Wales under the supervision of the earls of Warwick and Northampton; the rearguard was under the command of the earls of Arundel and Stafford, and the bishop of Durham; while the king commanded the centre. Arundel had at his disposal a contingent of 304 men: himself, one banneret, 41 knights, 105 esquires, and 154 archers.[64] It now seems that Arundel's division played a decisive role in securing the victory since, with Northampton, he was able to assist the Prince of Wales when he was pressed by the French forces. During the campaign Arundel was also empowered to issue grants in the king's name. After their victory, the English troops continued their march towards Calais to which they laid siege, in which Arundel took an intermittent part. In January, February, and April he was in England, possibly to report to parliament on the progress of war, but he was back at Calais on 16 May when he received his wages; he was then back again in England and due to return to Calais at the end of June.[65] Calais eventually surrendered on 4 August 1347.

Soldiers looting as depicted in the fourteenth century
(British Library, Royal MS 20 C VII f.41ᵛ)

Meanwhile, in Brittany, Northumberland's successor, Sir Thomas Dagworth, had captured Charles of Blois on 20 June 1347. Blois was sent to the Tower of London, where he joined David Bruce, king of Scotland, who had been captured at the battle of Neville's Cross on 17 October 1346.

The siege of Calais was of particular significance for Arundel for it seems to have caused the death of John de Warenne, earl of Surrey. Certainly Warenne had to abandon the siege, possibly because of the arduous nature of the campaigning, to return to England, where he died in his castle of Conisborough at the end of June 1347, aged 61. Edward III used the Warenne inheritance cleverly, splitting it up so as to recompense the most worthy military leaders of the Crécy-Calais campaigns. Arundel was granted the Sussex, Norfolk, and Marcher interests. Both Derby (also earl of Lancaster since 1345) and Salisbury's son and heir, William, were particularly interested in the old Lacy inheritance centred around the hundred of Ewyas Lacy in Herefordshire, which, in 1319, had been granted to Warenne who in turn had granted a reversionary right to Salisbury in 1339. Edward, however, granted these lands to Warenne's widow who leased them to the Black Prince, and Lancaster only obtained the Norfolk portion of the Lacy inheritance. Thus in one stroke Arundel became, territorially, the most important magnate after the Black Prince and Lancaster.

The victories of Crécy and Calais were of great importance for they made of Edward III a powerful monarch and enabled Lancaster, Northampton and Sir Thomas Dagworth to restore the English position in Aquitaine and Brittany. But by this stage little was left of the alliances Edward had built up in the Low Countries. As soon as the siege of Calais was over Pope Clement VI busied himself in trying to secure an extension of the truce concluded there. On 15 May 1348, a procuration was issued to John de Charlton, who had been sent to the curia to renew the truce for one year. The extension was arranged by the pope, and a final peace agreement was to be confirmed by a solemn embassy around Michaelmas. On 28 July, Edward III requested safe-conducts for the bishop of Norwich, Bartholomew de Burghersh, and the earls of Lancaster and Arundel. But in the event, the embassy was never sent, due to the outbreak of the Black Death and turbulent events in Flanders. Indeed, the Flemish popular revolts proved a powerful factor of instability within that region. On 25 September 1348, the earl of Lancaster was therefore appointed lieutenant to Flanders.

A fresh embassy to Avignon was planned in 1350. On 18 June, Edward warned the pope that he would send the same delegation as in 1348. On 28 July they were given the procurations empowering them to negotiate at the curia, and letters of protection were requested on 30 August.[129] The delegation's departure had been delayed by Spanish attacks on the south coast, but eventually the threat was removed in August 1350 by an English naval victory off Winchelsea in which Arundel took part, which became known as the battle of *Les Espagnols sur Mer*.[66] The envoys eventually left England at Christmas. The following year, Arundel was commissioned to arrange for a final peace agreement with Scotland and the ransom of their king, David II. Similar commissions were issued to Arundel again in 1354 and 1357.

On 6 December 1352, Pope Clement VI died, and the conclave of cardinals elected Innocent VI, who was also eager to secure a permanent peace agreement between England and France. On 26 January 1353 the pope sent his envoy, Guy de Boulogne, to Paris to inform Lancaster and John II of France of his desire for a permanent peace. A new peace conference was called to assemble at Guines in the spring. The English envoys, Arundel, Lancaster, Sir Guy de Brian, Simon Islip, archbishop of Canterbury, William Bateman, bishop of Norwich, and Michael de Northburgh, bishop-elect of London, were granted their procurations on 19 February. On 10 March, the truce was extended until 1 August, and the envoys were to meet, on 20 May, near Guines to pursue the peace talks. However, Edward III had to postpone parliament until 29 August, due to initial low attendance, and the conference was postponed until April 1354, when a draft of a peace agreement was compiled.

Lancaster arrived at Avignon with 317 men on 30 October 1354 and stayed until 28 March 1355. Arundel arrived in support of Lancaster on 6 November 1354 with a retinue which although it was smaller (175 men), was by far the more impressive in its display of power, wealth, and authority. Arundel stayed until 8 March 1355. Although he and Lancaster were received at Avignon with great honour, it must have been apparent that the pope was biased towards the French. The chronicler Thomas Walsingham was not exaggerating when, commenting on those discussions, he affirmed that in fact the French were in league with the pope and had no intention to come to any compromise, which proved very frustrating to Edward III. Even though the English may have felt some exasperation, it was the French who technically repudiated the terms agreed at Guines. Thus the parties were only able to prolong the truce until midsummer 1355.[67]

A short period of warfare followed, between the summer of 1355 and the spring of 1357. It was not unexpected, as parliament had granted a three-year subsidy to fund a large scale campaign in 1352. The initial plan had presumably been to have three simultaneous expeditions leaving England, but in the end there were to be only two, as Edward had to march to Scotland in the winter of 1355-56 to recover control over Berwick. This was settled in October 1357 when a truce was agreed. Of the two expeditions that left England, the first, under the command of the Black Prince, was to operate in Aquitaine, while Lancaster, heading the second, was to co-operate with Charles of Navarre in Normandy. As a safety net, in the Black Prince's indenture it was agreed that if he needed help, Lancaster, Northampton, Arundel, March and Stafford were to come to his rescue with an armed force. The earls of Warwick, Suffolk, Oxford, and Salisbury were to be in the Prince's army, while Northampton, March, and Stafford were to accompany Lancaster to Normandy.[68] The highlight of the 1356 campaign was the capture of King John II of France at the battle of Poitiers. Now in a position of renewed strength Edward III sought to establish his complete hegemony. As early as May 1358, he was again on the outlook for allies. Arundel was appointed plenipotentiary, with Sir Guy Brian and Sir William Thorpe, to negotiate an alliance with Wenceslas, duke of Luxemburg, Lorraine, Brabant, and Lemburgh, and marquess of the Holy Roman Empire.[69]

Half of Brittany and most of Aquitaine were now in English hands, and Normandy was under the control of Anglo-Navarrese forces. King John II was still a prisoner in London where, ultimately, he was to die in captivity, on 8 April 1364. Furthermore, France was on the brink of civil war, with the Jacquerie of 1357-58 openly opposing the Dauphin and the municipality of Paris.[70] One of the English demands of the second treaty of London of May 1359 was the enormous ransom of £700,000 for the return of King John, which the French had not wished to accept. The treaty as it stood with its strict conditions was, not surprisingly, utterly unacceptable to the French since it permitted much of western France to be annexed to England. Thus Edward resolved to embark on a further great expedition to France with a military campaign that was to bring him to Reims Cathedral for his own coronation.

On 4 November 1359 the English campaign set off from Calais, where Edward had spent some time organising his troops into three columns. The first, under his command, included his sons Lionel of Antwerp and Edmund of Langley, as well as the earls of Richmond, Warwick, Suffolk, Salisbury and Oxford. The second was under the command of the Black Prince, and included John of Gaunt and the earls of Northampton and Stafford. The third and last column was intended for Lancaster, but was meanwhile put under the command of the earl of March.[71] Arundel was in England from January to March 1360, with the bishop of Worcester, the abbot of Evesham, and William de Shareshull, to treat with the counties of Gloucester, Hereford, Shropshire, Stafford, Worcester, and Warwick for the array of men;[72] clearly Edward relied on Arundel, now in his early 50s, to negotiate with Parliament the troops and money necessary to a successful outcome of the war. The campaign was ultimately a failure, however, and Edward's troops fled before a coronation at Reims could be secured. On 8 May 1360, once the chevauchée was over, a peace agreement was secured at Brétigny, which was to mark the beginning of the longest period of peace between England and France since 1337.

The treaty was formally ratified at an official ceremony on 24 October 1360, at the church of Saint-Nicholas at Calais, with Arundel among the magnates

The rolls of the Brétigny Treaty, as well as many documents relating to the conference, were preserved in a specially made chest today known as the Treaty of Calais Chest and preserved at The National Archives in Kew. The lid of the chest is decorated with the coats of arms of Arundel (just discernable on the left), the Dauphin, England, France, the Black Prince, and one unidentified. The front panel is adorned with the coats of arms of John of Buckingham, Sir Guy Brian, and two unidentified ones[77]

present.[73] Earl Richard left Arundel for Calais on 24 August 1360 to finalise arrangements with the French, arriving the next day and remaining until 21 October. The following day he was back again in Arundel.[74] It is possible that he returned to England to report personally to the king on the progress of the negotiations and then later returned to the Continent for the ratification. Significantly, while Arundel's coat of arms appears on the chest that contained the treaty's rolls, Lancaster's does not.[75] Lancaster returned to England in November and shortly afterwards fell ill, possibly of the plague, dying on 23 March 1361 at Leicester Castle.[76] Arundel hence replaced Lancaster as guarantor of the treaty's terms and thus his coat of arms replaced the duke's on the chest.

In 1362 Arundel was among the commissioners appointed to find a settlement with Charles of Blois to end the Breton civil war, and in 1365, after King John II's death, Arundel was also appointed to examine the question concerning the payment of the remainder of the late king's ransom.[78]

Arundel's engagement in diplomacy continued right through the 1360s. In 1366, he and the archbishop of Canterbury were empowered, as deputies of the earl of Hereford, to treat with King David of Scotland; this secured the Treaty of Annandale. It may be that Arundel had been involved in the Scottish negotiations since 1364.[79] His involvement is not surprising, given his considerable influence within the royal council and his life-long involvement on the Scottish front. At this time much of Arundel's time and energy was also channelled into a dispute with William de Lynne, bishop of Chichester, who had secured a papal summons for Arundel to appear before the pope in the summer of 1364.[80] The dispute between the two men had begun in 1363 over some unpaid dues. Lynne began litigation against Arundel in England, but as the bishop was then excommunicated by the episcopate over this issue, he took his case to Avignon against the king's will. This sparked a controversy over the prerogative of English royal courts over papal courts which was only resolved with the publication of the second Statute of Praemunire of 1365 which reaffirmed the authority of royal courts over papal courts.

The renewal of military hostilities between England and France in the 1370s increased the Crown's dependence on Arundel. It was his wealth that helped to finance a great part of the renewed war effort, and he continued to be involved personally in the military campaigns. As early as 1367, Earl Richard had been appointed arrayer of troops in Sussex and his marcher lordships, thus clearly keeping him at the head of England's war machine.[81] By the early 1370s he was the only magnate left from the group of the king's friends who had gathered around him in the 1330s; the earls of Salisbury, Lancaster, and Surrey had died in the 1340s, Northampton in 1359, and the duke of Lancaster in 1361. By the 1370s Arundel was in his mid-60s, and it is possible that his role in any military campaign would have been that of a commander rather than a combatant, and it was perhaps in this capacity that he agreed to accompany the king on the planned but abortive campaign of 1372.

Significantly, Arundel's best friends were to form the clique around the king in the 1370s, and they had their own vested interests in a renewal of war with France. Arundel's influence and that of his friends were certainly key factors in the council's decisions during that period. These men included Sir Richard Lescrope, Sir Guy Brian, Sir Roger Beauchamp, and Sir Hugh de Segrave, but his closest friend was Sir William Latimer whom, in his testament, he called 'my dear brother'.[82] Guy Brian was a veteran soldier closely connected to the court, where he had been steward of the king's household. On 26 May 1376 he was chosen to be a member of the new royal council, along with the new earl of Arundel and Sir Roger Beauchamp. Sir Roger, kinsman to the earl of Warwick, had been a servant in the royal household since 1337, and had been steward to Queen Philippa and governor of Calais. Sir Hugh de Segrave had also served Queen Philippa, to whom he had been a squire in

1369. Before November 1372 he became seneschal of John of Gaunt's household in Gascony, and he was steward of the Black Prince's lands from October 1372 until 1376, when he acted as one of the prince's executors.

In the years after the death of Queen Philippa (d.1369), Edward progressively withdrew from court into the inner circle of his household, that small group of personal followers who, incidentally but not completely unexpectedly, were later suspected of using their position to enrich themselves. The most prominent members of this group were the king's mistress, Alice Perrers, Richard Lescrope, William Latimer, and John, lord Neville. Lescrope was treasurer from 1371 until 1375, when he took up the joint wardenship of the west Marches against Scotland.[83] Latimer had become chamberlain in 1371, and was regarded as the real political leader of the group around the king. He had enjoyed a distinguished military career, firstly under the Black Prince at Crécy aged only 16 and, from 1360 to 1367, in Brittany. In 1368, Latimer was appointed keeper of Bécherel, and of Saint-Sauveur-le-Vicomte in 1370, and he was known to be a wealthy man. John Neville, who was Latimer's son-in-law, became steward of the household in 1371, but was also wealthy in his own right, mainly through his inherited estates in Durham and Yorkshire.

Both Latimer and Neville played a leading part in the organisation of the war after 1369, and as both were experienced soldiers and diplomats it seems natural that such a role would have been given to them. They took up a dominant role at court from 1369 to 1376, together with a small group of chamber knights, and a London merchant, Richard Lyons, who became a member of the king's council — an unusual distinction for a man of his status and background. Lyons lent considerable sums to the Crown, up to £50,000, and must have had some dealings with Arundel, although no such connection can be established. It was the unsuccessful conduct of the war that became the downfall of this group of courtiers. They were also widely unpopular for the rumours of corruption and extortion that fuelled popular anger. Arundel himself could claim detractors among the Londoners. On 14 October 1372, the wealthy London poulterer Richard Donmowe was arrested and imprisoned for 'opprobrious words spoken openly in contempt of the Earl of Arundel'.[84] In April to July 1376, the accusations against Latimer and Lyons, supported by Lescrope's testimony, formed the basis of the ruthless attack launched upon them by what became known as the Good Parliament.[85] However, Arundel was not to witness his friends' downfall: he died on 24 January 1376, in his castle at Arundel.

Earl Richard II had chosen to be buried in the chapter house of Lewes Priory in Sussex, instructing that wherever he died his body should be brought there as soon as possible, instead of the traditional Fitzalan burial place, Haughmond Abbey in Shropshire. This was a testament to his desire to assert his and his family's authority and lordship over the eastern part of the county of Sussex,

The Buck brothers' engraving of Lewes Priory and Castle (in the distance) in 1737

which was largely dominated by a number of mighty gentry families rather than one powerful overlord. In his testament Arundel requested to be buried next to Eleanor of Lancaster. Indeed, his funeral was to resemble that of his wife, who had died four years previously on 12 January 1372. There should be no men-at-arms, horsemen, hearse, or any other display apart from five candles with mortars (the spikes on which the candles would be placed). The Black Prince's funeral, for example, that same year, was highly elaborate — as were those of many other nobles and knights — although his tomb inscription reflected very similar sentiments of penitence and humility to those found in the wills of Arundel, Lancaster, and later John of Gaunt.[86] This is often the case with such testamentary instructions; although they appear to express humility, in reality they only reflect how the testator wanted to be remembered. The Black Prince composed his own epitaph in the hope that people would remember him the way he wanted them to rather than as the war-mongering thug he was. The epitaph is undoubtedly a good example of medieval spin-doctoring.

Arundel's provision of 500 marks for the expense of his funeral shows that the occasion was in fact to be grand, not humble. Pious instructions were common, but rarely followed in practice. In 1393 Earl Richard III instructed that his funeral be the same as his father's; and other family members gave similar instructions as is shown by the examples of Agnes, lady Arundel (d.1401), widow of Sir William Arundel K.G., and of Archbishop Arundel.[87]

The alleged tomb of Arundel and Eleanor, known as the Arundel Tomb, is a controversial funeral monument. The tomb of Earl Richard II and Countess Eleanor was moved to Chichester Cathedral, where it stands under the arch between the fourth bay of the north aisle and the nave, when Lewes Priory was bought by Thomas Cromwell during the Dissolution. It is a table tomb on which recline a knight and a lady.[88] The male effigy is represented as a knight dressed in full-length armour, with a lion rampant emblazoned on his breast-plate, his head resting on a great helm which carries a lion's head within a

The Arundel Tomb, Chichester Cathedral, with the alleged effigies of
Richard II Fitzalan, earl of Arundel and Surrey and of Eleanor of Lancaster

coronet, whilst a reclining lion supports his legs. The lady lies to his right, her head turned slightly towards him; her legs are crossed and her feet rest on a lapdog. The two effigies are holding each other's right hand. Although this is often taken to be a gesture of affection, in fact it suggests the symbolic representation of the two figures' marital union before the altar. It would be more likely to represent affection if they were holding left hand to right hand.

The problem with the identification of the tomb is that there is nothing to suggest that the male reclining figure is that of Arundel — lions rampant were common heraldic figures — nor is there anything to suggest that the two effigies did belong together or did originally hold hands. The matter is further complicated by the evidence from Arundel's testament suggesting that, by 1375, Eleanor already had a tomb of her own and that his own tomb, who was still to be made, should not be higher than hers.[89] If the original tomb had been intended as a joint tomb, there would have been no need to specify this.

In 1843 the Dean and Chapter of Chichester decided to restore the statues, which had suffered considerable decay. By then the knight lacked both arms from below the shoulders and had a broken dagger sword and right spur; his lion's head crest was broken and his face was disfigured, as was that of the lady, whose right hand was also missing. The restorer, Edward Richardson, who had already been in charge of the restoration of the crusader effigies at Temple Church in London in 1842, largely recreated a new table tomb and then posed the two effigies on it. Richardson assumed from the position of the lady that she may have been holding hands with the male effigy. In this respect the position of the lady's arms and hands resembles that of the brass of Sir John Harsick and his wife at South Acre in Norfolk.[90] Joint effigies holding hands were far from exceptional and Arundel's bears a striking resemblance to that of Thomas Beauchamp, earl of Warwick (d.1369) holding the hand of Katherine Mortimer, which used to be before the high altar of St Mary's Church in Warwick — this tomb is now in the chancel which, along with the body of the church, was rebuilt by Earl Thomas's son, and completed around 1394[91]. The restoration of the Arundel Tomb was completed by Richardson's invention of the right gauntlet in the knight's left hand, almost to suggest that there was no doubt that the two effigies must have been holding hands. From this point of view it also bears striking resemblance to the tomb of John Beaufort, duke of Somerset (d.1444) and Margaret Beauchamp (d.1482) at Wimborne near Kingston Lacy in Dorset, where the effigies hold hands and the male effigy also holds a gauntlet in the left hand.[92]

The Arundel male effigy is, nonetheless, that of a knight in armour which can be dated to the reign of Edward III as it bears great resemblance to the effigy of the Black Prince in Canterbury Cathedral. This suggests that they may have come from the same workshop of Henry Yevele or that, indeed, the Arundel Tomb may have been completed after that of the Black Prince, whose funeral took place in 1376. If one is to assume that the Arundel Tomb is indeed that of Earl Richard II and Eleanor, based on the dating of the tomb, the location in Sussex, and the lion rampant on his breast plate (although this was also, notably, used by the Percies who were significant Sussex lords), one must still wonder why the tomb has joint effigies rather than separate ones as Arundel's testament of 1375 suggests. If the commission had been changed this could only have happened after his death, presumably by his executors or his children. To add further complication there is a reference to a ship, on 20 January 1375, carrying two tombs for the earl of Arundel and Eleanor and one stone for the bishop of Winchester.[93] It is possible that these were, in fact, two blocks of stone — one for the sarcophagus and the other for the effigy. However, if one accepts the theory of a joint tomb, it is possible that a new tomb was commissioned, possibly to reflect a change in tastes and fashion. If the commission came from Arundel's son and heir, this tomb may also have had the purpose of asserting and acknowledging the marriage between Eleanor and Arundel. For Earl Richard III this may have been of particular importance since, soon after the death of his father, his half-brother Sir Edmund Arundel began reasserting his right to the Arundel inheritance and the fact that the annulment of 1344 has been misguided, if not illegal.

From the evidence available it is unlikely that the Arundel Tomb is that of Earl Richard II and Eleanor, unless the commission was changed after his death, but no evidence of this survives. It may be that the knight's effigy is that of Arundel, but that the image of the lady, which cannot be identified, does not belong to it and the present tomb is only a nineteenth-century fabrication. When in 1955 the poet Philip Larkin wrote his poem *An Arundel Tomb* he rightly pointed out that 'Time has transfigured them into/ Untruth. The stone fidelity/ They hardly meant has come to be/ Their final blazon'.

The Rich Earl and his wealth

Such was the renown of Earl Richard's wealth that in 1364 the abbot of Cluny had urged Edward III to prevent Arundel from travelling to the papal Curia at Avignon for risk of his being taken prisoner by the Compagnies, the bands of mercenaries which, having been left without occupation after the peace treaty of Brétigny, terrorised the south of France.[94] The trip was presumably linked with the papal summons Arundel had received regarding his dispute with William Lynne, bishop of Chichester. But the abbot of Cluny's concern was not completely selfless. He also hoped that if the earl would not undertake the journey he could represent him at the curia and, of course, be rewarded accordingly.

The fame of Arundel's wealth may have to do with the fact that much of it was in hard cash, a luxury other magnates did not have and which sets Earl Richard apart from the norm. At his death, Arundel had £72,173, of which £60,180 was in cash readily available in his treasuries. An exact calculation of Arundel's wealth is nonetheless predicated on the impossibility of accurately valuing the vast amount of furniture, jewellery, tapestries, and other paraphernalia that he bequeathed at his death, even if his executors valued his most precious gold and silver plate at £1,148.[95] The Arundel hoard was phenomenal, and even the Crown usually had far less. Indeed, the last time such a treasure was held by the Crown was at the end of Edward II's reign when it had amounted to £69,052, of which £65,536 was in silver coins.[96] Arundel's treasure is also particularly significant when compared with the Crown's revenue from taxation. If the king was able to expect about £38,000 from a single direct tax such as a tenth and fifteenth in time of peace, this amount could increase to £78,250 for the fiscal year of 1350-51. As for the widely unpopular third lay poll tax imposed in December 1380 it had been expected to yield £66,666.

Arundel thus had substantial riches at his disposal. It was the earl's good working relationship with Edward III that allowed him to become as rich as a king and to be tolerated as what is sometimes simplistically termed an over-mighty magnate. Certainly many of the favours granted were given because of his power and influence. It is undeniable that he must have used his vast wealth as a tool for political leverage to exert influence and pressure on members of the local and national government. Though no direct evidence survives of such activities, it is worth recalling that he instructed his executors to distribute, if

Two views of Arundel Castle
The painting at the top, by James Canter c.1770 complements
the lower drawing by S.H. Grimm of 1781. Both show the ruined 12th-century
keep and the gatehouse on the left. The other buildings shown are later

it proved necessary, 5,000 marks worth of bribes in the curia to prevent any attempt by his bastard, Edmund Arundel, to assert his claim to the Fitzalan inheritance, and it has also been suggested that Arundel similarly distributed a great deal of money in the curia to secure the bishopric of Ely for his son Thomas.[97]

The minutiae of Arundel's testament regarding the distribution of his monies, jewels, plate and other movables highlight his obsession with wealth. He bequeathed about £27,168, almost all the cash readily available at the time of his death in Arundel Castle.[98] In comparison, John of Gaunt, duke of Lancaster, the other great magnate of the time, left only £6,707 in his 1399 Will.[99] Arundel's wealth was in part due to his miserliness. He appears to have invested less in building works and the patronage of the Church and the arts than some of his fellow magnates. But he was an aristocrat, and was thus expected to live magnificently. He bought fine tapestries and silverware some of which he commissioned in London, Chichester, Arras, and Paris.[100] Through his will he financed the construction of a chantry known as the Fitzalan Chapel (see chapter 4), which can be admired at Arundel Castle to this day and in which a daily service in memory of the earls and their ancestors is still held. Earl Richard undertook extensive building work at Shrawardine Castle in Shropshire, and at Arundel, where he built a range on the west side of the south bailey incorporating a great hall, and the south range was converted into private rooms for family and guests, while on the east side of the courtyard were added lodgings for retainers. Not much is known about the interior, but the timber roof apparently resembled that at Windsor Castle. The works at Windsor were mainly supervised by William Wykeham, bishop of Winchester and master of the king's works.

All that remains of Shrawardine Castle, one of a pair of castles built to guard a ford across the Severn. Destroyed by the Welsh in 1212 it was rebuilt by the Fitzalans who renamed it Castle Isabel, and in the 1390s Castle Philippa

The bishop was among the largest ecclesiastic overlords in Sussex and thus naturally within the sphere of the earl of Arundel's authority and lordship, so it would certainly be possible that Wykeham made, or suggested, the designs for Arundel Castle. A badly damaged document, probably dating from the second half of the fourteenth century, records some extensive works carried out there and at a new house in Tortington; notably, repairs with plaster of paris made to the fireplace in the lord's chamber, a delivery of sea charcoal needed for works in the castle and the bailey, deliveries of carts of lead from Apuldram near Chichester, new locks with keys, a delivery of Purbeck stone, 5,000 nails ordered in London for construction at the castle, repair works at the portcullis, as well as a new boathouse.[101] At Shrawardine Castle, a fragment of an account of works for Michaelmas 1343 records the construction of a new chamber for the earl as well as of a new hall.[102]

At Oriel College Oxford, where his son, Thomas Arundel, was studying in the 1370s, Arundel sponsored the construction of a new chapel. The construction of the Oriel College chapel began after 22 March 1373, when the licence was granted. The works were finished in 1379, but remodelling works of 1621 left nothing of the original chapel, although it has been argued that possibly as early as 1420-21 a new chapel may have been consecrated in place of the original 1373 building as a new licence was granted in 1437. This is not certain,

View of Oriel College by John Bereblock, 1566 (Bodleian Library, MS Bodl. 13)

but the original chapel apparently stood on the north side of the quad, while by 1566 it stood opposite the gate of Corpus Christi College. If the chapel was reconstructed, some of the stained glass from the original chapel was preserved and transferred into the new building and was then described by Anthony Wood in about 1668. The windows, opposite Corpus gate, bore the arms of Earl Richard II and his wife Eleanor of Lancaster, and the royal arms of France and England, since Oriel was a foundation of Edward II. Another window bore the arms of the Beauchamps, with the inscription 'Ricardus comes Arundellie et Thom[masus] filius ejus ep[iscop]us Eliens[is] Istam Capellam construi Fecerunt'. In the north windows of the chapel were the arms of Earl Richard III and his wife Elizabeth de Bohun, Joan Fitzalan, Sir John Arundel and his wife Agnes Maltravers, Alice Arundel and Thomas Holland, earl of Kent.[103]

This iconographic programme is compelling and was surely intended to commemorate the earl's family, as well as his achievement in securing dynastic alliances with some of the most powerful families of his time. It was the celebration of a family and the mark of its might. This programme is not atypical, and is reminiscent of the contemporary, and probably better known, Etchingham church in Sussex erected by Sir William Etchingham to commemorate his family.[104] A further example of this genre, which unfortunately has not survived, existed in St Mary's church of Warwick, where the tomb of Earl Thomas Beauchamp (d.1369) and Katherine Mortimer was also conceived as a family monument, to judge from the figures of their sons and daughters in heraldic robes which originally filled the chancel windows. The windows were smashed by Parliamentary troops in 1642. The fact that the arms of Beauchamp are also present in Oriel college chapel highlights the close links between these two families, which can also be seen by the choice of Sir Richard Beauchamp as one of Arundel's executors.

That such heraldic windows were important in the affirmation of family bonds and power is demonstrated by another example that has survived in St Mary's church, Hopesay (Salop). The fragment there, preserved in the quatrefoil above the sub-arches, represents the arms of Arundel and Mortimer,

The Arundel Window at St Mary's Church, Hopesay, with the arms of Arundel on the left and Mortimer on the right

63

commemorating the marriage, in 1391, between Earl Richard III and Philippa Mortimer of Wigmore, dowager countess of Pembroke.[105] As Hopesay was a short distance from Clun this was a clear signal to the people of the region that the two families were now one. The last time this had been so was in the thirteenth century, when John III Fitzalan had married Isabella Mortimer of Wigmore.

Religion and family were hardly separate spheres for noble families. Indeed it was common that cadets would be destined for a career in the Church. In 1373, Pope Gregory XI had exhorted Thomas Arundel, when elected bishop of Ely at the unprecedentedly young age of only 20, to follow his father's 'example in defending ecclesiastical liberties'.[106] This statement was not intended as a simple compliment to his father's having obtained the bishopric for his son, but indicated the true nature of the relationship between the pope and Arundel. Certainly as one of the top diplomats of his time, and a wealthy one at that, Arundel was undoubtedly able to use to advantage his proximity to the papal curia. Arundel's generosity towards the Church was commensurate with his wealth. In 1355, whilst at the curia, he obtained an order to the archbishops of Canterbury and York to 'cause the feast of that saint [St Augustine] to be celebrated as a double in all churches of the realm, and servile work to be ceased ... whereas honour is due to St Augustine the apostle of England, who converted the English race to the Christian religion, and gave it the catholic faith, and first erected the English Church'.[107]

Earl Richard II also looked after his two brothers who had joined the ecclesiastic hierarchy. The eldest, Edmund (1319-1349), had been warden of the hospital of St Nicholas in Portsmouth and had also studied at Oxford.[108] In July 1339 he was king's clerk, and in 1342 Arundel petitioned the pope to grant him the reservation and prebend of Salisbury, in addition to a prebend in York and the wardenship of the hospital in Portsmouth, which he then already held.[109] By 1347 he was treasurer of Chichester, probably of the cathedral, and Arundel petitioned the pope for a dispensation for him to be elected bishop. He died, however, in 1349, probably of the plague.[110] The second brother, Michael, followed a similar career. He became a monk of St Martin's, possibly the Benedictine priory of St Martin in Dover (today Dover College), where he was a secretary and, probably as of 1345, also administrator of the monastery's possessions, as well as bailiff of Atherington in Devon.[111]

Arundel's readiness to lend money to the Crown, his fellow magnates and his affinity, as well as to merchants and people of his lordships, prevented him from becoming resented for his wealth. Between September 1369 and September 1374, for example, he advanced the Exchequer loans totalling £58,666, which financed the renewed war with France. The fourteenth century is peopled with bankers, financiers, and merchants who eventually faced bankruptcy: families such as the Bardi or the Peruzzi, or merchants like Michael de la Pole of Hull and Richard Lyons formed the financial elite of their time, but their dealings with the Crown eventually brought about their ruin.[112] Arundel's dynastical and political status perhaps protected him, to a great extent, from such a fate since his status enabled him to recover any money he lent within the terms of the agreement.

An inventory of creditors compiled after Arundel's death in 1376 shows that he lent to a wide range of people: the princess of Wales owed 1,000 marks for which she had pledged a brooch;[113] 1,500 marks was owed by chief justice Richard le Scrope; and 3,000 marks by Bishop Thomas Arundel. The latter sum was withheld by Arundel in his testament, hence, the bishop was awarded 3,000 marks less than his brother John.[114] Two sums not recorded on this inventory are 4,250 marks owed by William Ufford, earl of Suffolk since October 1371,[115] and another sum of £1,000 owed by Thomas Beauchamp, earl of Warwick since July 1372.[116] It is likely that these sums had been contracted to finance the military campaigns of 1372, which may explain why Earl Richard II allowed those debts to remain unpaid for so many years. It was, indeed, increasingly difficult for the Crown to find willing creditors and it is possibly a sign of Earl Richard III's unwillingness to lend money on his father's scale that he decided, in 1376, to recover these two long overdue debts.

Arundel's loans to the Crown and fellow magnates allowed the realm to conduct war, while on a smaller scale credit enabled local commerce to flourish. To perpetuate his loans Earl Richard II founded two chests of £100 each in Arundel and Oswestry, and one of 100 marks in Clun for the poor merchants of those communities.[117] The administration of these chests was assigned to the warden, the mayor, and some competent people of the town, whereby merchants in need of cash could borrow up to 20 marks. A merchant taking out a loan was to give a security of double the borrowed sum; if he did not pay the money back by a given date, his deposit would be sold, the borrowed amount returned to the chest and the remainder, if any, returned to the merchant. It is not possible to tell how well this system worked, but it was quite common for merchants themselves to leave at their death sums of money to be given to similar charitable funds, or to be distributed among poor households or neighbours. The practice was common also among the aristocracy as is illustrated by the example of Elizabeth de Burgh, the foundress of Clare College Cambridge and a patron who employed a great number of craftsmen and gave business to a number of merchant communities. In her testament, dated 25 September 1355, she ordered that the residue of her estate should be distributed between various charitable works, including a bequest to merchants who because of 'weakness', possibly due to illness or old age, had been bankrupted.[118] Similar funds were also managed by London guilds and companies.[119]

In his role as a lender Earl Richard II may have been personally in charge of authorising large loans to the Crown, the members of the royal family and his fellow magnates, who would turn to him on a personal basis to ask for money. For smaller investments Arundel used agents and officials to administer his wealth. On 30 January 1350, Thomas de Batesford, for instance, was given £300 'to traffic for the earl's profit, and to render account to him therefore when required paying the said sum with the profit thereof to the earl at Midsumer next' (24 June).[120] Batesford was a well-connected and experienced man when it came to money matters. In the 1340s he had been sheriff of Norfolk and Suffolk, in 1342 collector of fines in Suffolk, and in 1349-50 he was collector of subsidy and of the tenth and fifteenth. Batesford also used to borrow money from other earls, such as £240 from Derby in 1342 and £100 from Northampton in 1346, both close friends of Arundel.[121] As a well-connected man in Suffolk and Norfolk Batesford proved an asset for Arundel when dealing in those areas, especially after 1347, when Arundel secured the Warenne manors in Norfolk centred around the lordship of Castle Acre.

The most prominent and most important of Arundel's financial agents must undoubtedly have been John Philpot. His original trade was as a fishmonger, and as a prosperous London merchant he became very prominent in city politics in the 1370s.[122] His work for Arundel guaranteed him the earl's patronage and many financial advantages. Philpot was in charge of selling the earl's wool in London: in 1376, for instance, he sold wool worth £2,722, from which he had already taken a commission of 25% from the net profit. He was also in charge of the collection of certain monies due to the earl, which in 1376 amounted to £161; and he also owed 900 marks to the earl on the latter's death.[123] In 1372 and 1374 he had acted as the earl's attorney for loans contracted by John of Gaunt.[124] Philpot's service to the Fitzalans certainly helped him in his own career and the accumulation of his own large wealth: in 1372 he was sheriff and also became an alderman, in 1378 he became mayor of London, and from 1377 until 1379 he and William Walworth were treasurers for war, handling some £200,000 of the Crown's money, a clear indication of their reputation for expert money handling.[125] In 1412 Philpot's widow, Margaret Stodeye, was assessed at about £122 yearly, making her by far the richest person in London.

Something of Philpot's character is revealed in the story that, as mayor of London, he fitted out at his own expense a fleet with which he sailed to attack a pirate who had been a continuous threat to the English coast. His feat was a triumph and he was celebrated like a hero. Furthermore, his role, in 1381, in assisting King Richard II against Wat Tyler was rewarded with a knighthood. Although Philpot's most important political and military feats came after 1376, some credit for his later prominence can certainly be given to his service in Arundel's time. Arundel's patronage may have been of some help in securing the position of sheriff in 1372. More importantly it must be recognised that

Arundel surrounded himself with talented and trustworthy people: Philpot is certainly the most dramatic example and he was duly nominated as one of the earl's executors. John Philpot remained closely associated with the Fitzalans, and after 1376 he was still welcomed by Earl Richard II's children: in October 1383, for instance, he enjoyed the hospitality of Thomas Arundel, in gratitude for which Philpot sent him some quinces and a mare.[126] It is possible that he continued to act as a financial agent or advisor to the Fitzalans. Philpot also remembered the late Earl Richard II in his will, bequeathing 10 marks to the endowment of a chantry in the house of St Pancras at Lewes Priory, where Arundel was interred.[127]

The people Arundel dealt with and employed to manage business are important, but so are also the locations where his business took place. London was certainly important for Arundel since he regularly had to attend court at Westminster or Windsor. Arundel Castle was only two days away, while his castle at Reigate could be reached on the same day.[128] Arundel also had a London hostel, Beaumont's Inn situated near Fish Wharf, not far from London Bridge, which he bequeathed to Sir John Arundel.[129] The inn probably came into the Fitzalan family through Eleanor of Lancaster, whose first husband had been John, lord Beaumont. As the inn was near the Thames, Arundel could commute by boat to the palace of Westminster.

After John Arundel's death in 1379, the inn possibly devolved to his wife, Eleanor Maltravers, although no mention is made of it in their testaments.[130] Somehow by then renamed the New Inne, it came into the hands of William Montague, earl of Salisbury who was in possession of it in 1397.[131] It is possible that the inn passed into the Salisbury family at the marriage of William's son, another William, to Earl Richard III's daughter, Elizabeth. Tragically, William was accidentally killed by Arundel on 6 August 1382 during a tilting at Windsor.[132]

There was another inn connected with the family, for in June 1385 Earl Richard III acquired 'Pulteneyesyn' from the master and chaplains of the London college of St Laurence of Pultney, in exchange for the advowson of Napton in Warwickshire.[133] Pultney's Inn was the former London seat of the wealthy draper Sir John Pultney (d.1349), who is also remembered for his other grand residence, Penshurst Place in Kent. For a while Pultney's Inn was occupied by the Black Prince before it was delivered, in 1359, to Sir Nicholas de Loveyne, the new husband of Pultney's widow. In 1366, at the death without issue of Pultney's son, the house passed to the college. This residence was known, in 1422, to be called 'My Lady's Inne of Arundel', possibly because Beatrice of Portugal, countess of Arundel, lived there. After her death in 1439, the manor came into the possession of her husband, John Holland, earl of Huntingdon, who sold it to William de la Pole, earl of Suffolk. In 1603, it was know as the 'Manor of the Rose', and it was situated not far from Beaumont's Inn. Excavation work undertaken in 1994-97 on the present site of Governor's House unearthed remains of the inn. The site is presently between Laurence Pountney Lane and Suffolk Lane, also known, in 1439, as 'Arundelleslane'.[134]

By the time of his death on 24 January 1376 Earl Richard II was undoubtedly one of the wealthiest magnates in England. His estates provided him with an income but it was certainly his skilled investments in trade, land and the lucrative money-lending market that made his fortune. It is nonetheless apparent that this powerful earl became as rich as he did because he did not lavish large amounts of his wealth on castle building, religious patronage or even the arts, like some of his contemporaries such as the duke of Lancaster and the earls of Bohun and Warwick. This explains why much of his wealth was in hard cash rather than land, bricks and mortar, or even a wondrous library of manuscripts.

The vast quantities of cash he could command made him powerful and towards the end of Edward III's reign the Crown had to rely heavily on his loans. The tenure of the earldom of Arundel by Earl Richard II was a pivotal moment in the family's history. He changed his marital alliance in favour of a union with the house of Lancaster, he chose to be interred in Sussex rather than Shropshire, and crucially, he doubled the size of the Fitzalan estates. The Fitzalans had now made it to the highest echelons of society.

4 The Appellant Earl
Richard III Fitzalan, earl of Arundel and Surrey
(1346-1397)

When Earl Richard III succeeded his father in 1376 he inherited estates worth at least £3,000 yearly and about £45,000 in hard cash, about half of his father's disposable wealth, the remainder having been divided among the other heirs. Like his father before him, Arundel was the wealthiest magnate outside the royal family.[1] He was already aged 30. With his brother Sir John Arundel (*c*.1348-1379) he had been knighted by 1369 and had served in Picardy as one of the royal household knights. In 1371 Richard served in the retinue of his brother-in-law Humphrey de Bohun, earl of Hereford (d.1373).[2] Earl Richard III and his sister, Joan, had been betrothed, in 1359, to the siblings Elisabeth and Humphrey de Bohun. Joan and Humphrey had two daughters: Eleanor married, probably in 1376, Edward III's son, Thomas of Woodstock (created earl of Buckingham in 1377 and duke of Gloucester in 1385), and in 1381 Mary married Henry Bolingbroke (earl of Derby, later duke of Hereford and then of Lancaster, and king from 1399). The unions were particularly significant because Elisabeth and Mary were the co-heiresses of the profitable Bohun inheritance. Thomas of Woodstock, hoping to secure the entirety of the estates for himself, had attempted to persuade Mary to become a nun, but John of Gaunt, duke of Lancaster secured her marriage, and her Bohun share, for his son Bolingbroke.[3]

Sometime before 1364 Sir John Arundel had married Eleanor Maltravers, one of the two granddaughters and co-heiresses of John, lord Maltravers (d.1364). Sir John's firstborn, another John, was brought up in the royal household alongside Prince Richard.[4] In October 1376, Sir John was appointed by Parliament to lead an expedition to France. He embarked on 7 November 1377, before the dissolution of the parliament, and returned the following year having relieved the fortress of Brest. John was summoned to parliament from 1377, the year in which he also became marshal, in succession to Henry Percy, earl of Northumberland, and the following year he was again appointed to this office. He drowned in the Irish Sea on 15 December 1379.[5]

Their younger brother, Thomas Arundel (1353-1414), had been destined by their father to a career in the Church and was sent, in the early 1370s, to study at Oriel College, Oxford. In 1373 his father then secured him the bishopric of Ely.[6] It quickly became apparent that he was a particularly intelligent man and he was to have a successful career both in the Church and in the government as archbishop of York (1388-96) and then of Canterbury (1396-97 and 1399-1414), as well as chancellor of England (1386-89, 1391-96, 1406-09, and 1412-13) (see chapter 5).[7]

Prince Richard was aged ten when he ascended the throne in July 1377, but the child king could scarcely hope to offer the same lordship as had his grandfather Edward III, and his father the Black Prince, who had led the great military campaigns of the 1340s and 1350s and who had also, crucially, managed the aspirations of the higher nobility in such a way as to give it a secure sense of function and place.[8] However, the Black Prince's own chequered success in the administration of Aquitaine, which bordered more than once on the disastrous, suggests that similar failures were likely to have occurred in England if he had become king. The failure of King Richard II to establish cordial relationships with many of the great magnates, especially his uncle Thomas of Woodstock and Arundel, and the failure of his guardians to mediate his authority effectively, were factors which culminated in the violent purging of the royal household in the Merciless Parliament of 1388.

Though the king's guardians shared the responsibility in the mismanagement which created the political divisions of the 1380s, it must also be accepted that the king's own character was a destabilising factor. He was emotional, over-impressionable, and prone to violence especially against his own magnates.[9] Furthermore, his highly developed aesthetic sense of refinement, whether in art or cookery, meant that he was not necessarily inclined to share the martial interests of his barons and magnates.[10] He certainly set a sharp contrast with the previous bellicose reign, but Christopher Fletcher's recent work on the manhood of Richard II has challenged many of the biased assumptions about this 'absolutist, handkerchief-waving dilettante'.[11] Indeed, many of the derogatory aspersions about Richard II which were elaborated after his deposition, including by Archbishop Arundel, were concerned with the affirmation of his youthfulness and its conventional lessons of inconstancy and sin. This was used in conjunction with a manly and chivalrous portrayal of King Henry IV's own spin-doctored image to justify the usurpation of the Plantagenet throne by the Lancastrian dynasty.

Richard's coronation was the first for half a century and naturally attracted enormous popular interest. Arundel participated in his hereditary role as chief butler, in the same fashion as his grandfather Earl Edmund had officiated 70 years earlier at the coronation of Edward II. He may have been somewhat disappointed though, for in June he had petitioned the king to be allowed also to bear the second sword at the coronation, since John, the heir to the earldom of Pembroke, was still a minor. He claimed this in right of the earldom of Surrey but the honour was instead granted to the earl of March.[12]

On Richard II's accession no formal regent was appointed. It was only the second time since the Conquest that a child had succeeded to the throne. In 1216, during Henry III's minority, William Marshall (d.1219) was appointed regent, but in July 1377 no candidate seemed to fit the purpose. The king's uncle, John of Gaunt, duke of Lancaster, had alienated elements in the political community by undermining the achievements of the Good Parliament of 1376.[13] Furthermore, Lancaster was alleged to have his own aspirations to the throne, although he refuted these during the following parliament on 13 October, challenging the slanderers who claimed that he wanted the Crown and demanding that they be condemned as traitors. The barons, prelates, and commons all quickly reacted anxiously to his speech, assuring him that of course he was free of blame and asking him kindly to forgive those who may have rashly spoken against his honour. With no regent, Richard II governed between 1377 and 1380 assisted by a series of councils. Though Gaunt was omitted from these councils, his two brothers Edmund, earl of Cambridge and Thomas, earl of Buckingham were included. Other magnates to be appointed, though they did not serve on all the councils, included Arundel and Edmund Mortimer, earl of March, who was married to Philippa, Edward III's granddaughter.[14]

In 1377-78, the expeditions that were staged to repel the Franco-Castillian forces which had ravaged the Channel coast in the summer proved largely ineffectual. On 5 December 1377, Arundel was granted his father's old office of the Admiralty of the West, and Warwick that of the North. Much of the ravages that occurred in East Sussex were blamed on Arundel, who, the following July, fled in panic from the county, leaving Lewes Castle undefended, even though in March he had been ordered to secure his castles against attacks.[15] The ease with which the castle was taken later in 1381, during the Peasants' Revolt, suggests a lack of investment in its upkeep and defence. To add insult to injury, Arundel then offered to send 400 lances to protect his tenants, but only if the latter paid the wages. The chronicler Thomas Walsingham commented that despite his illustrious ancestry, Arundel showed utter incompetence.[16] Again, in 1378, Arundel and Salisbury were largely blamed for the failure of the siege of St Malo and Harfleur, from which ports the attacks against Sussex were directed.[17] Arundel was nonetheless reappointed to the royal council, which he had temporarily left during the fighting.[18]

In 1377, the first poll tax had been introduced to help finance the wars with France and the campaigns in Scotland, Wales and Ireland. It was unpopular but tolerated, though the increases in tax in 1379 and 1380 caused considerable unrest. In 1377 the king's jewels were handed to Arundel and the bishop of London, who had mediated a loan of £10,000 for the king from a number of

London merchants, including Nicholas Brembre, William Walworth, and John Philpot.[19] In March, Arundel and his brother John had already lent 5,000 marks to Edward III, showing a willingness to continue their father's commitment to the Crown's wars, though this was to be the last generous loan until 1395 when Arundel lent 2,000 marks towards a royal campaign in Ireland.[20] Arundel's unwillingness to make any further advances to the Exchequer on the scale of his father highlights the fact that there was no one in government capable of leaning on him sufficiently to make a loan, especially to a government to whose policies he was increasingly opposed. In January 1380, Arundel was appointed with the earls of March and Stafford to a parliamentary commission to examine royal receipt and expenditure. But there were also calls on Arundel to strengthen his military leadership since Sussex had again been ransacked by Franco-Castillian forces. As in 1377, the abbot of Battle Abbey led the resistance in Sussex, organising and paying for his own troops. Arundel's failure to defend his county was blamed for much of the damage, since his attitude discouraged less important men from resistance.[21]

The unpopular taxations and the unsuccessful military campaigns that were supposed to guarantee the safety of the English coast acted as catalysts for the considerable popular unrest which erupted in Essex and Kent in May 1381, soon to be known as the Peasants' Revolt.[22] By 10 June, the groups which had

The death of Wat Tyler (British Library MS Royal 18.E.i.f.175)

risen in these two counties converged and organised an advance on London, where they arrived two days later under the leadership of Wat Tyler. The king had already retreated for safety to the Tower of London, where he was joined by Archbishop Simon Sudbury, the chancellor, Robert Hales, the treasurer, and the earls of Arundel, Oxford, Warwick, Salisbury, and Derby. While the king then met the motley rebels at Mile End on 14 June, a splinter group made their way to London where they pillaged and destroyed the palace of Savoy, the richest mansion in England, which the dukes of Lancaster had erected at considerable expense (it allegedly cost as much as £35,000[23]). John of Gaunt, having heard of the revolt, had fled to Scotland, while his duchess was chased in a panic through the Midlands to Pontefract. The rebels then made their way to the Tower, where the drawbridge was down and little resistance was offered. They plundered the Tower, gained access to the royal chamber, and eventually found Sudbury and Hales in hiding in the chapel of St John in the White Tower. Both were beaten and dragged out to Tower Hill, where they were beheaded.[24] Henry Bolingbroke, the heir of the duke of Lancaster, against whom much of the rebels' anger was directed, had also been left behind at the Tower. Henry was seized and nearly suffered the same fate as Sudbury and Hales, but was saved by the intervention of John Ferrour, a former soldier and pensioner of the Black Prince.[25]

Once Richard II had succeeded in appeasing the rebels, he appointed Arundel as chancellor in place of the executed Archbishop Sudbury. For three days, 14-16 June, he held this office, as Anthony Goodman commented, 'for the invidious task of issuing the charters and liberties extorted from Richard'.[26] After that the seal was handed to Hugh Segrave, steward of the household. The earls Arundel, Buckingham, and Warwick showed unequalled support for Richard II during the revolt, and subsequently managed to suppress its remnants in the Midlands and Sussex. At this point in time there was no sign of what was to follow, which was to antagonise these three lords for the remainder of the reign.

In 1381, parliament entrusted Arundel and Sir Michael de la Pole, the chancellor, with the duty of residing in the household and counselling and governing the king.[27] The following year saw the beginning of Richard II's prodigal distribution of royal favours, among whose recipients, incidentally, was Arundel, and for which the Lords Appellant were subsequently to reprimand the king. Earlier, in September 1381, a fine of £100 had been remitted, and in February 1382 Arundel was granted goods which had been forfeited within the lordship of his brother Bishop Thomas. The earl of Warwick was similarly granted gifts and favours, and in 1382 the king acted as godfather to the earl's son, Richard.[28] Later, in July 1384, the nobility and the royal couple gathered at Arundel Castle to celebrate the marriage of Arundel's daughter Elisabeth to Thomas Mowbray, who had been created earl of Nottingham the previous year. But the graciousness and good humour of the celebration could not overshadow the fact that the king's relationship with Buckingham and Derby had grown sour, due to growing tension between himself and John of Gaunt.

The failure of the English army in Flanders in 1383 was followed by the first concerted protest against Richard's manner of government. In May 1384, at the Salisbury Parliament, Arundel blamed the decline of the realm on bad government:[29]

> You are aware, my lords, that any kingdom in which prudent government is lacking stands in peril of destruction; and the fact is now being illustrated before your eyes, since this country, which, as you know, began long ago through bad government to lose strength, is at present almost in a state of decay. Unless remedies are promptly applied for its relief and it is speedily rescued from the stormy whirlpool in which it is engulfed, there is reason to fear that it will very soon suffer enormous setbacks and crippling losses, leading to its collapse and the removal (which God forbid!) of all power to come subsequently to its aid.

Hearing this, the king, 'white with the passion which, at these words, pervaded his whole being', scowled at Arundel and told him to go to the devil.[30] The situation was only saved by the duke of Lancaster who was able to calm the king by glossing what Arundel had said. In the following parliament in November, the Commons complained that the king had followed bad counsel and that his household was badly ordered. This only confirms that Arundel and Michael de la Pole's supervision of the household had been half-hearted at best and that they were, in fact, partly responsible for the situation. This may also explain why the king was outraged at Arundel's remarks. De la Pole was the son of a wealthy and prominent wool merchant of Hull and in 1383 married Katharine, daughter of Hugh, earl of Stafford (d.1386). That same year de la Pole was appointed chancellor and in 1385 he was granted the earldom of Suffolk, which caused much uproar among the nobility. Thomas of Woodstock, in particular, had hoped to be allocated revenues from the Ufford inheritance. Originally it had been planned that this inheritance was to be closely linked with the Fitzalans since Earl Richard II had obtained for his daughter, Eleanor, who died sometime before 1376, the marriage of Robert Ufford, the eldest son and heir of Robert Ufford, earl of Suffolk (d.1369), but Robert died before his father and hence the title passed to his brother William (d.1382), and then eventually, to Michael de la Pole.[31]

The tensions between the king, the magnates, and the Commons continued well into 1385 and 1386, when they were prominently displayed during parliament. In October 1386, Richard II held out against the so-called Wonderful Parliament, which requested the dismissal of ministers. Lords and Commons sent Gloucester, created a duke the previous year, and Bishop Thomas Arundel as delegates to the king at Eltham, where the duke allegedly threatened Richard with deposition. The king agreed to attend parliament and on 23 October Suffolk delivered the Great Seal to Richard II who, the following day, handed it to Bishop Arundel and Gloucester, while Suffolk was impeached.[32] At this stage Gloucester and the Arundel brothers were heading not a long-matured 'opposition party', but a movement in parliament of fickle public opinion. On 20 November, a Continual Council was appointed without which the king was not to govern. Significantly it contained only two of the five future Appellants, Gloucester and Arundel. Bishop Arundel was appointed chancellor and included in the council, and as a supporter of his brother in the following years may, at times, be regarded as the 'sixth Appellant'.[33]

Richard II soon retired to Windsor, leaving the council permanently resident at Westminster, and for the next eleven months the king toured the country trying to raise supporters and preparing to recover his authority by force. The attack on the ministers in 1386 had been primarily a criticism of their conduct of affairs, their corruption, and their inefficiency. That in 1387 it developed into a constitutional conflict was largely due to the fact that Richard II chose to take a stand on his royal prerogative.[34] By the letters which granted the council its commission it was only empowered to act in domestic affairs, but from the beginning it acted as if it had wider competence. Over the winter, with the approval of parliament, the council began to make diplomatic and military preparations to launch an expedition to serve in the Channel under Arundel. On 10 December 1386, he was appointed admiral in the north and west, and a week later he was retained to serve the king with 2,500 men for three months from 1 March. By then Arundel had assembled 60 ships at Sandwich. This was less than a quarter of the 250 ships which the French had assembled off Cadzand in the Dutch province of Zeeland; but during the course of the fight a number of German and Dutch ships deserted to join Arundel. The sheer number of ships, rather than Arundel's skills, enabled the earl to win the battle in what was the worst disaster to befall French or Flemish shipping at sea in the second half of the fourteenth century.[35]

Arundel's victory also won him widespread popular support since one of the most widely noted effects of his victory was the sudden drop in wine prices. Between 8,000 and 9,000 tuns of wine were captured and subsequently sold in England for 4d a gallon, a fraction of the usual price.[36] Arundel's success at sea was crucial for it delivered England from the threat of invasion for the remainder of the reign. This should, however, not detract from the failure of the later stages of the campaign whose objective was to undermine Burgundian authority in Flanders. Though Burgundian government was temporarily shaken, no shift in the balance of power between England and France came about.

Arundel's victory was short-lived since the king had used his tour of the country to rally support and recover authority. In August 1387, the judges advised the king that in their opinion the 1386 commission was derogatory to the king's prerogative, and that its instigators deserved capital punishment.[37] The commission of 1386 was due to relinquish its power in November 1387, clearly suggesting that Richard was preparing an offensive against those who had so limited his power. Any impression that the Appellants' coalition was fully formed from the start is incorrect. Only Gloucester, Arundel, and Warwick initially worked together, the first occasion being in October 1386 at the Wonderful Parliament. But it was only from the autumn of 1387, when Richard II ordered Henry Percy, earl of Northumberland to have Arundel arrested at his castle of Reigate, that the three acted strongly in concert. Their junior partners, Derby and Nottingham, joined them in December 1387.[38]

The three senior lords each had their own reasons for resenting the court at the eve of the Wonderful Parliament since over the previous three years they had seen their influence on policy steadily diminished. The strategy they had advocated of taking an aggressive line against France had been disregarded in favour of a policy of conciliation which had weakened the realm and left it virtually defenceless, at least until 1387 when Arundel was finally able to secure an end to the attacks on English soil. Gloucester, furthermore, was dependent for his income on Exchequer goodwill. Small wonder that he became jealous of courtiers like de la Pole and Robert de Vere, earl of Oxford, who were showered with royal favours. For his part Warwick had seen his lordship progressively eroded by Richard II's ostentatious recruitment of the earl's retainers and men in the Midlands in 1387, directly challenging

A stone pyramid that covers the entrance to a basement room is all that now remains of Reigate Castle

the earl's local pre-eminence. Of three senior Lords Appellant, Nigel Saul notes that only Arundel 'took his stand out of genuine concern at the direction of policy'. As for the junior Appellants, Henry Bolingbroke and Thomas Mowbray, they probably harboured resentment against Robert de Vere, who had monopolised the king's favour. Thomas Mowbray (1366-1400), created earl of Nottingham in 1383, Earl Marshal in 1386 and duke of Norfolk in 1397, was the great-grandson of Thomas Brotherton, earl of Norfolk and Marshal of England, a half-brother of Edward II.[39] Henry Bolingbroke in particular faced a challenge from de Vere on the Lancastrian domains in the north-west where de Vere and his deputy Sir Thomas Molineux had recruited those who bore a grudge against the Lancastrian lordship, thus maintaining a position within the palatinate in independence of John of Gaunt and his affinity.[40]

Arundel, whom Northumberland had been unable to capture at Reigate, now joined forces with the other lords and, before 13 November, met Warwick and Gloucester at Harringhay Park, north of London.[41] The following day they moved to Waltham Cross. That same day all the members of the council met the earls at Waltham to arrange a meeting with the king. It was at this meeting that the lords made their first formal submission of the appeal of treason. The appellants' grievances were directed against a number of courtiers, including Robert de Vere, earl of Oxford, created marquess of Dublin in 1385 and duke of Ireland the following year, and the chancellor Michael de la Pole, created earl of Suffolk in 1385, who were accused of having encroached the royal prerogative and, through their counsel, of having enriched themselves at the expense of the realm, that is to say the other magnates and especially Gloucester, who as a son of Edward III, had to rely largely on the Exchequer for his income. Three days later, on Sunday 17 November, the three men, now known as the Lords Appellant, rode to Westminster to meet the king, and when they entered the Great Hall the three of them prostrated themselves before him. Richard, Lord Scrope, who had been deprived of the office of chancellor in 1382, speaking on their behalf, reaffirmed their opposition to the five they had accused of treason — Robert de Vere, Michael de la Pole, Alexander Neville, archbishop of York, Robert Tresilian, chief justice of the King's Bench, and Sir Nicholas Brembre, former mayor of London — and confirmed that they intended to proceed against them by way of appeal. Richard II assented to the petition and assigned a hearing in the next parliament, due to convene in February 1388.[42]

This escalation had caught the king and his courtiers unawares. De la Pole and Neville fled abroad, whilst de Vere was sent to Cheshire to mobilize an army to come to the king's rescue. By mid-December he had gathered about 3,000-4,000 men ready to go south. This news reached the Appellants from Arundel's garrison at Holt, in the vicinity of Chester. Gloucester and Arundel were in favour of deposing Richard, while Warwick, whose position in the end prevailed, argued that their quarrel was with de Vere, not the king. The three lords assembled their force and moved out of London to meet de Vere's army. On 12 December they were met at Huntingdon by Derby and Nottingham. On 19 December the Appellants met de Vere's force in the north Cotswolds, where he was defeated. Upon hearing the news, the king retreated to the Tower of London with a number of his councillors, to await his fate. On 30 December the five lords entered the Tower with 500 armed men. Though what happened next has been the subject of intense debate, it is commonly agreed that the lords rebuked the king for his duplicity and misgovernment and deposed him for two or three days. This blow to his prestige was to leave a profound mark on Richard II, who in later years was to become much preoccupied with his regality and its affirmation.[43]

The crisis also exposed the division that threatened the Appellant coalition. Derby and Nottingham were less hostile to the king than the three senior lords, since their grievance was mostly with de Vere, and they disagreed with Gloucester's plan to remove the king. Richard noticed these divisions and persuaded Derby and Nottingham to dine with him when the other three had left his chambers at the Tower. On 1 January the Appellants made their way to Westminster and assumed control over the royal household by purging from it a number of royal servants and arresting others.[44]

The trial of the five accused opened on 3 February 1388 in the White Hall at Westminster. The aim of the appeal of treason was to set out the offences of which the appellees stood accused; most of the clauses were concerned with the undue influence they had exerted over the king to their own personal gain, as well as Richard's defiance of the council of 1386-87. The emphasis was put on the appellees who had used their undue influence to encourage the king to take military action against the Appellants.[45] The aptly-named Merciless Parliament concluded in May with the execution of a number of members of the court's inner circle. On 1 June the king entertained the lords at a banquet customarily given at the end of a parliament, and two days later they attended a solemn mass in Westminster Abbey that was to mark their symbolic reconciliation. During the service the king renewed his coronation oath and the lords their oaths of allegiance, in view of the events which had taken place in the Tower the previous December.[46]

The royal Christmas celebrations of 1388 were kept at Eltham in Kent. They were a stark contrast to those of the previous dark year. As the Westminster chronicler noted, 'numerous tourneys and pleasant pastimes suitable of the season' marked the festivities.[47] The following May the king held a council at Westminster at which he declared his intention of ruling in person now that he had come of age and proceeded to dismiss a number of officials whom he had been forced to accept by the Appellants. Thomas Arundel, who had succeeded

Alexander Neville as archbishop of York in 1388, was dismissed as chancellor.[48] The Appellants had been caught unprepared by Richard's assumption of power and reshuffle of the council. That same month the admiralty of the West was granted to Huntingdon and that of the North to Lord Beaumont, thus prematurely terminating the grant which in March 1388 had been made to Arundel for five years. Three weeks later Arundel obtained royal licence to go abroad on a pilgrimage to the Holy Land, but soon afterwards the licence was revoked.[49] It was a sign of the dramatic change that Richard II had been able to bring about that a man who had recently been at the peak of influence contemplated leaving the realm on a prolonged and dangerous expedition. On 9 July, the king dismissed from his household more people whom he considered to be closely associated with the Appellants. The political outlook remained uncertain.

During the next few years the Appellants were eclipsed at court and disappeared from the lists of those present at council meetings. In November 1389, John of Gaunt returned from France after an absence abroad of over three years. He soon met the king at Reading, where Richard II adopted the duke's livery collar of Esses to signify their new-made concord. At the same great council meeting the king pardoned the Appellants and at the parliament which met in January 1390, Lancaster and Gloucester were formally appointed councillors.[50] On 24 July, Lancaster welcomed guests to a magnificent hunting party at Leicester. Among the guests were the royal couple, the dukes of York and Gloucester, the earl of Arundel and his brother Archbishop Thomas, and the Earl Marshal. The event turned out to be of great significance for when Lancaster asked the king to pardon one of his dependants, John Northampton, the king cleverly replied that it was not in his power to make such a grant. Well aware of the king's predicament, Gaunt retorted that 'On the contrary ... you could do that and more. God forbid that your power should be so cramped that you could not extend grace to your liege subjects when the circumstances call for such action.' Richard's reaction showed his resentment at the exile endured by some of his own friends: 'If I can do what you say, there are others who have suffered great hardship; so that I know what to do for my own friends who are now overseas.'[51] This marked the beginning of a new understanding between Richard and Lancaster.

In 1391, Arundel married Philippa Mortimer, dowager countess of Pembroke, thus considerably extending his power in the Welsh Marches.[52] Next to his own lordships Arundel controlled a third of the lordship of Abergavenny after the death of its lord in 1389; and from 1384-93 he chaired the consortium that administered the Mortimer inheritance.[53] Between August and December 1394, Arundel also vigorously pursued cases in the King's Bench for the assignment of Philippa's dower lands in Ireland, Herefordshire, Pembrokeshire, and the March of Wales.[54] This showed that despite Arundel's temporary exile from court his lordship and influence remained considerable. On 14 February 1392, he was reappointed to the great council which had been taking measures to prepare a campaign against the French. Archbishop Thomas Arundel had also been readmitted to court the previous September, and had once again become chancellor.[55] The possibility of an imminent war and its concomitant financial and political difficulties undoubtedly forced Richard II to reunite the baronage and the body politic.

Once more the king desired to settle for peace with France. However, Arundel and Gloucester were joined by the commons in their concerns, since the French demanded that the English king should renounce all right or claim to the French throne and therefore that he should also drop the fleur-de-lys from his coat of arms. Regarding the English territories in France the French demanded that Normandy and Artois should be surrendered, and that Aquitaine be granted to the duke of Berry with a reversionary right to the duke of Lancaster and his heirs who would then hold it as lieges of the king of France.[56] A truce was agreed in the meantime, until the demands could be considered and be submitted to parliament for discussion. In January 1393, parliament met at Winchester and approved the continuation of the peace negotiations, Lancaster and Gloucester being appointed to a new delegation to treat with the French.[57] That same year the people of Cheshire rebelled, complaining that Lancaster, Derby, and Gloucester intended to surrender to the French demands. It was this episode that made government aware of the scale of the popular opposition to peace. Gloucester, who had been appointed justice of Chester in succession to Robert de Vere in 1388, was thus placed in the position of having to suppress the rebels. Arundel, who, like Gloucester, must have sympathised with the rebels failed to come to Gloucester's assistance despite residing at nearby Holt Castle with an armed force at the time of the revolt.[58]

In the parliament that followed in 1394 Arundel was accused of supporting the Cheshire rebels. Arundel launched a characteristically rash verbal assault against the king and Lancaster, complaining among other things that Richard II and his uncle were too intimate, that the king and members of his retinue should not wear the duke's livery collar, and that Lancaster was so over-bearing in meetings of the royal council that other lords dared not speak their minds. Arundel was perhaps angling for support, but his attempt backfired; he received no backing from his fellow lords and was forced to make a humiliating apology to Lancaster in full parliament. On 30 April 1394 he took the precaution of securing a comprehensive pardon from the king.[59]

However, on 3 August, Arundel and the king clashed again when the former arrived late for Queen Anne's funeral at Westminster Abbey, and then promptly asked leave to depart. Arundel had undoubtedly shown little sympathy for the king, who was so grief-stricken upon Anne's death that he had the palace at Sheen, where she died of the plague, razed to the ground. So incensed was the king that he seized a baton from an attendant and struck Arundel on the head with it so forcefully that he fell to the ground with blood streaming over the floor.[60] Arundel was then imprisoned in the Tower of London for a week, and only released on a bail of £40,000, an amount which suggests that Arundel was still extremely wealthy.[61] Nor did his relations with the king improve thereafter. He continued to raise objections to the terms of both the peace negotiations with France and the conditions attached to the 28-year Anglo-French truce of 1396.

On 10 July 1397, without any warning, Richard II ordered the arrest of the three senior Lords Appellant. Warwick was arrested at a banquet in London to which he had been lured by the king. Gloucester was seized at his castle of Pleshey, near Chelmsford in Essex, and Arundel was persuaded by his brother Archbishop Thomas to give himself up at Reigate, after the king swore he would not suffer any bodily harm. Arundel reluctantly obeyed and was placed in the custody of Thomas Mowbray, his son-in-law, and sent to the Isle of Wight.[62] The reason the king gave for the arrest was that the lords had recently committed offences including plotting against the king; it was emphasized that these accusations had nothing to do with the revolt of 1387-88. However, it is clear that the king was moved by revenge as well as concern at his inability to control his own barons. The German electors whose envoys were sent to Richard to offer him the imperial crown implied that he was not fit to wear it if he could not control his own subjects at home. What is certain is that by 1397 Richard was experiencing renewed criticism of his style of government, which at times was described as tyrannical.[63] The Appellants' arrest was his reaction to the mounting pressure he was experiencing.

Two months later, in September, Gloucester, Warwick, and Arundel were put on trial by appeal in parliament. Arundel was brought into parliament on 21 September to face his accusers. He conducted himself with a degree of courage and defiance which clearly made a strong impression on the chroniclers of the time, for several of them included vivid descriptions of the events:[64]

Then, once they had pledged themselves to prosecute their appeal, Richard earl of Arundel was brought to trial dressed in a red robe and scarlet hood; and immediately the duke of Lancaster said to Lord Nevill, 'Remove his belt and hood,' which was done. But when the articles were read to the earl, he vigorously denied that he was a traitor, and claimed the benefit of the pardon which had previously been granted to him, declaring that it was never his intention to withdraw himself from the king's grace. The duke of Lancaster said to him, 'Traitor, that pardon is revoked'. 'That is a lie', replied the earl, 'I was never a traitor'. 'Why did you ask for a pardon then?' said the duke of Lancaster. 'To silence the tongues of my enemies', replied the earl, 'of whom you are one. And I tell you this for sure, that when it comes to treason you need a pardon more than I do'. The king said to him, 'Answer your appeal.' The earl replied: 'I can see perfectly well that these people presenting these appeals and accusing me of treason are all liars. I never was a traitor. I insist on claiming the benefit of my pardon, that pardon which you, of your own volition, within the past six years, at a time when you were of full age and free to act as you wished, granted to me'. 'I granted it on condition that it was not to my own prejudice', replied the king. 'Thus the grant is invalid,' said the duke of Lancaster. 'I tell you this,' replied the earl, 'I knew no more at the time about that pardon than you did, and you were out of the country.'

Then Sir John Bussy said, 'That pardon is revoked by the king, the lords, and us, the faithful commons.' 'Where are those faithful commons?' retorted the earl, 'I know you and your crew well enough, and why you have gathered here – not to act in good faith, for the faithful commons of the realm are not here. They, I know, are grieving greatly for me. But you, as I know only too well, have always been false.' Then Bussy and his fellows cried out, 'You see, lord king, how this traitor is trying to stir up trouble between us and the commons of the realm who have remained at home.' 'You are all liars,' replied the earl, 'I am not a traitor.'

... Then the earl of Derby rose to his feet and said to him, 'Did you not say to me at Huntingdon, where we initially gathered in rebellion, that before doing anything else it would be best to seize the king?' 'You, earl of Derby, you are lying through your teeth', replied the earl. 'I never considered any action against our lord king except what was in his interests and to his honour.' Then the king himself said to him, 'Did you not say to me in the bath-house behind the white hall, at the time of your parliament, that there were a number of reasons why my knight Sir Simon Burley deserved to die? To which I replied that I could see no reason why he should die – but even so you and your fellows treacherously put him to death.'

... Then the duke of Lancaster passed sentence of death on him as follows: 'Richard – I, the steward of England, do adjudge you a traitor, and I condemn you, by the final and definitive process, to be drawn, hanged, beheaded, and quartered, and your lands, entailed and unentailed, to be confiscated.' In recognition of his birth, however, the king ordered him to be beheaded only.

Gloucester did not face the charges brought against him since in the summer he had been despatched to Calais, where he was allegedly murdered by Thomas Mowbray, earl of Nottingham. It is undeniable that Mowbray and Thomas Holland, earl of Kent, Arundel's nephew, were moved by their desire to advance their interests through the downfall of the Appellants. Both clearly coveted Arundel's fortune and hoped to capitalise on the Appellants' demise to advance their territorial interests and influence. Warwick so prostrated himself before the king, 'like a wretched old woman, he began to weep and sob and wail', that he was reprieved and banished to the Isle of Man.[65] To contemporaries his performance must have been a saddening sight to end an otherwise brilliant military and political career.

Arundel's performance was quite the opposite. Thomas Walsingham described how the earl hardly reacted at his death sentence, his face not more changing colour than if he had been invited to a banquet. When he was escorted from the hall he turned towards Mowbray and Holland and warned them that it would not be long before the same fate would befall them. When he was brought to the site where the execution was to take place, he tested the blade with his finger and jovially commented on the sharpness of the blade. His head was severed with a single stroke.[66]

In the wake of his triumph King Richard rewarded his chief supporters and, at the same time, remodelled the peerage. On 29 September 1397, among those elevated was Nottingham, who became duke of Norfolk, Huntingdon, now duke of Exeter, Derby duke of Hereford, and Kent duke of Surrey. All the new dukes or earls were duly endowed with forfeited lands of the Appellants to a level appropriate to their new dignity. Huntingdon was given Reigate and the bulk of Arundel's Sussex properties, and Thomas Percy, who had become earl of Worcester, was given Arundel's Welsh Marcher property.[67]

The chronicler Adam of Usk commented on Arundel: 'Would that I might be deemed worthy to accompany his soul, for I have no doubt that he has been admitted to the fellowship of the saints.'[68] Indeed, not only did Arundel face his accuser and his execution with great poise but at the precise moment his head was severed a miracle is said to have occurred. His body rose to say the Lord's prayer before falling to the ground again, which led the Commons immediately to declare him a martyr, even organising pilgrimages to his tomb in the Austin Friars Church in London.[69] For fear of popular revolt, the king, to whom Arundel's ghost had appeared in nightmares, ordered that the grave be covered by a pavement, and all markings erased.[70] Another tomb was later erected by Arundel's son, Earl Thomas, on the north side of the choir; it was said to be 'a sumptuouse toumbe of marble stone'.[71]

That Arundel was buried in London is interesting in itself, for in his testament he had expressed the wish to be buried in Lewes Priory where his parents and his brother, Sir John Arundel, were interred.[72] The Austin Friars church had been founded, in 1252, by Humphrey de Bohun, earl of Hereford and rebuilt a century later by his successor and namesake. The steeple, rebuilt in 1362, was considered among the tallest and finest in London. The church was remarkable in its size, exceeding even cathedrals such as Exeter, Ely and Winchester, and hence became a favourite burial place for many aristocrats. It survived the Dissolution relatively unscathed, so Arundel's tomb could still be seen in the early seventeenth century, but in 1865 a fire completely destroyed the nave and the church was rebuilt. By the late nineteenth century only some slabs of Purbeck marble were still visible, and the brasses had gone.[73] Eventually the church was completely destroyed by bombing in 1940; the present neoclassical church is entirely modern, but still on the original site not far from the Bank of England.

The Austin Friars church was under Bohun patronage, through Arundel's sister Joan Fitzalan, dowager countess of Hereford, which may explain why his cult was so quickly promoted and encouraged. Furthermore, as one of the largest and most visible of the city's churches its famous spire became the beacon around which his cult was celebrated. Not surprisingly, Richard II ordered that Gloucester's body be interred at Bermondsey Priory in Surrey, in the obscurity of the suburbs, rather than in Broad Street with Arundel.[74] But despite all the king's efforts to eradicate the cult it survived until about 1404, when the last references to Arundel's miracles are mentioned.[75]

Earl Richard's cult is also of interest since it appears that at about the same time an attempt was made to promote his grandfather, Earl Edmund, as a martyr to King Edward II's cause.[76] Traces of the cult have survived in a Psalter which was once in King Henry IV's library, possibly through his wife, Mary de Bohun, whose mother, Countess Joan Fitzalan, commissioned part of the imagery (see images pp.29-30). Of course, as Earl Edmund's granddaughter and Earl Richard III's sister it was in her family's interests to promote Edmund and Richard as true martyrs to their kings' causes. It is evident that the cults of Earl Richard and Earl Edmund are closely linked to the long tradition of English political saints. Since not all noblemen were seen as saints, but almost all saints came from the nobility, the fabrication of Earl Edmund's martyrdom and the promotion of that of Earl Richard enabled the Fitzalans to underline their political agenda. Thus the family participated in the mystical propaganda of its martyrs, which allowed them to portray themselves as the legitimate councillors of kings. The association of Earl Edmund's cult with Psalm 5 in the Egerton Psalter and St Edmund of East Anglia particularly emphasizes the role of the just councillor, betrayed by those wicked and deceitful courtiers whose monopoly of the royal ear and favour turned the king away from his legitimate councillors. The association of these themes with the political events of the 1386 Commission, the 1387-88 Appeal of Treason and, earlier in the century, the 1310-11 Ordinances is clearly directed towards justifying the Fitzalans' right, and duty to intervene in matters of royal prerogative.

The Fitzalan Chapel, Arundel
Earl Richard is undeniably best known for his role as one of Lords Appellant which determined the last ten years of his career, but he also deserves to be remembered as the builder of his most enduring monument, the Fitzalan Chapel at Arundel Castle. After his father's death in 1376, much of Arundel's energy

was spent on the execution of his father's will and in particular the construction of the chantry he had requested. The reason for its foundation was that when, in 1344, Earl Richard II had secured the annulment of his marriage to Isabella Despenser he had been required to found three chaplaincies as penance.[77] It is rather remarkable that Earl Richard II never completed the penance, suggesting a mixture of superficial piety and niggardliness which moved him to post-

The Fitzalan Chapel with the tomb of Henry, 15th duke of Norfolk (d.1917) in the foreground and Earl Thomas (d.1415) and Beatrice of Portugal (d.1439) in front of the altar (Arundel Castle Trustees Ltd)

pone it for as long as he could. Only later, in 1355, when Arundel was on an embassy to the curia, did he obtain papal authorisation to found this college in the chapel of his castle.[78] As a matter of fact the castle already had two existing chapels. The chapel of St George was in the south-east wing of Arundel Castle, to which had already been transferred the service of the other castle-chapel, St Martin-within-the-Keep.[79] By the time of Arundel's death, however, little work had been done. He thus left 1,000 marks to buy lands or rents worth 107 marks yearly to maintain six chaplains and three children who could read and

Roof bosses from the Fitzalan Chapel, drawn by S.H. Grimm in c.1781. When Grimm visited Arundel in May 1780 he drew bosses from the original ceiling of the late fourteenth century. This contained some 75 bosses with a central line of angels bearing musical instruments, and lines either side of various figures, notably old men with beards. Over the windows were small single heads, some wearing mitres. This ceiling was replaced in 1782, and again sometime between 1886 and 1902, when 38 of the original bosses were retrieved, some from an outhouse in Poling, and reinstated. The bosses at the bottom are in a different style, possibly indicating that they were in the Lady Chapel which was added on the north side, probably in the early 15th century (British Library, Add. MS 5674 f.22)

sing reasonably well.[80] When one of the chaplains became too weak or ill to carry on with his duty, he could retire and reside in the priory of Tortington, which lies on the west bank of the river Arun south of Arundel.[81]

Earl Richard III changed the foundation plans by rebuilding the Benedictine priory of Arundel and its attached parochial church of St Nicholas, both of which were in a state of decay and had been left 'utterly desolate', the monks having withdrawn to their motherhouse, the French abbey of St Martin, in Séez.[82] These monks had also been among the beneficiaries of Arundel's will to the tune of 100 marks together with lands which he had bought from Tortington Priory. These grants should have secured a chaplain in charge of celebrating masses for his soul in perpetuity.[83] That the changes in the foundation had not been an easy decision for Earl Richard III is shown in his 1392 will. He was worried that he had not fulfilled his father's last wishes precisely, but hoped nevertheless that the changes he had made were all for the better.[84] On 1 April 1380, Arundel obtained royal permission to dissolve the priory, then in the king's hands, and to attach its revenues to the new college, subject to an annual payment of 20 marks, and the first statutes were issued on 24 May 1380.[85] A new church and conventual buildings, the first ready in 1380, were built to provide enough space for the thirteen clerks.[86] At the Dissolution the college was valued at £168 yearly.[87] Much later the foundation was restored by Henry, duke of Norfolk (d.1917), who began large-scale rebuilding works at the castle in 1877.[88]

The new foundation comprised three parts. The first was a parish church for the townspeople of Arundel dedicated to St Nicholas, as the previous church had been. The second was the collegiate chantry chapel, separated to the east by an iron grille, and nowadays known as the Fitzalan Chapel, which later became a burial place to the earls of Arundel. Earl Thomas was the first to be buried there, in front of the high altar, in 1415. Accommodation for the twelve priests and a house for the master were provided in a two-storeyed quadrangle to the south-east of the chancel, which still partly survives. The third part of the foundation was an almshouse, or *Maison Dieu*, for the old and infirm, which occupied a further quadrangle to the west of the parish church.[89] The church was built on a cruciform plan, whereby the collegiate chapel housed the high altar and the choir. The nave, which was completed after 1381, was built under plans by Henry Yevele, who is also known for his work at Westminster Abbey and Canterbury Cathedral.

The corbel heads in the nave's walls may be Yevele's personal work, and some may be the caricature of members of the collegiate community as well as of the comital family. Other images such as carved wooden bosses represent, for instance, the head of a youthful bishop, which could be a reference to Thomas Arundel who had been elevated at a very young age.[90] The iconography of the wall paintings is also interesting, in particular the two fragments of fourteenth-century fresco. The two fragmentary wall paintings are, over the north door, the Seven Deadly Sins or Pride and her Six Daughters, representing a large central figure with, proceeding from various parts of the body, dragons in whose mouths are depicted scenes of the deadly sins; while on the north wall of the north aisle is represented the Wheel of the Seven Corporal Works of Mercy arranged in a circle around the figure of an angel or a saint.

It is a common observation that the complexion of a life is in great measure decided by the particular circumstances that surround it. Arundel lived in a time and reign very different from the previous one he had known when his father was still alive. M.A. Tierney was undoubtedly too rash in branding Earl Richard as the earl of Arundel who 'became the leader of a faction, a conspirator against the authority of his sovereign, and has left a name sullied by reproach, if not by crime, to darken the more honourable achievements of his life'.[91] Arundel was a religious man much concerned with the memory of his father, as well as a family man. His role as one of the premier earls of the realm in terms of wealth and influence naturally predestined him to become a companion and councillor of his king. Arundel's interests and political convictions, however, were at times diametrically opposed to those of Richard II and his court. The extraordinary drama between the king and Arundel at Queen Anne's funeral only confirmed that no reconciliation between the two men would ever be possible. The consequences of the events of 1386-88 were too far-reaching for the king simply to forgive and forget, whilst Arundel's composure at his execution suggests that he may truly have believed that his deeds had been in the realm's interests. Richard II's overthrow by Henry Bolingbroke in 1399 partly vindicated the death of one of the most vociferous critics of the Ricardian regime who truly became the people's martyr to the Appellant cause.

5 The Last Earl
Thomas Fitzalan, earl of Arundel and Surrey
(1381-1415)

Thomas Fitzalan was the second son and surviving heir of Richard III Fitzalan, earl of Arundel and Surrey, and Elizabeth de Bohun. On the execution of Thomas's father in 1397, the castle and honour of Arundel was granted to King Richard's half-brother John Holland, duke of Exeter, to whose custody the 16-year-old Thomas was committed. Exeter's treatment of Thomas was at best callous, Thomas, for example, allegedly being forced to black his jailor's boots.[1]

Thomas was held prisoner at Reigate Castle but within a few months had escaped and joined his uncle, Archbishop Thomas, in Cologne.[2] At the fall of the Lords Appellant in 1397 Archbishop Thomas had been deposed from his see of Canterbury and translated to St Andrew's in Scotland — that is to say, as far away as possible from Westminster. However, at the end of October 1397, the prelate left England in order to plead his case with the pope in Rome.[3] In this he was not successful, and he spent the following months in Rome, Florence, and Cologne before, eventually, moving to Paris to join those who had gathered round their fellow exile, Henry Bolingbroke, son of John of Gaunt, duke of Lancaster. In the months, and indeed years, that followed the fate of the two Fitzalans was closely linked to that of Bolingbroke. The two families were also tied by the marriage of Henry and Mary de Bohun (d.1394), the niece of Archbishop Thomas; and the fact that the heirs of both families had been affected by their fathers' exile.

Henry Bolingbroke was exiled in September 1398 and left for France the following month. On his father's advice he settled in Paris, where he was welcomed by King Charles VI and his uncles, and it was there that he heard the news of his father's death on 3 February 1399. During this time Bolingbroke had been allowed an annuity of £2,000 which enabled him to maintain himself in style at his residence, the Hôtel de Clisson in what is now the Rue des Archives. The French court was broadly favourable to Henry and saw his exile as unjust, especially when in March 1399 his inheritance was declared forfeit and his exile extended from ten years to life.[4] That autumn, his wife having died five years earlier, Henry began negotiating for the hand of the daughter of John, duke of Berry, King Charles's uncle, which would have given him a powerful ally in his campaign to recover his inheritance. However, King Richard II had a strong ally in Berry's brother, Philip the Bold, duke of Burgundy, and used this influence to thwart Henry's intentions, for Philip was eager to maintain good relationships with England in view of his Flemish interests. In 1369 Philip had married Margaret of Flanders, and thus in 1384, when her father died, he became count of Flanders. Since 1392, when Charles VI's madness no longer enabled him to carry out his duties, Philip had furthermore effectively taken control of French government and was thus able to prevent the proposed union between Henry and the duke of Berry's daughter Mary.[5]

Philip the Bold faced mounting threats from his nephew Louis, duke of Orléans, whose intention it was to increase the size of his own dominions into Italy and Périgord, on the borders of English-held Aquitaine. At this stage, Louis had a strong supporter in his uncle the duke of Berry who, as lieutenant general of all regions south of the Loire since 1380, was in control of the government of Languedoc. Orléans' expansionist intentions were clearly not amenable to the English. By 1399, it had therefore become clear to Duke Louis that if he was seriously going to pursue his territorial expansions he needed to put an end to the understanding between Burgundy and Richard II. In the spring of that year Louis approached Henry Bolingbroke and, on 17 June, whilst the dukes of Burgundy and Berry were absent from Paris for the summer, the two men entered into a treaty of friendship. Bolingbroke and Orléans were able to approach and obtain unhindered the blessing of notable figures including Duke Louis's brother, Charles VI.[6] Although the terms were innocent enough it was clear that Henry was counting on Louis to assist him in regaining his inheritance. It is doubtful whether at this stage Bolingbroke had any design on the Crown.

In May 1399, King Richard II had informed his father-in-law, Charles VI, that he was leaving England for an expedition to Ireland. Henry Bolingbroke must have realised that this provided an opportunity to strike. By late spring Archbishop Arundel and his nephew, Thomas, had joined Henry and his retainers in Paris.[7] Henry and his entourage then left for Boulogne where a fleet, which had been sent from England by his sympathizers, awaited to bring him home. Though the preparations had been secret, the movements of sizeable numbers of men and ships alerted the duke of Burgundy and Edmund, duke of York, the keeper of England during Richard II's absence. Nevertheless, at the end of June Bolingbroke landed at Ravenspur in Yorkshire. By 16 July he had secured the support of the most powerful northern lords, including Henry Percy, earl of Northumberland and his son Henry Percy, known as 'Hotspur', who had become increasingly disillusioned with King Richard's handling of northern affairs.[8] Having officially obtained the support of Percy at Doncaster, Henry began slowly moving south. Richard II had been informed early in July of Henry's invasion but reacted slowly and inappropriately. Possibly on the advice of Edward, duke of Aumerle (formerly earl of Rutland), the king called off a speedy return to England. Instead he sent the earl of Salisbury with a small retinue to north Wales around 17 July. Salisbury was, however, unable to muster the Welshmen. In part they did not trust him but, more importantly, they believed that the king must have been killed, assuming that if he was alive, he would have returned to England to face Bolingbroke himself.

By 27 July Bolingbroke had caught up with the forces of the duke of York at Berkeley. It is likely that York had been unable to hold his troops together and that a great number had already deserted him. York therefore offered his capitulation to Henry and the following day the two men moved towards Bristol. There the constable, Sir Peter Courtenay, surrendered immediately on receiving York's orders. By the time the king did return at the end of July he was left with little support. By early August the king was at Carmarthen and in a changing and febrile mood. Initial plans to move through Glamorgan and meet Bolingbroke in battle were abandoned, and so was the plan to link up with Salisbury's forces in the north. Eventually, as rumours of a plot to capture him began circulating, Richard II fled to the north in the dead of night disguised as a priest, with a small group of men including the dukes of Exeter and Surrey, Thomas Despenser, earl of Gloucester and the bishops of Carlisle, Lincoln and St David's. When the king's flight was discovered, Thomas Percy, earl of Worcester (brother of the earl of Northumberland) and steward of the household broke his rod of office in tears and told the king's followers to disperse.[9] He must have known that the end of the reign was now near.

The king managed to reach Conway, Chester having already fallen to Bolingbroke, but was now forced to negotiate. On 11 August he agreed to meet the earl of Northumberland and Archbishop Arundel. It is generally accepted that Northumberland told Richard that Henry was in favour of a peaceful settlement if three conditions were met: first, that Henry's inheritance should be restored to him; second, that parliament should be summoned and that Henry should preside over it as steward; and thirdly, that the dukes of Exeter and Surrey, the earl of Salisbury and a number of other royal councillors should be put on trial for treason. By 15 August an agreement was reached and the king and Northumberland travelled to Flint where the earl entertained the king; but as both were aware, the king was now effectively the earl's prisoner. The following day Bolingbroke entered Flint. In the morning Richard II met with Archbishop Arundel, the duke of Aumerle and the earl of Worcester who reassured him of Henry's intentions. After lunch Henry entered the castle where he met Richard II in a courteous encounter and, later that afternoon, they set out for Chester, Richard's heartland. The reception there was much cooler than at Flint. Richard was taken straight to the highest tower of the castle and entrusted, no doubt to his horror, to the sons of the late duke of Gloucester and earl of Arundel, men he had had executed in 1397.[10]

On 19 August, Duke Henry issued summonses in the king's name for a parliament to meet at the end of September. The entourage left Chester and about 1 September arrived in London, where Richard was dispatched to the Tower, of which Thomas Fitzalan was appointed governor.[11] But towards the end of August it had become apparent that Henry's intentions were changing, especially with the appointment of a committee to enquire into the legitimacy of placing him on the throne. The committee's role was to legitimise the entirely illegitimate act of deposition by finding precedents that would suit the occasion.[12] Henry knew that Richard was vengeful and could not be trusted; the punishment the king had inflicted on the Lords Appellant in 1397 was sufficient reminder of what could befall him.

On 29 September, under pressure, the king read out a schedule by which he resigned the crown in favour of Bolingbroke. The following day parliament was dissolved and a new assembly summoned in the name of Richard's successor. On the opening day, on 6 October, Archbishop Arundel, who had resumed his chancellorship, gave an address on the text *Vir dominabitur populo* ('The man shall reign over the people'), in which he praised the qualities of the duke of Lancaster, denounced King Richard's crimes, and called for the replacement of the childlike Richard with the manful Henry.[13] After the address, parliamentary proceedings were adjourned for a week until after Henry's coronation.

St Edward's Day (13 October) was chosen to be the coronation day. The 'young and agile' Thomas Fitzalan, knighted the previous day, officiated in his hereditary role of chief butler.[14] It was, however, only on 28 November, with the judgement on his father reversed, that Arundel was granted livery of his inheritance, two years before the end of his technical minority.[15] Given Henry's tenuous if not spurious claim to the Crown, changes were made to the ceremony to introduce additional attributes of legitimation, including the use of a closed imperial crown with arches in the shape of a cross, and the use of a phial of oil said to have been presented to St Thomas Becket by the Virgin Mary. It seems that King Richard, who had come across the phial a year or two previously, had asked Archbishop Arundel to anoint him with it. Arundel had refused, and yet, ironically, he was willing to use the oil to anoint Richard's supplanter.[16]

The question remained, in the wake of Henry's accession, as to what to do with Richard who, aged 32, was likely to live for some time, and might have become a rallying figure for any disaffected lords. Following the reopening of parliament and Henry's refusal to try Richard, Archbishop Arundel and Northumberland asked the lords what should be done with the deposed king. It was agreed that he should be imprisoned in a secret and secure place. At the end of October he was, therefore, removed from the Tower and eventually confined at the Lancastrian fortress of Pontefract. However, Richard's removal from London and King Henry's favourable treatment of his courtiers did not prevent a group of them hatching a plot in early December. The earls of Salisbury, Huntingdon, Rutland and Kent, and Lord Despenser, who had been degraded from their titles and deprived of some of their lands by parliament at the beginning of November, planned to seize the king and his sons during the New Year celebrations at Windsor and to release Richard.[17] King Henry, who had learned of the plot, immediately returned to London to gather troops and close all the ports. The dissidents precipitately launched the so-called Epiphany Rising of 1400 and declared Richard as king, but their support was threadbare due to the breadth of popular support for the new king.

On 8 January the earl of Salisbury was captured at Cirencester and lynched by the townsmen. A number of other captives were brought for trial to Oxford where they were executed and then, the chronicles tell us, 'their bodies, chopped up like the carcasses of beasts killed in the chase, being carried to London, partly in sacks and partly on poles slung across pairs of men's shoulders, ... were later salted to preserve them'.[18] On 15 January Lord Despenser was seized at Bristol and killed; while the earl of Huntingdon was captured at Pleshey, where in 1397 King Richard had captured Gloucester, and beheaded on the orders of Joan Fitzalan, countess of Hereford, Bolingbroke's mother-in-law.[19] Possibly to reward Thomas, earl of Arundel, for his support during the rising, the king admitted the earl to the Order of the Garter that same month.[20] Another to be similarly rewarded was the king's half-brother Sir Thomas Beaufort (later earl of Dorset from 1411 and duke of Exeter from 1416) who was also granted forfeited Holland manors in Kent, Sussex, and Hampshire.[21] It is possible that Arundel may have been the recipient of equal generosity.

Within two weeks the first rising to challenge Henry's rule was over. The king sent news of the events to Archbishop Arundel who announced the victory to Londoners in the form of a sermon on the theme 'I bring you tidings of great joy'.[22] On 16 January Archbishop Arundel led a procession through the city to give thank to God and on 8 February, the royal council agreed that if Richard was still alive he should be kept securely. If, on the other hand, he was already dead, his body should be shown to the people. The implications were clear; it was necessary to do away with Richard. By 17 February he was dead, probably through a combination of voluntary and inflicted starvation.[23]

The last two years of Richard II's reign had brought about a dramatic change in the English political landscape. It had also shaken the foundations and the traditional bonds of loyalty in Wales. The events of the years 1397-99 had a devastating impact on the role and position of the Welsh community and its leaders. Three of the great Marcher lords forfeited their lordships: Thomas of Woodstock, duke of Gloucester (Caldicot and Huntingdon); Thomas Beauchamp, earl of

Warwick (Elfael and, until 1396, Gower); and Richard III Fitzalan, earl of Arundel and Surrey (Bromfield and Yale, Chirkland, Oswestry and Clun). The vacuum of lordship was accentuated by the natural deaths of Roger Mortimer, earl of March, who held sixteen Marcher lordships, in July 1398, and John of Gaunt, duke of Lancaster and lord of Grosmont, in February 1399. Finally there was the exile for life of Thomas Mowbray, duke of Norfolk (Gower and Chepstow), and Henry Bolingbroke, heir to Gaunt's estates and to the lordship of Brecon through his late wife, Mary de Bohun. Into this vacuum of power in the Marches King Richard installed his own favourites — Lescrope, Despenser, Exeter, and Aumale. The Welsh historian Sir Rees Davies noted that 'the seismic impact of these changes extended much further than a mere title to lordship; the ties of service and reward, often carefully cultivated within families over generations, had suddenly been severed'.[24]

A sense of discrimination grew among the Welsh. They were disenchanted by the fact that no Welshman had been knighted (as had happened in the reign of Edward III), and that low-born men were promoted and noblemen overlooked. On 16 September 1400 the storm broke when Owain Glyn Dŵr was proclaimed prince of Wales by some of his followers at Glyndyfrdwy in Denbighshire. Thus began a revolt which engulfed much of Wales during the next few years. The rebellion hence came to dominate the life of Thomas Fitzalan, earl of Arundel, since not only did it break out in the middle of his lordship, but its leader was also one of his affinity. Owain's family had filled conspicuous offices in the administration of the Fitzalan lordships – Owain's father, Gruffudd, had been steward of both Oswestry and Chirk in 1348, and there is evidence to suggest that his father before him, also named Gruffudd, may have held the same office.[25]

Little is known of Owain's early years. He was born in the 1350s and his position in Welsh society was determined by his ancestry and his descent from the Welsh princes of Powys, Deheubarth, and Gwynedd. But his illustrious descent did not hide the fact that his estates only yielded about £70 yearly. Although by Welsh standards this made him wealthy it did not allow him to cut much of a figure with his English neighbours. In 1387 Owain was but one of the 127 squires in Arundel's retinue, a painful reminder that by the standards of the English political society his position was modest. Until 1400 he pretended no greater title than lord of Glyndyfrdwy. However, Owain's ancestry and choice of bride certainly secured him a position in the more exalted Welsh circles. Marred ferch Dafydd was the daughter of Sir David Hanmer whose family had settled in the Marches during the Edwardian conquest. In September 1381 Hanmer was appointed joint justiciar of south Wales and by 1383 he was chief justice of the King's Bench and was also appointed to the king's council. Hanmer was also a legal adviser to John of Gaunt and the earl of Stafford, and was a member of the councils of the earls of Arundel and March. However, his

All that remains of Owain Glyn Dŵr's home of Sycharth in Cynllaith Owain

death in 1387 put an end to any influence he may have had to promote Owain's career.[26]

Owain Glyn Dŵr's revolt drew immediate support from among the tenantry of Arundel's lordships and its main targets were English towns in north-east Wales. Nine men from Yale took part in the initial attack on Ruthin on 18 September 1400, and Holt was one of the boroughs attacked in the following days.[27] Oswestry was also severely hit, and so were Ruthin, Denbigh, Rhuddlan, Flint, and Welshpool. The outbreak was deemed sufficiently serious for Henry IV to divert his army which was journeying home from Scotland, where it had

The remains of Oswestry Castle, perched above the town

been employed in securing the Scottish Marches of Henry's new kingdom. It arrived at Shrewsbury on 26 September from where it conducted a fast punitive campaign into north Wales. By mid October much of the initial revolt had been suppressed, and by 23 October the relief force assembled at Chester

*Holt Castle as it might have looked in 1400 at the time
of the Glyn Dŵr rising (top) and as it appears today (bottom)*

had been disbanded and the garrison at Flint Castle reduced to ten men.[28] The local revolt was suppressed and the submission of some of the leading rebels, including Glyn Dŵr's sons, may have given the English the false impression that what looked like a localised episode was over as quickly as it had begun. Henry IV's swift and forceful intervention certainly demonstrated that any rebellions that appeared to threaten his rule would not be tolerated.

The government was magnanimous in extending a pardon to all Welshmen who submitted, but it also rubbed salt in the wounds of discontent by holding judicial sessions in north Wales and exacting large subsidies. It also went some way towards granting the Commons' demands in the Hilary Parliament of 1401 for Welshmen to be forbidden from acquiring land in England or in English towns in Wales and from becoming burgesses. Englishmen were also to be protected from conviction at the suit of Welshmen in Wales.[29] In March the first statutes and ordinances were issued declaring the Welsh *de facto* second-class citizens.

The Welsh response came quickly. On Good Friday (1 April) 1401, while the garrison was at prayer, Conway Castle was attacked and captured by Glyn Dŵr's cousins, Gwilym and Rhys ap Tudur, who had led the revolt on Anglesey the previous September.[30] Owain himself, who was still on the run, now emerged from hiding to lead the revolt in the uplands of mid-Wales. The capture of Conway had no immediate widespread military impact, but psychologically it had profound effects. It had probably only been intended to secure for Gwilym and Rhys the pardons denied to them for their role in the September 1400 rebellion; but it showed the vulnerability of English strong-holds. While the justiciar of north Wales, Henry 'Hotspur' Percy, seems to have been willing to accede to the Welsh terms, the government, furious at the ineptitude of the English commanders, refused any negotiations. It was not until late May or June that the castle was finally handed back, and pardons were issued in early July.[31]

The earl of Arundel took part in several campaigns against the rebels in the following years but after the initial outbreak of hostilities, Bromfield and Yale seems to have lain outside the mainstream of events. However, this did not alter the fact that Arundel's lands had been ravaged, and their profitability affected. Furthermore, many of Arundel's tenants, alienated by the increased pressure applied by the earl's officials to the collection of rents and dues, joined the revolt.[32] This pressure was one of the elements forming the prelude to the uprising of 1400. The lordship of Chirk was no exception and the progressive increase in the level of arrears in the 1390s was accompanied by clear signs that the lord was intent on halting this process of decay by persisting with the collection of revenue, accompanied by the exaction of fines and rents. However, the collection of arrears remained a problem, and arrears increased from £375 in 1397-98 to £663 in

1399-1400 when only 14% of lordship's expected revenue was delivered to the receiver. The revolt and its support by the local tenantry had profound effects on seigniorial revenue. By 1403-04 no revenue at all was collected in Chirk. Similarly affected were the Lancastrian lordships of Cydweli, Brecon, and Ogmore which reported no yield; by 1405 no revenue was reported in Monmouth; and in 1406-07 no revenue was apparently collected from any of the Lancastrian estates.[33]

For the next six years Arundel fought to reassert the king's authority in north Wales, as well as his own. On 26 July 1402 Earl Thomas was appointed the king's lieutenant in the northern Marches of Wales whilst Edmund, earl of Stafford was granted a similar appointment in the southern Marches.[34] South Wales was put under the control of Lord Grey of Codnor and the area around Welshpool under that of Edward, lord Charlton. Henry IV made these appointments in direct response to the Percies' increasing power and influence, and the king's growing distrust of their motives. In November 1401, Henry had appointed Thomas Percy, earl of Worcester, as lieutenant in south Wales and governor of Prince Henry's household. But in 1402 the Percies' stated wish to negotiate with Glyn Dŵr made the king suspect that they were conniving, and so he replaced Percy with the earl of Stafford.[35]

In March 1403 the king appointed Prince Henry as his lieutenant in Wales above all other commanders, with his own army of 500 men-at-arms and 2,500 archers. By then Henry IV's relations with the earl of Northumberland were moving towards crisis point. Henry refused his demand for £20,000 owed for the wardenship of the northern Marches, and also frustrated his ambitions to secure the lands of the earl of Douglas in south-western Scotland, where Northumberland owned the castle, constabulary and forest of Jedburgh, making him a powerful English magnate on Scottish territory. Northumberland's ambitions were partly kept in check by Henry IV's attempt to counter the Percies' authority by extending royal favour to Ralph Neville, earl of Westmorland.[36] In mid-July, as Henry was marching northwards with an army, Hotspur and his uncle, Worcester, came out in revolt in Wales. Hotspur raised Cheshire in the name of King Richard II and Mortimer, the boy earl of March who was the nephew of Hotspur's wife. The earl of Worcester, as the prince's steward, suborned over a thousand men from the prince's army to join Hotspur at Shrewsbury.

Henry IV arrived at Shrewsbury on 22 July having discovered that Glyn Dŵr, Edmund Mortimer, Hotspur and Northumberland would be there to meet him in battle. The following day the two forces met on the field, although there was no sign of Glyn Dŵr. The king's army was organised in three divisions under himself, Prince Henry, and the earl of Stafford, and earned a hard-fought victory. Hotspur was killed, and Worcester taken alive but later executed, whilst Northumberland fled north but submitted, on 11 August, to

*Owain Glyn Dŵr
when at the height of his power,
as depicted on his seal*

Ralph Neville, earl of Westmorland. Northumberland was stripped of his estates and offices but, on the king's intervention, parliament pardoned him in February 1404.

Following the battle Arundel was retained to guard the Welsh Marches, an appointment renewed in October 1403.[40] However, the suppression of Percy rule paralysed the Crown's offensive in Wales for eighteen months, during which time Glyn Dŵr was able to extend his control in the south of Wales. In July 1404 Owain signed a military alliance with France which sent troops in August 1405, taking Carmarthen and other castles on their progress to the English border. Now that Glyn Dŵr's control was more secure he called for his own parliament to be held. The first was held at Machynlleth in 1404 and the second at Harlech in July 1405, while his chancery issued documents in his name, as prince of Wales.[41]

A new offensive into Wales under Prince Henry was planned in March 1405, but was primarily conducted by the marcher lords Arundel, Warwick, and York, and Lords Grey of Codnor and Charlton of Powys.[42] Thomas, earl of Arundel, was specifically appointed to the north and Edward, duke of York, to the south while Prince Henry had general oversight of the war. While the lords were in charge of the military activities, Prince Henry was called to the north where a revolt had erupted. Later in June, Arundel was called from Wales to assist Prince Henry in suppressing this rising led by the earl of Northumberland and Archbishop Richard Scrope of York. Earl Thomas and Thomas Beaufort, the king's half-brother, were hastily invested with authority as constable and marshal to pass judgement.[43] When Archbishop Arundel heard of Scrope's surrender and capture outside York, and the king's intention to execute him, he rode all day and the following night from London in a bid to rescue his fellow prelate. On 8 June Archbishop Arundel warned Henry IV of the consequences that the execution of an archbishop could bring, and advised him to leave judgement to the pope or parliament. The king assured Archbishop Arundel that nothing would be done without his consent, but while he slept, exhausted by the journey, Scrope and the 19-year-old Thomas

Mowbray, Earl Marshal were beheaded. Archbishop Arundel was so shocked by this deception that he had a nervous breakdown.

This episode marked the beginning of a deepening rift between the primate and his nephew, since Archbishop Arundel now considered Earl Thomas to be among those who had deceived him and had Scrope killed. The pope pronounced sentence of excommunication on the perpetrators, but Archbishop Arundel decided not to publish the sentence, thus unofficially accepting Scrope's execution as legitimate. This decision marked a drawing together of the king and the archbishop.[44]

The northern rising had posed no real military threat, but it highlighted the persisting complaints and threats against Lancastrian rule. Scrope's rising in part reflected the continuing hostility of the Church towards the high levels of taxation. Whilst the Church had played its part in accepting and legitimising Henry IV, the Crown's mounting insolvency created tensions in parliament.

The rebellions and wars that confronted Henry IV between 1399 and 1405 certainly proved costly. The earl of Northumberland had received at least £40,000 in less than four years for the defence of the north; while the cost of all domestic departments in the royal household stood at £41,700 yearly in 1399-1403 and £32,300 yearly in 1403-06.[45] At the same time the forfeitures that had resulted from the various rebellions had considerably increased the Crown's estates, thereby greatly increasing the king's direct influence in local affairs. There could be no more threats in the Marches of Wales since almost all the lordships were in the king's hands: the Despenser lands in Glamorgan, the Bohun lordship of Brecon, the Hastings lands in Pembroke, the Mowbray lordship of Gower, the Lancastrian estates, and the Mortimer lordships. To their north Henry IV was already powerful through the royal lordships of Chester and Flint. The only independent Marcher lords remaining were the earl of Arundel, his brother-in-law William Beauchamp, baron Abergavenny, and the Greys of Ruthin, all faithful Lancastrians.[46]

The earl of Arundel's position was therefore particularly significant in the Marches. On 3 October 1405, Arundel was appointed keeper of the town of Shrewsbury and the Marches of Wales with full powers to do everything necessary for their safety.[47] The following month the king also saw that Earl Thomas was provided with a bride, Beatrice, an illegitimate daughter of John I, king of Portugal. The union was arranged at the urging of Henry IV, who defrayed the costs, as a means of strengthening the alliance with Portugal where his sister Philippa was queen.[48] Nonetheless, the union remains puzzling. Beatrice's bastardy was in itself not an issue, but she brought no lands with her, although the amount of her dowry is unknown, and may have been substantial. It seems that half may have been paid up-front while security for the unpaid moiety was advanced by Portuguese merchants in the shape of merchandise. It was only in October 1410 that 500 marks, still outstanding from the unpaid moiety, were received by Arundel from Martin Alfonsidinis, a Portuguese merchant, by receipts of the late Sir John Velasci of Almadana.[49]

Over the next four years Arundel increasingly attached himself to his cousin Prince Henry, becoming his principal retainer in 1407, and distanced himself from the court where his uncle's influence prevailed, having been estranged from the archbishop since Scrope's execution in 1405. Archbishop Arundel, having served twice as chancellor in the previous reign, accepted the seal of office for a third time on 30 January 1407. At the same time, in Sussex Earl Thomas was challenged by the growing influence of Sir John Pelham, treasurer of England and counsellor to Henry IV, who held custody of the Mowbray castle of Bramber and the Lancaster castle of Pevensey. And between 1407 and 1409, disputes arose between Earl Thomas and his uncle over lands in Kent and Sussex.[50] For a time, therefore, Earl Thomas' influence was limited. However, his association with Prince Henry was to prove significant especially

Thomas Arundel, archbishop of Canterbury, surrounded by four Benedictine monks, as depicted in a manuscript (Bodleian Library, MS Laud misc. 165 f.5r)

since in the period from 1406 to 1411, Henry IV was forced both by parliament and by his declining health to surrender much of the business of government to the council. Although Prince Henry had been head of the council since late 1406, he seems to have delegated much of the work to Archbishop Arundel, partly because Prince Henry was still largely concerned with affairs in Wales.[51]

For eighteen months Archbishop Arundel as chancellor remained the effective head of the council. In June 1408 Henry IV had a seizure after which he was never the same man again. In the winter of 1408-09 he was again severely ill for several weeks and his will was made with the archbishop as witness. This illness brought Prince Henry and his half-brother, Sir Thomas Beaufort, to the king's bedside, and from that moment the prince began re-asserting his authority in the council, especially now that the Welsh revolt had come to an end with the capitulation of Harlech and Aberystwyth in 1408, even though Glyn Dŵr was still considered an enemy on the run.[58] Mounting divisions over the conduct of government within the council finally came into the open on 11 December 1409 when Sir John Tiptoft resigned as treasurer, followed ten days later by Archbishop Arundel as chancellor. This marked the displacement of the king's friends by the group of younger nobles who had been the companions of Prince Henry in Wales: the earls of Arundel and Warwick, Lord Charlton of Powys, Lord Grey of Codnor, and Lord Grey of Ruthin.

The bridge between the king and the prince was formed by the Beauforts, the king's three half-brothers through Katherine Swynford, John of Gaunt's third wife. Henry Beaufort, bishop of Winchester was one of the prince's advisers, while Thomas Beaufort was in the king's household. The third brother was John Beaufort, earl of Somerset. Certainly there were strong tensions at work. In February 1407 the king had confirmed the Beauforts' legitimation, although, probably at Archbishop Arundel's request, a clause was added which excluded them from claiming the Crown.[52] Prince Henry completed his control over government with the appointment, on 6 January 1410, of Lord Scrope of Masham as treasurer, and when parliament opened on 27 January Thomas Chaucer, the poet's son, was chosen as Speaker. His appointment was notable since he was the first cousin to the Beauforts through his mother, Philippa Roet, sister of Katherine Swynford.[53]

The prince's administration was thus installed and its first challenge was to deal with the Commons and a request for taxation. The prince's demands were partly granted through a subsidy voted on 8 May 1410; although the amount was less than Prince Henry and his council had hoped for, it was at least a sign that parliament had cautiously welcomed his rule. The following month, on 14 June 1410, Arundel was appointed along with his uncle, Archbishop Arundel, to borrow money in the king's name, probably because it would take some time for the first instalments of the subsidy to be collected, but the promise of the subsidy could be used as guarantee for loans.[54] Earl Thomas's position in council certainly brought him personal advantages and in February 1411 he was able to secure a royal grant regarding goods which had been forfeited from his father in 1397 and had still not been returned.[55]

For nearly two years, from January 1410 to November 1411, Prince Henry and a council consisting of his friends administered the realm in the king's name. The most pressing problem they faced was the re-establishment of the king's finances, which had been depleted by a decade of military activity in Wales and on the northern Marches. However, in 1411 a second problem assumed growing significance — the internecine struggle between the Armagnacs and the Burgundians for supremacy over the French Crown. Since

1392 Philip the Bold, duke of Burgundy, had had control over government, as King Charles VI had been prone to periods of mental instability. Philip's own interests were held in check by the king's brother, Louis, duke of Orléans who, following Duke Philip's death in 1404, took over complete control of the government. Whilst Duke Philip had been the king's uncle, Duke John the Fearless of Burgundy, as the king's cousin, had less influence. Duke Louis thus took control of the royal council and the realm's finances. This put him in conflict with John the Fearless. On 23 November 1407 Orléans was murdered on the streets of Paris by Burgundy's men. Duke John was initially forced to flee Paris, but the murder quickly led to his gaining control over the government and the capital, where he had built a network of alliances among the burghers and the members of the university.[56]

In 1410, however, those opposed to Burgundian rule began to assemble around Charles, the new duke of Orléans and his allies the dukes of Bourbon, Berry, and Alençon, and Louis II of Anjou, king of Sicily. Under the leadership of Bernard of Armagnac, Duke Charles' father-in-law, they became known as the Armagnacs. In July 1411 the Burgundians approached the English to suggest an alliance against the Armagnacs, a proposal which met a favourable response. The duke of Burgundy offered his daughter, Anne, in marriage to Prince Henry, and negotiations were carried out by ambassadors who included Thomas, earl of Arundel. At the same time, negotiations were also held with the duke of Berry who had approached Queen Joan asking her to see that her husband, Henry IV, would not intervene in the quarrel.[57]

A crucial point for the English was the fulfilment of the terms of the 1360 Treaty of Brétigny by which France had conceded Aquitaine in full sovereignty to the king of England if he renounced his claim to the French throne. The treaty had never been fulfilled since no English king had done so. Although now all parties expressed the desire for peace, the English were not prepared to include the Burgundians' allies, since this would have meant implicit recognition of Owain Glyn Dŵr. But the question the king and his council put to the Burgundians was unequivocal. In exchange for assistance against Orléans would they give military assistance to the English king to recover lands wrongfully withheld in France?[59]

Arundel now became closely involved in the implementation of the pro-Burgundian policy. Ships were prepared to lead a military expedition to France. It is possible that Henry IV himself intended to lead the expedition but, probably because of ill health, he did not do so, and in September 1411 Arundel took the king's place. Although not officially authorised by the king, the expedition was thus led by one of the prince's closest associates. While the duke of Burgundy faced Armagnac pressure in Vermandois in northern France and Paris, Arundel led his force to Arras in October. Thence, in conjunction with the Burgundian army, Arundel moved towards Paris where on 9 November at

St Cloud, south-west of the capital, they launched their attack on the Armagnac forces, who had hoped to isolate and capture the city. The duke of Burgundy was able to muster additional support among Parisian citizens. The Armagnacs, already under siege by the English, and now surprised by a second attack by Duke John's forces, broke ranks and fled to the nearby convent and castle, but were finally forced to surrender to the English. A few days later Arundel was feasted in the Louvre by the duke of Burgundy. Arundel was well rewarded by the duke and among the gifts he is likely to have received were a ring, a golden heron (*unum sarpe de auro*), a gold cup, and a fur jacket embroidered in gold.[60] Arundel and his men stayed some time in France and returned to England in January 1412.[61]

It is possible that their sojourn was connected with the events that were unfolding in England. At the same time as the English and Burgundian forces were triumphant at St Cloud, parliament was meeting at Westminster. In a surprising turn of events the Commons asked the king to thank the prince and his council for their work and effort. It was announced that 30 November 1411 was to mark the end of Prince Henry's rule. It is likely that the Beauforts' proposal that the king should be deposed in favour of his heir was too much. Parliament's dismissal of the proposal enabled the king to secure the Commons' assurance of their loyalty and the grant of a new tax to spend as he wished. Archbishop Arundel was recalled as chancellor and his follower, Sir John Pelham, as treasurer. For the rest of the reign the king ruled on his own authority and no council was appointed.[62]

With the dismissal of the prince's council at the end of November 1411 Arundel had no further political or military role until Prince Henry's accession as king in 1413. Henry IV's resumption of power in December 1411 implied that he was now taking responsibility for war policy. His favourable position towards the Armagnacs, allies of his Gascon subjects, was diametrically opposed to Prince Henry's favourable treatment of the Burgundians. By June 1412 the relationship between father and son had reached a nadir. However, it was soon to be mended. From October the king's health deteriorated sharply and although he spent Christmas at Eltham Palace with his wife, by the end of January he was a dying man, unable to stand or speak. He died on 20 March.

On 10 April, the day after Henry V's coronation, Bishop Henry Beaufort was recalled as chancellor and Archbishop Arundel was dismissed.[63] Thus ended the period of his influence. On 19 February 1414, aged 61, he died, having suffered a stroke, and was later buried in Canterbury Cathedral.[64] For Adam of Usk the archbishop had been 'the strength, lamp and wisdom of the people, the light and delight of church and clergy, and the unshakeable pillar of the Christian faith'.[65] Archbishop Arundel had been a considerable force in disentangling what was considered to be genuine piety from the new English

Lollard heresy which developed in England from the 1380s. The Lollard ideal was part of a larger trend of anti-clericalism in the late fourteenth century that affected members of the lay nobility. Arundel was able to strengthen the Church by securing the support of the State over the issue of heresy. Especially after the statute *De Haeretico Comburendo* of 1401, which ordained the death penalty for heresy, the established Church became an efficient organ of discipline and inquisition.

The new reign, which marked the end of the archbishop's influence, promoted his nephew's rise to great power. As part of his new government, Henry V appointed Thomas, earl of Arundel treasurer of England, an unusual appointment for a magnate.[66] The following day, Arundel was also appointed constable of Dover Castle and warden of the Cinque Ports, offices which had been held by Prince Henry himself since 1409.[67] A further sign of royal favour came on 9 October 1413, when Arundel was granted keeping of the king's park of Guildford, close to the earl's residence of Reigate Castle, with the right to hunt, the right of warren, and the right to fish in its fisheries, so long as he paid the wages of the parker and the other staff and looked after the upkeep of the king's hunting lodge.[68]

Arundel was an active member of the new royal council, involved in the reform of royal finance and the preparations for re-launching the war with France. Between 1413 and 1415, Arundel made loans to Henry V totalling £2,969 — £2,000 more than any other lay magnate during the whole reign.[69] This shows not only Earl Thomas's ability to come up with large sums of cash, but more importantly that among the magnates he was one of the most significant supporters and beneficiaries of the new regime. Nonetheless, compared to that of his grandfather and father, Thomas's wealth must have been modest since it is unlikely that he was ever able to recover all the monies forfeited in 1397. Furthermore, Arundel's estates were now less profitable and, especially in the Marches, the levy of rents and farms had been hampered by the Welsh revolts. His favour at court under Prince Henry must have brought certain advantages, and it is possible that his marriage to Beatrice of Portugal was also financially advantageous.

Arundel's royal favour and influence with Henry V was certainly high, yet this did not inhibit the king from a formal demonstration of royal authority at the centre of Arundel's lands in Shropshire. In the aftermath of Glyn Dŵr's revolt Arundel's retainers, John Wele, captain of Oswestry, and Richard Lacon, captain of Clun, had restored the earl's authority with systematic harshness. Arundel's absence in England encouraged them to practise extortion and intimidation on their own account, thereby provoking resistance from the followers of Arundel's rival, John, lord Talbot. In November 1413 Henry V bound both lords by recognisances to keep the peace, and in the summer of 1414 he conducted a tour of the west Midlands to suppress disorders. On 15 June Arundel's officers (Lacon, Wele, and others) were indicted at Shrewsbury for offences over the preceding years, and Arundel was made to stand surety for them. Although they were eventually pardoned and Lord Talbot dispatched to Ireland, King Henry had shown himself determined to discipline magnate feuding. The settlement of disorder in Shropshire, as elsewhere, was facilitated by recruitment of troublemakers for the military expedition to France.[70]

The Armagnac and Burgundian feuding had already invited English intervention as has been recounted. However, even if there were legitimate premises for intervention in France, there was still a risk that a military campaign might end in utter failure, like the interventions of the previous century. It was therefore necessary to prepare the ground carefully. Henry could justify either a claim over the lands conceded in the unfulfilled treaty of Brétigny, or a claim to the Crown of France, which Edward III had never renounced. Between 1414 and 1415 negotiations were held with the Armagnacs, but these were a charade since Henry V was meanwhile also seeking an alliance with John the Fearless, duke of Burgundy.

The king was, however, soon to realise that Burgundy was an unreliable ally. In July 1414 Armagnac troops besieged the duke of Burgundy at Arras, the duke finally agreeing to a truce in September. This was followed on 13 March 1415 with a peace agreement. As part of the settlement, Burgundy was pardoned for the sake of re-establishing peace among the royal princes, and thus forced to end his negotiations with the English.[71]

During the two years that Henry V was negotiating with the French, he had also started making preparations for war on a grand scale. Since Calais in 1347, no major French town had been captured. Henry ordered bows and arrows to be stockpiled at the Tower; guns were forged at Bristol, and siege engines, scaling ladders, battering rams, and 100,000 gunstones were ordered. Fifteen warships were constructed, to be led by the flagship, the 540-ton *Trinity Royal*. The transport was to be provided by a fleet of 1,500 ships, half of them hired from the Low Countries. The king also made jewels available for security of the army's wages. On 13 May he commanded Richard Courtenay, bishop of Norwich and keeper of the royal jewels, to hand them over to Arundel as treasurer, so that they might be given out to the captains as surety.[72] On 11 August 1415, with an army of 10,000 men, the fleet sailed from Southampton for Chef de Vaux near Harfleur.[73]

Arundel's retinue was among the largest and the fact that it matched in number those of the dukes of York and Dorset, the king's relatives, was a clear recognition of his prominence as one of the king's closest companions and also of his martial abilities and experience as a commander. His retinue of 400 men was composed of his banneret, Sir Reginald Cobham, three knights (Sir John Mortimer, Sir Robert Moton, and Sir Robert Morley), 95 men-atarm (including John Cosoun, Arundel Herald) and 300 archers. The king's brothers, the dukes of Clarence and Gloucester, had retinues of 960 and 800 men respectively. After that followed the other earls of the royal family: March (220), Cambridge (210), and Norfolk (200); and the other earls: Suffolk (160), Oxford (140), and Salisbury (120). John Holland, earl of Huntingdon and Henry Percy, earl of Northumberland had comparatively small retinues of 80 and 24 men respectively, which may be explained by the fact that they had not yet been fully restored to their possessions following their forebears' treasonable acts a decade earlier.[74]

The English besieged Harfleur and the town surrendered on 22 September. This was significant because Harfleur commanded the mouth of the Seine and passage along the English Channel. For Henry V it was another Calais, in that, as with the earlier English 'victory', it was intended to be the first step in a large design, but had a heavy impact on the troops. Many died from sickness during the siege, in all likelihood caused by dysentery. On 15 September the bishop of Norwich had died followed, three days later, by the earl of Suffolk. A third of the army had to be sent home at the end of September, including the duke of Clarence and the earls of March and Norfolk (the Earl Marshal). They survived but Arundel, who had returned to England on 28 September, died on 13 October aged 34.[75] The difference was, according to the chronicler Thomas Walsingham, that unlike the other magnates, who died of disease, 'the earl of Arundel, so it is said, was poisoned'.[76] Though there is no other evidence suggesting that this had been the case, it is nonetheless significant that the death of Henry V's closest companion and confidant, and one of the leading commanders of the campaign, may have been seen as murder, possibly by way of infected drink or food. Arundel's death and the loss of the other commanders, however, did not stop Henry V's resolve to continue his progress into France.[77] Following Arundel's death, his men had joined the royal host.

After Harfleur the king was urged to return to England because of the heavy losses he had incurred, but he decided nonetheless to march through Normandy to Calais, a journey of 144 miles. A garrison under the earl of Dorset was left at Harfleur, and on 8 October an army of almost 6,000 men, mostly archers, set off along the coast. At this stage they were probably not seeking to bring the French to battle. Henry V looked to cross the Somme at Blanchetacque, but the ford was taken by the French, forcing the English to follow the river until they reached an unguarded ford near Nesle. In the meantime the French had moved towards Abbeville, thus blocking the English advance to Calais. It was now clear that they had to engage in battle.[78]

On 24 October the two armies faced each other at Agincourt in Picardy over a muddy and slippery field. The site provided poor fighting conditions for the heavily armoured men-at-arms and cavalry. Since the English were outnumbered by three to one and had a long march behind them the conditions on the ground assumed great importance. Each army waited all morning to see what move the other side would make. Henry V broke the deadlock and ordered his men to advance until they were 200 yards short of the enemy, within range of the English arrows. The archers also fortified their positions with sharpened stakes driven in the ground. When they opened fire a hail of arrows fell on the French, who were forced to charge their positions. Encountering the arrows and fearing to impale their horses on the stakes the cavalry started to back away in confusion, only to meet their own men-at-arms advancing on foot. Heavily armoured men and horses lost their balance and fell in the mud, and the restricted space became a killing field, the English slaughtering the French with their knives and clubs.

Within an hour it seemed as though the English had won, since two French lines of men-at-arms had been destroyed. However, a third remained, though they retreated from the field of battle rather than entering the fray. It is probably at this stage that Henry V considered that what looked like a victory could still be turned into defeat. He had a large number of prisoners, unarmed yet still in their armour, and a few men guarding them who could not be spared. Thus the king took the controversial decision that, contrary to chivalric ethic, the prisoners would be killed. When the knights refused to do this, the archers were ordered to shoot the prisoners. Over 1,000 of them did, nonetheless, survive and were later taken back to England for ransom, including the dukes of Orléans and Bourbon, and the counts of Eu, Richemont, and Vendôme.[79] The slaughter of the French army had profound effects on French government; the death and capture of the royal princes, most of the military commanders, and almost all the bailiffs of northern France precipitated the country into an even deeper political crisis.[80]

The English victory at Agincourt was the last great battle of the Hundred Years war, and ranks on a par with Crécy in 1346 and Poitiers in 1356. From 1413 Henry V began a methodical conquest of Normandy and northwestern France. There was little resistance since most French noblemen had died at Agincourt or were held hostage. The murder in 1419 of Duke John the Fearless by the Armagnacs also brought to Henry's side Duke John's son and heir, Philip the Good. By 1420 the French were forced to sign the Treaty of Troyes, which disinherited the dauphin, gave his sister Catherine in marriage to Henry V, and declared the latter heir of Charles VI of France. But Henry V and Charles VI both died in 1422, and the dauphin was crowned Charles VII by those French, mainly in the centre and south, who did not recognise the Treaty of Troyes. Henry's infant heir became Henry VI of England as well as France under the eye of his uncle John, duke of Bedford, who continued the English war effort in France.

Though Arundel died short of a personal triumph at Agincourt, his men fought a legendary battle. But men at this time, as at all times since, knew that war was a deadly game. Earl Thomas's testament and codicil, both in

Latin, were dated 10 October 1415, three days before his death.[81] The testament was to be executed in conjunction with a will (*voluntas*) which Arundel had composed in French the previous 10 August at Chichester before crossing for France. In the traditional format Arundel made provision for masses and pilgrimages for his soul and the construction of a new chapel near St Mary's Gate in Arundel, which he had promised to make a long time ago. He also instructed his executors to pay the wages of his servants and military retainers at Harfleur. To his sister Elizabeth, duchess of Norfolk and Elizabeth Ryman, the wife of one of his executors, Earl Thomas made a special grant of £40 and 50 marks respectively for 'the good and diligent work and service' which they performed during his illness. Both ladies also witnessed the testament.[82]

On 6 December 1415 Arundel's properties and estates were taken into the king's hands;[83] and on 18 January a commission was issued to have all charters and other muniments regarding the Fitzalan estates delivered to the Chancery.[84] In his testament Earl Thomas had granted all his property in England and what was left in France to his wife; hence, on 10 April 1416, the king ordered to deliver to Countess Beatrice and the other executors various jewels, goods and chattels including the gifts he had been given by the duke of Burgundy in 1411, as well as a wide collar powdered with pearls, semi-precious stones and sapphires, a great brooch with a diamond, a brooch and a gown of cloth of gold furred with ermine which he had of the king's gift, a ceremonial Garter gown furred with miniver, a crimson mantle of estate furred on the outside with ermine, twenty pairs of shoes, ten shirts, twelve breeches, a banner embroidered with the earl's arms, and five tapestries of worsted.[85]

In February 1416, a commission had been issued to investigate why the tenants of the Fitzalans' Welsh Marcher estates were refusing to pay rents and dues to Countess Beatrice and Arundel's executors.[86] The tenants asserted that since the lands were now in the king's hands, the dues should be paid to him and not Arundel's executors. They said that they wanted to ensure that the money would go towards paying the late earl's soldiers in France and thought that if they paid the money to the king this would happen more speedily. A number of Arundel's men who fought in France, especially the archers, came from his Marcher estates, and their relatives were understandably anxious that they were paid their wages. It was in the tenants' interest to insist that their rents and dues be used for this purpose, rather than being diverted to Countess Beatrice's coffers and those of the other heirs and creditors.[87]

Earl Thomas had had no legitimate heirs with Countess Beatrice, although he fathered an illegitimate son called John by an unknown lover. His estates therefore passed to the closest male heir of the line of Sir John Arundel (d. 1379). On 22 July, John Arundel, lord Maltravers (d.1421) was granted full livery of the Arundel estates.[88] However, the mixture of different legal arrangements that were undertaken to keep the family's control over the estates had its dangers. Earl Richard II had held the estates both in tail male and in fee which meant that once the family became extinct in the main male line the inheritance had to be divided between the heirs of the next surviving male line.

The lordship of Chirk should also have passed to John Arundel, but its descent is more obscure, because when Earl Thomas had drawn up his will on 10 August 1415 he enfeoffed the castle and lordship of Chirk and a number of manors in favour of his illegitimate son, John.[89] Later, on 10 October, Arundel granted to Countess Beatrice control (*gubernacionem*) over his son and the estates he had granted him until he was of age. If John was to die without male heirs and before Countess Beatrice, then the lordship would revert to her for the remainder of her life. If both were to die, then the feoffees were to sell the lordship and manors, giving preference to John, lord Maltravers. Nothing more is known of Earl Thomas's illegitimate son, neither who his mother was nor when he was born, but he may never have inherited the lordship for, although in 1416-17 the lordship remained an Arundel possession, the following year it had been granted to certain feoffees for the king's use. It would seem that Countess Beatrice was not granted the boy's wardship nor that of his lands and that therefore Chirk was taken into the king's hands. Nor was Beatrice allowed dower in Chirk when she sued for it in 1436.[90] The lordship's strategic value was far too significant for Henry V to miss the opportunity to acquire it for his own personal use. It remained in the king's hands for most of the fifteenth century but was frequently granted to royal creditors; in 1437, the lordship was part of the dower of Joan of Navarre, the Queen Mother.[91]

The title to the earldom of Arundel was disputed between John, lord Maltravers and the Mowbray family, and eventually passed in 1431 to John's son, another John (d.1435).[92] The lands which had been inherited from John de Warenne, earl of Surrey (d.1347) were again separated from the main Fitzalan inheritance. These lands, comprising the lordship of Bromfield and Yale and various possessions in Surrey and Sussex, passed to Earl Thomas's three surviving sisters, Elizabeth, duchess of Norfolk (d.1425), Joan, baroness of Abergavenny (d.1435), and Margaret (d.1422), wife of Sir Roland Lenthall; the lands thus became attached to the inheritances of their respective families. The earldom of Surrey, also part of the Warenne inheritance, reverted to the Crown.[93] When, in 1483, John Howard (d.1485) was created duke of Norfolk as reward for his support of King Richard III, the earldom of Surrey was bestowed on the former's son and heir, Thomas Howard (d.1524).[94]

On 24 February 1416, the king granted licence to Countess Beatrice to sue for her dower as soon as the inquisition into the earl's estate had been completed.[95] However, she was not legally entitled to dower because she was an alien. Two days later, therefore, the king ordered Henry Kays, keeper of the Hanaper of Chancery, to deliver to Countess Beatrice letters patent confirming that the king had taken her homage and that, despite being born in Portugal, she was now to 'be held, entreated and ruled as his liege woman born in England and not otherwise', thus enabling her to sue for her dower without any legal impediments.[96] In July 1418, however, she complained that she still had not

*Above and overleaf: The alabaster tombs of Earl Thomas
and Beatrice of Portugal in the Fitzalan Chapel at Arundel Castle
(Arundel Castle Trustees Ltd)*

obtained her dower in the Welsh Marches, although Arundel's three sisters had already received their inheritance.[97] It also appears that a new challenge to her titles was made in 1421, following the death of Earl John of Arundel, for on 14 July an Act of Parliament was issued confirming her naturalization.[98] Countess Beatrice remarried in 1433 when King Henry VI granted her licence to marry John Holland, earl of Huntingdon (d.1447).[99] She died on 23 October 1439 at Bordeaux without issue.[100] Her heirs were found to be John Mowbray, duke of Norfolk (d.1461), Edward Neville, lord Bergavenny (d.1476) and his wife Elizabeth, and Edmund Lenthall (d.1447). Partition of the dower lands was made in Chancery on 12 July 1440 and attached to the inheritances of these three branches of the family.[101]

Countess Beatrice was buried with Earl Thomas Fitzalan in the Fitzalan Chapel at Arundel, where their alabaster tomb can still be admired. The tomb was probably completed after Countess Beatrice's death in 1439. It is a large tomb chest with double effigies, all of alabaster, originally painted and gilded. The effigies lie with their heads protected by elaborate canopies and resting on cushions held by angels. Earl Thomas's effigy is crowned and prominently displays the Lancastrian collar of esses with tiret and trefoil. Beatrice's effigy is also crowned and she wears a crespine and an elaborate veil as well as a necklace. The earl rests his feet on a horse, presumably because the horse featured on the Fitzalan coat of arms as a supporter, while his wife's feet are flanked by little dogs. In niches round the sides are twenty-eight priests symbolic of the canons of Arundel College, which had replaced Arundel Priory in 1380 under the instigation of Earl Richard III. The metal hearse fence round the tomb, one of only three extant in England, is contemporary and the ten uprights have spikes on top for candles.[102] The tomb is particularly notable because of its striking resemblance to that of King Henry IV and Joan of Navarre at Canterbury Cathedral. The association was undoubtedly intended to highlight Arundel's own royal connections through his cousin Mary de Bohun, Henry IV's first wife and the mother of Henry V. If the design had been the choice of Countess Beatrice, herself of royal stock, it was also a way to immortalize Thomas and herself as the premier comital couple of the age.

13 October 1415 marked the end of the Fitzalan ascendancy. Earl Thomas's own tomb, of regal proportions and iconography, is the symbol of his prominence and that of his family. Thomas could claim to be heir of a long line of lords and earls who had, without exception, fought for their kings defending their interests in the Marches of Wales and Scotland, and on the Continent. The imposition and consolidation of English rule in Wales and the assertion of the English claim to the French throne owed much to the military, as well as financial, support the Fitzalans were able to muster for their respective kings. Earl Thomas did not fail to rise to the challenge of defending the honour of his family and performing the burdensome duties which his ancestry and name

had bestowed on him. Nonetheless, he failed his family by not producing a legitimate heir. The result was the end of Fitzalan power. As the Hundred Years war drew to an end, one of its principal actors died with it. The Fitzalans were no more.

6   The Fitzalan Estates

The Fitzalans' titles to the earldoms of Arundel and Surrey betray their English heritage, but their power-base really lay in the Marches of Wales, not least because this area provided most of their income. The interest of their English estates resided in the fact that their associated titles elevated them into the higher nobility thus conferring on them specific privileges and authority. It is, therefore, not much of a surprise that the Fitzalans were greatly concerned with the consolidation and augmentation of their estates since they constituted the family's main source of income and power. To maintain the profitability of these estates, and to secure influence over their tenants, they had to be efficiently managed.

The Marches, in particular, were considered hugely profitable by English lords. The most prominent fourteenth-century Marcher families such as the Fitzalans, the Mortimers, and earlier in the century the Clares, could count on an average of £2,000 each yearly, while the Black Prince received £5,000 yearly from his principality and Flintshire. Later in the century the pre-1399 Marcher estates of the duchy of Lancaster yielded about £1,189 and the following year, with the inclusion of Brecon, about £2,594, while the estates of the Mortimers of Wigmore yielded about £2,409 in the March and £1,000 in England in 1398.[1] £1,000 per year was also what the Fitzalans could expect from their English estates from the 1350s to the 1380s.

English lords like the Black Prince, the Fitzalans and the Mortimers used their position in Wales as overlords and justices to maximise their revenue by imposing law, order, and fines on local communities. Earl Richard II in particular owed his powerful position to Edward III who allowed him to hold the lordship of Bromfield and Yale, and the lordship of Chirk, next to those of Clun and Oswestry. Furthermore, Arundel's appointment as justice of north Wales in 1334, and then life-justice from 1337, shows how royal favour could help Marcher lords to accumulate enormous power.[2] It was, however, not possible to further one magnate without depriving another: so Marcher politics were an integral part of the English political chessboard. The power which lords like Arundel or March could wield in Wales was unequalled throughout England. This is the reason why Wales and the Marches became one of the premier playgrounds of English politics.

The Warenne inheritance

Though the Arundel inheritance propelled the Fitzalans to the top of the higher nobility, it was only under Earl Edmund that the change in the family's fortunes took place. Earl Edmund is an especially important link in the territorial expansion of the Fitzalans in the fourteenth century for it was on his watch that the Warenne inheritance and the Mortimer lordship of Chirk were legally bound to the family's estates, even though it was not until 1347 and 1354, respectively, that those estates were at last successfully integrated into the main Fitzalan inheritance. Earl Edmund truly laid the foundations on which his son, Earl Richard II, built his financial and territorial empire. Earl Edmund achieved this by capitalising on his favour and influence in court circles which enabled him to secure power, money, land, and first-class brides and grooms for his offspring.

When Earl Edmund married Alice de Warenne in 1306, no one could have foreseen that her brother, John de Warenne, earl of Surrey (d.1347), would die without legitimate heirs. The descent of the Warenne inheritance to the Fitzalans was therefore rather fortuitous, as had been that of Arundel, but it had also been the object of the Fitzalans' close attention: they actively ensured that in the event that Warenne was to die without legitimate heirs their family would have a secure claim to his estates. A settlement of the Warenne estates was reached on 14 May 1326, when John de Warenne surrendered and released to Edward II various of his possessions; then, on 17 May, the king regranted them to Warenne and his wife, Joan de Bar in tail male with remainder to Arundel and his wife Alice and to their son Richard II and his wife Isabella Despenser.[3] This was a clear sign of Arundel's importance at the close of this reign since Warenne would have preferred to settle his lands on the illegitimate children he had had with his mistress. But Warenne's position under Edward II was not one of favour. Later, in 1328, having regained a position of prominence under the new regime of Queen Isabella, Warenne was regranted his estates.[4] The execution of Earl Edmund in November of that year did not, however, result in a resettlement.

Twenty years later, in 1346, John de Warenne became increasingly concerned about the preservation of his name as he had no legitimate heirs. On 1 April 1346 he granted his estates to Edward III, who was then to grant them to one of his children or any person of his choice on condition of preserving the name of Warenne.[5] This was contrary to the 1326 settlement which made Arundel the main beneficiary. Earl Richard II therefore petitioned the king who then delayed and finally abandoned the feoffment. On 12 December Edward formally renounced and quashed the recent surrender and re-grant, claiming that he had not been fully informed concerning his father's grant, and that he could not allow this grant to be superseded — especially as he was not willing to refuse Arundel his inheritance.[6] When Warenne died, on 30 June

1347, his family became extinct in the direct line and the Warenne inheritance was split up. The political pressure exercised by the Fitzalans was instrumental in preventing Warenne from settling his estates on the illegitimate issue he had had with Matilda de Nerford. In 1347 her sons were formally disinherited and exiled into a monastery.[7]

At Warenne's death several parties had interests in his estates. Edward III cleverly used the inheritance by dividing it in several parts so as to reward his most worthy military leaders of the Crécy-Calais campaigns which was just coming to an end. Arundel obtained the East Sussex, Surrey, Norfolk, and Marcher interests centred around Lewes, Reigate, Castle Acre, and the lordship of Bromfield and Yale, respectively. Arundel's brother-in-law Henry, earl of Lancaster, tried, albeit unsuccessfully, to recover part of the Lacy inheritance which had been granted, in 1319, to John de Warenne, who in turn granted a reversionary interest in it to William Montague, earl of Salisbury in 1337. In September 1347 Salisbury's son and heir, another William, and Lancaster submitted a petition to the king. But the lands were granted to Joan de Bar, now dowager countess of Surrey, who leased them to the Black Prince, who in turn surrendered them to Salisbury after the countess's death in 1361. Lancaster only obtained the Norfolk manors of the Lacy inheritance by virtue of the claim he had through Earl Thomas of Lancaster, who had married Alice, daughter of Henry de Lacy, last earl of Lincoln, who died in 1311.[8]

The Warenne lordship of Bromfield and Yale was initially taken into the Black Prince's hands, for he claimed it as part of his principality of Wales. He granted the lordship to Arundel on 8 August on a security bond of £2,000 until it was ascertained whether Joan de Bar was alive. As a matter of fact she was, and therefore had a right to her dower. On 27 August, the Black Prince ordered delivery of the lordship to Joan, having taken her fealty. On 1 December, Joan obtained licence to grant the lordship with its castle to Arundel, in exchange for £400 yearly from his lands in Shropshire and £500 yearly from his lands in Sussex, but with a reversion to herself if he were to pre-decease her. These transactions allow for an assessment of the value of Bromfield and Yale in 1347 at £900 yearly, which is more plausible than the sum of 2,000 marks estimated by the Black Prince's officials. In 1351 the lordship was estimated at £851, which might have resulted from losses due to the Black Death; in 1391 it was valued at £1,105, and in 1397 at £966.[9] On 18 August 1360, Edward III further granted Arundel the right to enter all the properties Joan held at her death without waiting for the normal inquisition to be held. He was also allowed to hold them in fee, despite some of the properties being held in chief.[10] Arundel, however, waited until Joan de Bar's death in 1361 before assuming the title of earl of Surrey.

The acquisition of the Warenne inheritance doubled the size of the Fitzalan estates overnight. The Fitzalan interests in the Marches were confined in the thirteenth century to the lordships of Oswestry and Clun, while the Warenne inheritance enabled that influence to be extended to Bromfield and Yale in the fourteenth century. These had been granted to John de Warenne (d.1304) by Edward I as a reward for his service during the conquest of Wales in the 1280s and 1290s. Although Earl Richard I had taken part in these campaigns, as the military base was in Oswestry, he was not among the beneficiaries of the conquest's spoils. Another family, however, to profit greatly from the conquest were the Mortimers, who were granted the lordship of Chirk. This was granted to Roger Mortimer junior (d.1326), the second son of Roger

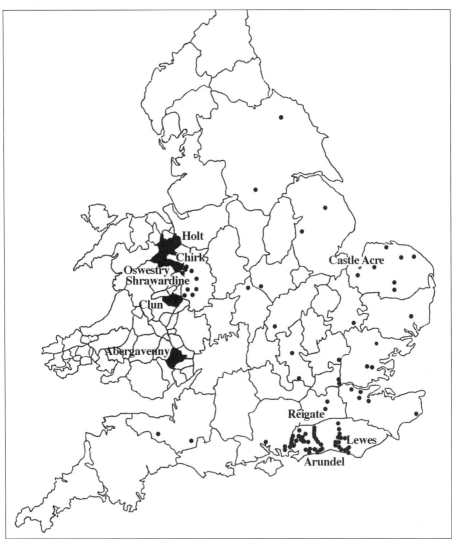

A broad impression of the location of the Fitzalan castles (given by name), lordships and most manors in 1399

Mortimer of Wigmore (d.1282). The fact that later the Fitzalans were able to unite these lordships under their control is of paramount importance in Marcher as well as English politics. The union of these territories into one dominion made of the Fitzalans the most powerful lords in the northern Marches of Wales.

The principal Fitzalan manors in Shropshire

The Lordship of Chirk

At Roger Mortimer's downfall, in January 1323, the lordship of Chirk was seized by royal officials, and it was granted to Arundel two months later. Chirk remained in Arundel's hands until 1326, when he was executed. Roger Mortimer of Wigmore (d.1330) success-fully petitioned to be reinstated into his inheritance as heir of his late uncle, Roger Mortimer of Chirk (d.1326); and his relation-ship with Queen Isabella also secured him Arundel's lordship of Oswestry.[11] Earl Edmund's tenure of Chirk, however, set a prece-dent for Arundel rule in the lord-ship. At the execution of Roger Mortimer and the forfeiture of his estates, in 1330, the lordship of Chirk was granted to Arundel, while the lordship of Denbigh was granted to William Montague, who had helped Edward III in his

coup to overthrow Mortimer. But Mortimer's son, another Roger, came of age in 1346, having distinguished himself at the battle of Crécy, and was admitted to the Order of the Garter with seizin of his father's lands. In 1348 he was then summoned to parliament as a baron, but most of his inheritance was only restored to him in 1354 when he claimed for a resettlement of his estates, and a reversal of his grandfather's judgement.

In April 1354 a decision by parliament conceded the reversion of all the Mortimer estates to the earl of March. An agreement, however, with the king's blessing, between Mortimer and Arundel settled

This page and opposite: Adam's Tower, the part of Chirk Castle that was built under Roger Mortimer of Chirk in the last years of the thirteenth century

that the lordship of Chirk should remain with Arundel as long as he could rule it efficiently. This was presumably the agreement that had been reached on 20 March 1354 when it was decided that the lordship would revert to Mortimer. The indenture sealing this deal was made in four copies, of which Arundel, Roger Mortimer of Wigmore, Sir Bartholomew de Burghersh and Sir John Beauchamp, the brother of the earl of Warwick, were to keep one copy each. It was stated that Edward III had seized the lordship of Chirk because it had reverted to him after the earl of March's forfeiture; thereafter he granted the lordship to Arundel. Because, now, March's heir, Roger Mortimer, had managed to secure the annulment of his uncle's attainder he was entitled to the lordship of Chirk. It was therefore agreed that the lordship would be released to Sir Bartholomew de Burghersh and Sir John Beauchamp, who were to keep it under the following condition: Roger Mortimer was entitled to obtain a reversion of it if he was able to compensate Arundel adequately to the full value of the estates. He was given two years to do this. If he was unable to find adequate compensation for Arundel, the latter and his heirs would be entitled to keep the lordship in perpetuity.[12]

Roger Mortimer was of course unable to compensate Arundel appropriately, and the lordship therefore reverted to him. This was clearly part of the deal, for both Arundel and Edward III knew that Mortimer would be unable to find the necessary funds. This new agreement was sealed in November with a settlement that Mortimer's son, Edmund, should marry Arundel's daughter, Alice. But, in the event, in 1368 Edmund Mortimer married Philippa, the daughter of Lionel, duke of Clarence and Elizabeth de Burgh, lady of Clare (the maternal aunt of Arundel's first wife Isabella Despenser). It is not clear when this marriage was arranged, but there is an interesting piece of evidence concerning a payment of £2,174 made by Edward III to the earl of March sometime in 1359-63 for the dower and marriage of his son.[13] Mortimer's loss of Chirk in Arundel's favour is a clear indicator of the importance and level of power the latter had acquired by this date. Even the Prince of Wales and the earl of Salisbury could not compete. Both had to return the lordships of Montgomery and Builth and the lordship of Denbigh, respectively, to Mortimer. The only allowance that was made to the Prince of Wales was that Mortimer was to hold the lordships from him rather than the king.

The 1354 restoration is quite significant as it shows the changes in attitude and legislation that had taken place in those years.[14] Although Mortimer was almost fully restored to his estates, another person who profited from the new 1352 Statute of Treason was Arundel himself, as will be shown.

When, in 1331, Earl Richard II had petitioned the king to be restored to his estates these were granted because the king wanted to show favour to all those who deserved it and, having great hope of good in Arundel, he granted him his estates as a reward for his role in bringing about the downfall of Mortimer and Isabella. On 8 February 1331, the charter of confirmation to his title and lands was granted.[15] In 1347-48 and 1350-51, the 1331 charter was re-examined on petition by Arundel because not all the property had been returned to him. The 1331 charter was nevertheless confirmed both times as it stood.[16] For Arundel the matter was, however, anything but satisfactorily settled. This may explain why he delayed giving his homage for Bromfield and Yale. Only in 1353, when he had been able to ensure that Chirk would be his, did he agree to give homage.[17] This delay is significant, but even more so is the fact that the future of the lordship of Chirk as a Fitzalan dominion undoubtedly depended on it.

These settlements were, however, also part of the major territorial resettlement Edward III was making during those years. That is why the restorations of 1354 can only be truly understood in the wider political context of the events preceding the judgements in favour of Arundel and Mortimer. They are, indeed, to be directly related to the 1352 Statute of Treason. After the political turmoil of 1340-41 created by the difficulty in financing the wars with France, the situation had been more relaxed in England, to the point that in 1352 it was decided to tackle the issue of treason, and thus newly define it under six articles:[18]

(1) compassing or imagining the death of the king, the queen, or their eldest son;
(2) violating the queen, the eldest unmarried daughter of the king, or the wife of the eldest son;
(3) levying war against the king or adhering to, or comforting his enemies;
(4) counterfeiting the royal seals or the royal money;
(5) importing counterfeit money into the realm;
(6) killing the chancellor, the treasurer or any of the judges.

In order to obtain agreement to this definition, Edward III needed a consensus from all parties, and it could be surmised that Arundel and Mortimer would be willing to give their support if this new statute was going to be useful to them. According to the new statute Arundel could claim that his father had not been guilty under any of the six headings and should not, therefore, have been condemned. The reasons why Mortimer's sentence should have been void is unclear as he was undoubtedly guilty under heading (3). But the political climate of the time was such that both obtained what they were aiming for. It was certainly not a simple decision for Edward III, for obviously the reversion encompassed problematic issues like the resettlement of landed interests. There were people Edward could afford to upset, like Salisbury for instance, but in the case of Arundel this was less simple. To secure the deal Arundel could do little but to accept, in the first instance, Mortimer's claim of Chirk, for this would simultaneously validate the reversal of his father's attainder. However, Arundel could not abandon the lordship without adequate compensation, hence the deal, whereby it was apparent that Mortimer would be unable to fulfil his side of the bargain. This episode further illustrates that Arundel was among those few English magnates Edward III could not afford, at this juncture, to alienate for whatever reason.

Arundel's estates had been granted back only as a mark of royal favour, not because they belonged to him by hereditary right. In 1354, he therefore petitioned the king anew in order to have an enquiry into the circumstances surrounding his father's execution which, he claimed, had been carried out without a fair trial. The subsequent enquiry uncovered a document that had inexplicably escaped previous attention, from which it appeared that nothing seemed to have justified why Earl Edmund should have been put to death without a fair trial. Parliament therefore declared that Arundel had been illegally executed, meaning that the present earl of Arundel had the right to hold all his estates and titles as if his father had died of natural causes.[19] Arundel had learned from the experience of men such as Montague who had been the beneficiaries of earlier royal grants which were later reconsidered. Under such circumstances the example of Chirk is quite telling. The change in emphasis on the declaration is extremely important for it prevented any possible challenge to the Fitzalans' rights over their estates.

Landed acquisitions

The acquisition in the mid-fourteenth century of the Warenne inheritance (1347) and the lordship of Chirk (1323 and 1354) are superb examples of how noble estates could expand to great proportions in the early fourteenth century. The lordship of Chirk along with the lordship of Bromfield and Yale gave the Fitzalans control over most of the former Welsh principality of Powys Fadog. This is undeniably one of the greatest success stories of aristocratic ascendancy in fourteenth-century England.

Another way by which estates could increase in size was by buying lands and manors directly. Such acquisitions enabled a family to choose their territory and area of influence more directly. From at least 1337 Earl Richard II began to acquire lands on a large scale, and particularly in Sussex;[20] his son, Earl Richard III, continued to purchase land, albeit on a much smaller scale.[21] In total Earl Richard II purchased twenty and a half manors and almost 2,000 acres of land worth 5,643 marks. The first recorded acquisition dates from 1337, when he bought Bilsham for 100 marks, followed the next year by another five manors; from this time onwards Arundel regularly acquired more and more land. These purchases do not only indicate active periods of financial investment and territorial expansion, but also suggest an increased availability of money in Arundel's coffers. The acquisitions are concentrated in the years of Arundel's campaigns in Scotland, Crécy and Calais, and then again in the years immediately after the Normandy campaign and the treaty of Brétigny-Calais. The chronology of these investments, coming right after active periods of conflict between England and France, suggests that Earl Richard II profited from war in the form of ransom money and booty.

One factor that helped Arundel to buy lands was the decreasing population. The pestilence of 1349 is recognised as one of the major causes of the decline but it is also true that in urban areas the population had begun to decline well before the pandemic reached England, supporting the existing evidence that in the south some lands remained untilled for lack of tenants.[22] This partly explains the paradox that as early as 1341 it was possible to see a progressive abandonment of arable land in Sussex, accompanied by a depopulation of certain areas. After the political turmoil of 1340-41, in 1341 parliament authorised the levy of a ninth on wool in order to rise taxes for war. The resulting tax returns, the *Nonarum Inquisitiones*, indicate that in Sussex land had gone out of cultivation in the early fourteenth century in at least 52 of the 271 parishes. Some 6,000 acres which were once cultivated were recorded in 1342 as lying untilled, and a further 4,000 acres had been flooded by the sea. The jurors who had been appointed to compile the parish returns had, as a point of comparison

The Fitzalan estates in Sussex

and guide, the assessment of the tenth of clerical incomes for 1291 which had been levied by Pope Nicholas IV. The jurors were then asked to explain the discrepancies in acreage and value between 1291 and 1341.[23] The highest concentration of untilled land was not in the Weald, but on the supposedly richer soils along the coast and around the South Downs because of fear of French attacks, rabbit burrows, poor soils, and the lack of tenants. The latter was seen to account for abandoned lands in the parishes of Goring, Hooe, Billingshurst, East Dean, Falmer, Friston, Iford, Houghton, Ninfield, Patcham, Rottingdean, Sutton, Up Marden, West Blatchington, Bepton, Cocking, Heighton, Street and Streat.[24] It comes as almost no surprise to see that the earls of Arundel, the local lords who had cash to spend, were able to acquire properties there, in Goring, Iford, Up Marden, West Blatchington and Cocking in particular.[25]

Through regular investments the Fitzalans increased dramatically the size of their southern estates and the impact of their lordship on the locality. In the 1380s this estate can be estimated, for Sussex alone, at 7,471 acres of arable, 6,350 acres of pasture, 615 acres of meadow, and a further 610 acres of unspecified land: a total of 15,046 acres, most of which was in demesne, over double in size the demesnes of the bishop of Chichester, Battle Abbey, and even Canterbury Cathedral Priory.[26] Earl Richard II also bought a number of plots of land in Arundel itself, suggesting that he was consolidating his holdings.[27] Some of the plots he bought were near the castle, so they may have been incorporated into his park; while others were small pieces of arable or meadow ranging from only two to six acres. It is noteworthy that he also purchased a number of mills nearby.

Comital lands were not entirely held by purchase, however, and the descent of the estates greatly depended on their legal status. Earl Richard II ensured that his son, Richard, was to inherit the family's estates by enfeoffing them — the lands would be granted to some trusted people, the feoffees, who would then re-grant them to the legitimate heirs once they came of age. This was particularly necessary to ensure that his first-born, Sir Edmund Arundel, was completely removed from the succession. Major transfers of land from one family to another rarely happened unexpectedly, as had been shown in the case of the Warenne inheritance. These transfers were usually carefully planned by arranging suitable marriages and the marriage contract therefore enabled the inheritance to be settled on husband and wife to form a jointure in land. If, in the worst case scenario, the only heirs were daughters, the lands and the titles would pass to their husbands, thus avoiding the concentration of lands, titles, and power within a small circle of noble families.

Due to Earl Edmund's sudden death in 1326 he had no time to leave any clear indication about what he intended to do with his estates or what type of enfeoffments he may already have carried out.[28] There is more evidence regarding his son's enfeoffments. When, in 1345, Earl Richard II married Eleanor of Lancaster, he made an enfeoffment of nearly all his lands, giving himself a life interest in them; this may well have been part and parcel of the marriage deal. The annulment of his marriage to Isabella Despenser the previous year had also automatically bastardised their son, Edmund.[29] Although the annulment did legally remove Edmund from the succession, it was still deemed necessary to ensure that the line of succession would be that of the second marriage. One could never be careful enough. There is no evidence, however, to suggest that there had already been an earlier enfeoffment in favour of Edmund which needed to be amended in favour of any new heirs. The reversion of Arundel's Sussex lands was granted, therefore, to Eleanor of Lancaster, while that of his Marcher estates was granted to his trustees, John de Alresford and John Sprot, chaplain.[30] This arrangement was changed in 1347 by a grant of the reversion to Eleanor's male heirs; this was presumably undertaken in view of the birth of their son, Richard. On this occasion Arundel's other son, Edmund

Arundel, asserted his own claim to the estates.[31] In 1356, a new re-enfeoffment was arranged to clarify the descent, as meanwhile Arundel and Eleanor had had more children; thus the estates were to descend firstly to Richard, then to John or Thomas. The number of feoffees was also increased from two to four: John de Alresford and John Sprot remained feoffees, as in 1345, and they were now joined by the chaplain John Vyncent and Sir Edward de St John, a major Sussex landholder closely associated with Earl Richard II's business and witness to charters on numerous occasions.[32]

Again, in 1366, two new re-enfeoffments were made which specifically included the Surrey, Sussex and Marcher estates that Arundel had inherited from John de Warenne in 1347.[33] This time the importance of the enfeoffments is apparent given the number and importance of the feoffees: Sir Edward de St John was appointed again, and was joined by John of Gaunt, duke of Lancaster; Humphrey de Bohun, earl of Hereford and father-in-law of two of Arundel's children; Sir Henry de Beaumont, an important knight and relative of Eleanor of Lancaster through her first marriage; Sir Roger Lestrange, the earl's brother-in-law, friend and executor; Sir Guy de Brian, Arundel's friend and executor; Sir Gerard de Lisle, the earl's brother-in-law and retainer; Sir Henry Percy, also a family member; Sir Thomas de Lodelowe; Sir John de Lodelowe; Sir John de Delves, the earl's steward in Chirk and Oswestry in 1348, before becoming Deputy Justice of north Wales; Sir Walter de Hopton, an influential member of the Shropshire gentry, in particular in Clun and Wem; William Banastre, Robert de Halsham, John Botiller, Sir Roger Dallingridge, John de Kyngesfold, and Henry de Wynnesbury, all important Sussex men and landholders.

The second re-enfeoffment of 1366 stated that the estates were to be held jointly by Arundel and Eleanor for life, with a life interest for her and the remainder to their son Richard or his brothers, John and Thomas or the male heirs of the bodies of their sisters Joan and Alice.[34] The feoffees of this arrangement were the same as in the first one. Earl Richard II had to sort out the legal descent of his estates, but that this was a legal technicality is demonstrated by the fact that by 1373 the Surrey, Sussex, and Welsh estates of the Warenne inheritance were already in the hands of the younger Richard III and his wife, Elizabeth de Bohun. By granting them the estates three years before his death Arundel showed that he wanted to ensure, at all costs, that the children of his second marriage would obtain his estates.[35] It may also indicate that as early as the 1370s Arundel had handed over most of the estate's management to his son. At Earl Richard II's death none of his estates was held in fee simple, and therefore no *inquisition post mortem* was made. As all the estates had already been enfeoffed with reversion to his son, Richard, the heirs did not need to claim their inheritance in the ordinary way, but they received, nevertheless, a royal letter patent pardoning them for entering on their estates.[36]

These arrangements did not solve all the problems that might have existed. In 1396, Earl Richard III secured a quitclaim from Philippa Sergeaux, Sir Edmund Arundel's daughter, over all the rights she still had over his father's estates.[37] The date suggests that he was concerned by the succession of his estates, even though Sir Edmund's branch did not have any claims to the main estate. It is uncertain whether on this occasion money was exchanged.

The following year Earl Richard III was executed, and the lands were seized by the Crown. Most were kept in the Crown's possession, and the Marcher lordships were annexed to the new Principality of Chester. The Sussex lands, including Arundel, and Reigate in Surrey, were granted to John Holland, earl of Huntingdon, who after Thomas Mowbray's downfall from favour was also granted Lewes and its pertaining manors; the Norfolk properties were granted to Edmund of Langley, duke of York; and the Shropshire lands to Thomas Percy, earl of Worcester. All the estates were restored to Earl Thomas Fitzalan in 1399.[38]

The Fitzalan inheritance illustrates how control over the devolution of a large estate could be withdrawn from the Crown. In this sense it is true that from the second half of the fourteenth century magnates were gaining a larger control over their inheritances.[39] However, the mixture of different legal arrangements that were undertaken to keep the family's control over the estates had its dangers: because Earl Richard II's estates were held both in tail male (by which only direct male heirs could inherit) and in fee simple (full ownership), ultimately, once the family became extinct in the main male line in 1415, the inheritance had to be dismembered and divided between his granddaughters and his grandson, through the line of Sir John Arundel (d.1379). This division put an end to over a century and a half of territorial concentration in the hands of the Fitzalans. What had become the largest estate held by a comital family in the fourteenth century was no more: the lordship of Oswestry went to a cousin of Earl Thomas, John Arundel, lord Maltravers (d.1421), and only legitimate male heir to the Arundel inheritance because at Thomas' restoration, in 1399, the descent of the earldom was limited to male heirs only, thus becoming an earldom in fee. The lordship of Bromfield and Yale, originally a Warenne holding, was divided among Earl Thomas's three sisters: Elizabeth, duchess of Norfolk, Joan, baroness of Abergavenny, and Margaret, wife of Sir Roland Lenthall; while the earldom of Surrey reverted to the Crown.[40] When, on 13 October 1415, Earl Thomas succumbed to dysentery, the Fitzalan inheritance died with him.[41] The vacuum of power left by the disappearance of Fitzalan lordship enabled the rise of the local squirearchy. Many of these families, who now looked towards themselves for leadership, were to emerge as gentry in the sixteenth century.

Seignorial administration and income

The lordships of Chirk, Oswestry, Clun, and Bromfield and Yale formed a financial unit in the Arundel complex of the north-eastern March of Wales.[42] Bromfield and Yale along with Holt were jointly worth £960 in 1397; the surveys of Bromfield and Yale also clearly show how dramatically the expected revenue from these territories increased, from £434 in 1315 to £1,105 in 1391, and £967 in 1397. Similarly, Oswestry was valued at £233 in 1351, £404 in 1362-63, and £376 in 1397; while Chirk produced annual receipts of £500 in the 1360s and 1370s but fell to about £375 from about 1381 onwards, to reach £414 in 1397. Clun was worth about £398 in 1351, £251 in 1397, and £256 in 1404.[43]

Marcher lordships were, therefore, handsomely profitable to their English lords; even though there was a decrease in revenue towards the end of the fourteenth century, these lordships remained at the heart of seigniorial income. Arundel's coffers in the March, probably at Holt and Clun, reported £19,000 in ready cash at Michaelmas 1370. By the following year Arundel held £21,109 there of which £11,193 was outstanding as loans, and in July 1375 he had £10,981.[44] When, in 1397, the Fitzalans' Marcher lordships were declared forfeit the king was able to levy a fine of £3,083.[45] The financial success of this seigniorial pressure was ultimately to fuel the discontent which erupted in 1400 under the leadership of Owain Glyn Dŵr, a man closely connected to the Fitzalans since his father had been their steward in Oswestry and Chirk in 1348, and therefore a direct witness of their imposing, if not overbearing, lordship (see chapter 5). However, by the time the revolt erupted, the decay of the Arundel lordships could already be witnessed in the reduction of seigniorial income. The pressure this caused ultimately triggered Owain's revolt.[46]

The Fitzalans' English estates were mainly centred on Sussex and Surrey, with some scattered manors in other counties, notably in Norfolk around Castle Acre, part of the Warenne inheritance. These became increasingly profitable during the fourteenth century, enhanced by Earl Richard II's purchases noted above. He could expect to receive about £1,100 in 1350, and his son about £970 in the 1380s.[47] Arundel thus showed a preference for his English estates which is hardly surprising since, as Sir Rees Davies once commented, 'good hunting was one of the few reasons, short of war, which could persuade the English nobility to visit their lands in Wales'.[48] Marcher lordships were the golden geese and playgrounds of the English nobility. The Fitzalans' Marcher lordships were, however, only located on the border of Wales and were thus spared the threatening environment and geography so little appreciated by the English. Medieval Oswestry was indeed one of the larger market towns and on one of the main routes into Wales thus becoming known, in the fourteenth century, as the 'London of Wales'; it was only once a traveller had passed Chirk to the south-west that one entered a very different country in terms of terrain, language, and people.[49]

The move of the traditional Fitzalan burial site from Shropshire to Sussex is indicative of the increased significance that their English estates acquired as the fourteenth century progressed. Nonetheless, under Earl Richard III, increasing attention and money was again spent on the Welsh borderland. He refurbished the castles of Shrawardine and Holt, which remained the main treasuries there, and he also renamed the former Castle Philippa, probably in honour of his new bride, Philippa Mortimer dowager countess of Pembroke, whom he had married in 1391. Earl Richard III's power in the Marches was unprecedented: apart from his own lordships he controlled a third of the lord-ship of Abergavenny after the death of its lord in 1389; and from 1384-93 he chaired the consortium that administered the Mortimer inheritance.[50] Earl Richard III's marriage to Philippa Mortimer only strengthened and sealed his supremacy within the country, and he certainly did whatever was neces-sary to obtain the control for which he had married Philippa. Between August and December 1394, he vigorously pursued cases in the King's Bench for the assignment of Philippa's dower lands.[51]

Seignorial power, influence, and income was centred around the manor, which was intended as a profit-making unit in a magnate's estate. The profits came from the production of consumables and livestock, but also from the services, rents and jurisdictional rights which were invariably attached to it. Manors were normally not held singly, like self-contained units cut off from the outside world, but in groups, even if these manors were widely scattered. When it became possible to acquire manors and lands within a small area, this enabled production to concentrate upon certain crops or livestock, and made organising the management simpler. This was particularly important in Sussex which was peculiar for its sheep-corn husbandry. The profitability of an estate

Gathering in the harvest under the supervision of the lord's official
(British Library, Royal MS Royal 2.B.vii, f.78ᵛ)

Ploughing (British Library, Add MS 42130, f.170)

as a whole was assessed not only in terms of cash surplus, but also in estimates of agricultural productivity and the amount of capital investment in stock and produce.[52]

Each Marcher lordship had a receiver who was in charge of rendering his own account for the lordship's revenue and who also often acted as chancellor and treasurer. There is no evidence, however, to suggest that the Arundel receiver benefited from such extensive powers. In the Marches the receiver's financial duties were to receive the issues of a lordship into the treasury from the various officials and to render his own account to the lord's receiver-general, making any necessary expenditure, and paying the expenses and fees of officials. In his role of chancellor he would have the custody of the records and seals, and would be responsible for the production of charters, writs, court rolls, fines, and amercements.[53] But, as the example of the dukes of Stafford shows, in the fifteenth century the distribution of administrative responsibility really lay with the dukes and therefore did change: while the first duke preferred a centralised administration in the hands of the receiver general, the second duke preferred a more flexible approach.[54] The Fitzalans' receiver was, furthermore, also responsible for the lord's agricultural interests. Large estates, with their units of manors and single productive units, were administered for the lord by his cohort of officials (bailiffs, reeves, and provosts) accountable to central officers such as receivers or the receiver-general.

A dog cart in a manuscript of the fourteenth century

A reaper's cart going uphill, as depicted in the Luttrell Psalter

This was all part of a wider organisation in charge of administering a lordship, honour or estate. For such an administration to work effectively the Fitzalans, like all their fellow magnates, needed an administrative framework that would enable their officials to be appointed, to levy their monies, and to be controlled effectively to minimize fraud and thus maximize profits. In 1365, for example, Nicholas Neweton, Nicholas de Wilcombe senior, and John Emmery were appointed as supervisors to survey the state of the Sussex manors of Bourne and Nutbourne.[55] Trustworthy officials and efficient control procedures were the minimum requirement for a well-managed estate, but the organisation of the Arundel estates depended on whether they were in the Marches or in England.

The lordship of Oswestry was organised into three main administrative portions: the Duparts, the Traean, and the borough of Oswestry with its liberties. The borough of Oswestry was in the charge of two bailiffs, one responsible for the burgage, rents and farms of demesne land, and the other in charge of the rents of the other lands and the perquisites of the borough courts. In the same manner the Duparts was allotted to two bailiffs.[56] The manors owned by the Fitzalans, whether they were held in fee or in demesne, had their own bailiffs and reeves and transferred their revenues to the receiver of Oswestry. In Ruyton, for example, the revenue was delivered to the receiver of the lordship of Clun until the 1330s and to the receiver of Oswestry thereafter. This example highlights perfectly the differences in manorial revenue and size. In the fourteenth century Ruyton was among the most valuable manors of the Oswestry lordship, worth about £60 per year in 1357-58 and £75 in 1388-96.[57] It had a borough, a castle, and its own market, and the manor as such consisted of ten townships (Rednal, Eardiston, Sutton, Felton, Shotatton, Haughton, Tedsmoor, Wikey, Shelwoke, and Cotton) which, with Ruyton itself, gave

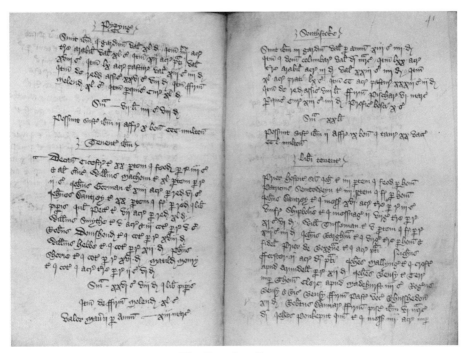

The Fitzalan Survey
showing the entries for Peppering (left) and South Stoke (right)
(Arundel Castle Trustees Ltd)

their name to Ruyton-XI-Towns. The other important manor of the lordship was Shrawardine. It was worth about £60 yearly, and its castle was among the Fitzalans' favourite residences in the fourteenth century, and may well have superseded Chirk and Oswestry in that respect.[58] The castle was certainly in use until the end of the fourteenth century and Earl Richard III made his will there on 4 March 1393.[59] Chirk Castle, meanwhile, had become the centre for the lordship's chancery and exchequer as well as a repository for its records. As the administrative centre of the lordship it had been built at the beginning of the fourteenth century by the Mortimers on plans resembling those of Edward I's castle of Beaumaris.

The lordship was subdivided in commotes, which in turn were subdivided into ringildries, thus using existing Welsh administrative divisions, under the responsibility of a ringild. At least until 1334 these officers were paid directly by the lord and later a system of farms was introduced. The same was the case in Oswestry.[60] This was certainly caused by a drastic fall in demesne revenues due to the heavy reliance on paid labour. Many other Marcher lords felt the same pressures on their demesnes and progressively throughout the fourteenth century, from Elizabeth de Burgh, lady of Clare to the earls of Hereford and the dukes of Stafford, demesne farming was abandoned in favour of farms. Far

*The Fitzalan Survey
showing 'The Extent of the Earl of Arundel's Lands.
The Earl of Arundel's Fees in Norfolk' (top half)
and the extent for the manor of Arundel (bottom half)
(Arundel Castle Trustees Ltd)*

from being a simple chapter in economic and agrarian history this dramatic development changed the character of lordship itself, undermining the meaning and role of the manor. The leasing of the demesne weakened in some measure the nature and impact of lordship and hastened the process whereby the lord became little more than an absentee rent-collecting landlord.[61]

The administrative function of the castle of Holt in Bromfield and Yale is better documented than the centres of Chirk and Oswestry, but it can be surmised that all three, as centres of Marcher baronial power, worked on broadly similar administrative frameworks. There were undoubtedly differences as, for instance, in the detail of the administration of law. Indeed, although the personnel of Chirk and Oswestry were often the same, the actual financial and judicial administration was distinctly kept apart. The body of the administrative personnel was mainly recruited by the lord and trained in his administration and could be composed of people from one lordship or another; local Welshmen could also be employed. Robert Eggerley was such a notable clerk who, born on one of Arundel's manors in Shropshire, then became receiver of Oswestry and Chirk from the late 1380s and authored the three surveys of the Arundel Marcher lordship.[62]

The central administration at Bromfield and Yale was composed of a steward, a receiver and other central officials (as at Chirk and Oswestry) based at Holt Castle. The three administrative divisions of the raglotries of Bromfield and Yale — the castle of Holt and Dinas Brân, the lands of Bromfield and Yale, and Wrexham — were each under the jurisdiction of a raglot, a keeper of the peace, and a coroner and escheator.[63] The term of lesser local officials, such as ringilds and reeves, usually coincided with the financial year. Local officials were normally chosen by the local community, but the appointment of important central officers was the preserve of the lord or his council. Also in Bromfield and Yale comparatively few offices were farmed out, mostly being supported by fees, and in the case of major local officers they were paid directly from the lord's coffers. In Denbigh, on the other hand, all the local offices were farmed out. It is possible that in Bromfield and Yale the offices at farm were not much sought after, and that the expected profits from them were too little to attract people willing to buy the farms, who might also have been worried by the possibility of losses. An officer was personally responsible for the issues of his bailiwick and any shortfall of the expected sum was carefully recorded at the foot of account rolls and then reported from account roll to account roll, year after year, sometimes for up to a decade.[64]

The chief officer on the Marcher estates was the steward or seneschal.[65] From 1322 until 1326 the administration of Chirk and Oswestry was often performed by the same person. Between the three north-eastern lordships there was also sharing of senior officials. John de Bourton had been steward of Bromfield and Yale in 1349, and had held the same position in Chirk and Oswestry in 1336-42

*The Fitzalan Survey
showing the extents of the manor of Stansfield (top)
and the manor of Bourne (bottom)
(Arundel Castle Trustees Ltd)*

and 1348-50. John Herlaston had been steward of Bromfield and Yale in 1387, and then in all three lordships in 1390.[66] Thus senior officials could be rotated between periods of office in the three lordships and show how a common administrative control could be achieved by the joint-tenure of certain offices. The steward and the auditors were the real managers of the Fitzalan estates. Although the functions of the steward are not precisely known, he was to act as if he was the lord in person and therefore had almost complete *carte blanche* over the administration of the estates, as well as the appointment or removal of farmers and officers alike. The steward was also in charge of dispensing the lord's justice in the lordships and was, in the survey of Bromfield and Yale, also styled as chancellor. The steward was therefore one of the most important officials on a lord's estate since he was expected to have legal knowledge to represent his lord in court actions, had supervision of his seneschaucy, and he was in charge of directing the work of the bailiffs.[67] The role of the steward was to manage the estate and ensure its productivity, whilst the receiver was in charge of the collection of rents and dues.

Little to nothing is known regarding the senior officials active in Sussex and Surrey, for only a partial list of receivers for Arundel has survived. It is possible that the receiver of Arundel was responsible only for that rape (Sussex being divided into the six jurisidictional units of the rape: Chichester, Arundel, Bramber, Lewes, Pevensey and Hastings), but was still considered a receiver-general, whereby he would still be accountable to a central higher ranking official, the treasurer of the household. Indeed, in 1408-09, clear distinctions were drawn between John Gobell, receiver of Arundel, John Bartelot, treasurer of Earl Thomas' household, and William Beche, who was the receiver of Lady Margaret Arundel.[68] For previous years the evidence is wanting. However, it is possible that William Herdwyck, who appears prominently in 1376 as being in charge of the earl's monies, may have had a role resembling that of receiver or treasurer.[69] William was a canon of Chichester Cathedral and undoubtedly an experienced administrator since he had been steward of Bishop Stratford's household as well as his executor in 1362.[70] Earl Richard II also nominated William to be one of his executors in 1376.[71]

The Sussex and Surrey estates were distinguished by three administrative units centred around Arundel, Lewes, and Reigate, each of which had at its centre a castle and borough, which are known to have been used regularly by the Fitzalans, and each of them had its own receiver.[72] The latter two were originally Warenne holdings which came to the Fitzalans after 1347, and it is possible that existing administrative divisions were maintained when the Warenne inheritance was absorbed into the Fitzalan estates. However, the absence of sources on Lewes and Reigate means that almost nothing is known about them. The seignorial records at Lewes Castle were destroyed in 1381 when the peasants stormed it.

Little, also, is known of the auditors who assisted in the administration of the estates, but some evidence suggests that the abbots of Haughmond acted in this function. Richard de Brugg, who may have been a monk at Haughmond when he was Arundel's auditor in 1334, was by 1346 abbot of the same, which shows how service and patronage were closely linked. This was certainly a position that would have suited Haughmond's other responsibility as keepers of the Fitzalan burials in their abbey. The abbey was also used on occasion as a depository for monies from the lordship, and the abbots were also sporadically in charge of transporting these monies to Arundel.[73] It is possible that the abbots of Battle and the priors of Lewes officiated in a similar capacity for the Fitzalans' southern estates. Battle Abbey was among the largest ecclesiastical landowners in Sussex, commanding large sheep flocks, and its abbots would have been perfectly suited to act as auditors for the Arundel estates. The fact that the abbot of Battle and the prior of Lewes, rather than the abbot of Haughmond, were appointed as executors in Earl Richard II's will may also indicate their acquaintance with the earl's administration.[74]

From 1322 until 1415, apart from the periods of forfeiture (1326-1330 and 1397-1399), all the officers of the Marcher lordships were appointed directly by the earls of Arundel. In particular the long career of Earl Richard II allowed the development of a consistent body of administrators, suggesting that this must also have been the case on the English estates. John de Delves, for example, was steward of Bromfield and Yale in 1348, before becoming deputy justice of north Wales; and Gruffudd, lord of Glyndyfrdwy and Cynllaith, had been steward of Oswestry and Chirk in 1348. The lords of Glyndyfrdwy are a good example of how the Welsh aristocracy was able to preserve part of their role in their Welsh baronies as performers of administrative duties.[75] In Bromfield and Yale as well there were some exceptional Welshmen who had prominent roles in the administration: Madog ap Llywelyn and Thomas ap Dafydd, for instance, were receivers in 1319 and 1351 respectively.[76] The stewards were often, but not always, high-ranking professionals, which was less often the case for the receivers.[77] In the Marches the receivers held office, normally, for periods averaging five years. Some, such as Alan de Thorp and Gruffudd Chastell, were beneficed clerks and had their own livings.

The offices of lower level than that of receiver were usually performed by members of the local landed families who had their own interests at heart, and often the manors would be farmed out to such people, who would thereby also be able to influence local justice to some extent through the manorial courts. The Gethins, for instance, were a prominent local landed family who in each generation had members holding the offices of ringilds, reeves and parkers.[78] Again, comparison with Sussex is difficult but it would appear that there officers of bailiwicks were appointed for an average of two years. As for the receivership of Arundel, at least in the 1350s and 1360s, it was based on the rotation from year to year between individual receivers, while from the 1370s onwards receivers held the office for three or four years in a row. Again, these positions were filled by local men. From 1352 until 1365, for instance, John Wilcok, John Dounton and Richard, rector of Tangmere all acted as receivers for a number of years. The case of Richard shows that, as in the Marches, some officials could be beneficed. Another notable example is that of Simon Bredon, fellow of Merton College, Oxford, who in 1352, in his capacity of rector of Rustingdon, was in charge of some of Arundel's monies, and by 1355 is said to have also been acting as his physician.[79] The Fitzalans were certainly demanding lords, but it was the income that the estate generated that enabled a magnate to finance all aspects of life pertaining to his rank and personal inclinations, ultimately aggrandizing his own person and family and, by default, also his affinity and entourage who were, or wished to be, associated with such a powerful and grand lord.

The accounts presented by these officials were an important aspect of the collection of revenues. They were not strictly intended to show the profit or loss of an estate; but they were to account for the revenue and expenses of an accounting unit, which would indicate the amount of money past and present officials owed to the lord.[80] Often arrears thus accounted for were reported from account to account, and sometimes paid off or sometimes reported over the years until they would on occasion be written off. Arrears were usually collected in the end, however, and should not be regarded as bad debts for which all hope of recovery had been abandoned, as the example of Angmering in Sussex illustrates. By 1365 arrears amounted to £120, and £145 by 1376, but by 1389 part had been collected and thus the arrears only amounted to 19s 8d, although a part had had to be written off. The account of Henry Janyn, bailiff of Angmering, accounted for £145 arrears by 24 January 1376. Just over half of this sum had been accumulated by Janyn's predecessors of nine years: Robert Anestetonne owed 20d, Philip Maister 45s 10d, John Brekepot £8, and John Pote £65. In 1376 it was decided to pardon the arrears of John Brekepot who had been imprisoned because of them, but was eventually freed and pardoned. It is unclear if he had been seized before or after Earl Richard II's death, but in any case the account clearly states that he was incarcerated on the earl's orders.[81] John Pote was pardoned £21, as the executors decided that his long service to the earl deserved such a reward: he had served as bailiff for four years at Ford, two at Strodlond, and two at Angmering. Robert Anestetonne and Philip Maister remained accountable for the full amounts. In total Earl Richard II's executors pardoned £94 so that in the end Henry Janyn only owed £8, and the earl's son, Richard III, who had also acted as one of his father's officials, owed £17.[82]

This is a prime example of how a magnate could educate his offspring in the management of the inheritance. There was nothing like first-hand experience on the ground to learn about the management of an estate, the difficulties of levying dues, and the working procedures of an official. It removed an over-reliance on officials and taught a magnate-to-be how important the work of levying revenues was in the preservation of the inheritance. It also meant that tenants would meet and know the future heirs and it enabled these heirs to visit the estates and know them more intimately. This was not absent lordship, quite the contrary. Arundel's second son, Sir John Arundel, also served his father and, at the latter's death in 1376, Sir John held 8,486 marks worth of receipts from the lordships of Arundel, Lewes, and Reigate.[83] This is quite extraordinary; no similar example is known among the other noble families.

The exploitation of the Estates

Besides the administrative control of an estate there was also the issue of its direct exploitation. Wool was an important source of income for the Fitzalans and their fellow magnates. The same was true for the Crown, which imposed export taxes on wool, particularly at the beginning of the Hundred Years war. In 1336 the export of wool was prohibited, and the king obtained from the merchants a subsidy of 20 shillings per sack (300 fells). The following year Edward III asserted his right, introducing a monopoly on the commerce of wool. In 1353 wool staples, or markets, were established at Newcastle, York, Lincoln, Norwich, Westminster, Canterbury, Chichester, Winchester, Exeter, and Bristol; for Wales at Carmarthen, and for Ireland at Dublin, Waterford, Cork, and Drogheda. For those towns without ports, neighbouring locations were assigned to which the wool should be sent for export: from York to Hull, Lincoln to Boston, Norwich to Yarmouth, Westminster to London, and Canterbury to Sandwich. Additionally, in 1363, a staple was also established at Calais where it remained until 1369, and then again from 1373. However, by the time the staples were established exports of wool had already begun to decline which had a dramatic impact on custom's revenue; it fell from £68,000, in the heyday of the Calais staple, to £12,000 in 1449.[84]

By the mid-fourteenth century the Arundels had ceased to cultivate their lands directly in the Marches of Wales, but like many other large landholders in the Marches they began exploiting their estates as centres for the rearing of large flocks of sheep. This specialisation in the lucrative production of wool is also seen on the Sussex estates. In 1349 Earl Richard II owned 12,974 sheep: most of them was concentrated in Sussex and Clun, where there were 6,625 and 3,089 sheep respectively.[85] Astonishingly, there was no sheep-farming on a seigniorial level in Chirk; this is especially surprising since sheep were at the heart of an integrated economy, providing manure for fertilising arable ground.[86] The territorial acquisitions undertaken by Earl Richard II considerably increased the number of animals and by the 1380s the Fitzalans' Sussex livestock amounted to 13,950 sheep, 908 head of cattle and 63 farmhorses, living on 6,350 acres of pasture.[87] The Fitzalans' estates were amongst the largest in the country and compare, in their extent and complexity, only with other great landowners such as Lancaster and Clare, or the large ecclesiastical institutions such as Canterbury, Westminster, and Winchester.[88]

In the Marches, such as in the lordship of Oswestry, certain manors were set up as specialist centres for the farming of sheep, while others concentrated on the production of those goods necessary to the farming of sheep. The most important among these manors were Sandford, Ruyton and Llwyn-y-mapsis in Sweeney. Ruyton had a regular large flock between 1336 and 1354, ranging from 515 to a peak of 973 sheep in 1340-41. At Sandford the rearing of sheep began only at the beginning of the 1380s when the lack of tenants and a decreasing income from rents encouraged Arundel to convert the demesne land into pasture, keeping a flock of around 300 sheep. This was a response to the fall in demand for land, and echoes the general trend seen on other estates where, progressively, during the fourteenth century demesne was given over to sheep.[89] Throughout England the fourteenth century saw a doubling of the numbers of livestock, which also meant that large areas of land were converted into temporary and permanent pasture. At Llwyn-y-mapsis a flock of nearly 600 head was kept in 1360-61.[90] But we have seen that the greatest concentration of sheep in the Marches was at Clun which could be down to the nature of the native Clun sheep, a light-weight breed which produced a fine, short-woolled fleece and was ideal for the poor soils of the south-west and central uplands. In 1371-72 the bailiff of Clun managed nine flocks of about 240 sheep each kept in seven different places.[91] He was in charge of buying and selling sheep, supplying the hay, and paying the seven shepherds, as well as arranging the washing and shearing of the sheep.

A sheepfold. Sheep were valuable for their meat, their wool and their milk (British Library, Add MS 42130 f.163ᵛ)

Sheep were also often transferred between flocks kept on various manors under the care of demesne officials. In 1372-73, for example, the bailiff of Clunton and Kempton handed over 240 sheep to the reeve of Bicton to stock a new grange and received in turn 237 hoggets from the reeve of Clunbury.[92] Similar pastoral patterns also appear in Sussex: at Angmering, in 1349-50, there was a flock of 528 sheep.[93] In 1356-57 their number had increased to 1,414 of which 30 had been brought from Cudlow, 20 each from Changelton, Wepham, and Peppering, and 16 lambs from Singleton.[94] Again, in 1375-76, of the 1,314 sheep 437 had been brought by Robert atte Grene, then the receiver of Arundel;[95] and in 1379-80, when some 1,673 sheep grazed on the lands of Angmering, again an important number came from other manors: 48 ewes from Poling and 57 from Lyminster, 244 hoggets from Heene.[96] Other notable examples are Preston (now part of Worthing);[97] and North Stoke where large numbers of carts of hay are accounted for and certainly destined for winter fodder.[98] In 1357-58, for instance, six carts of hay were sent to Peppering to feed the lord's sheep and cows.[99] The role of these manors was also determined by the size of their estate, and although the average estate had 100-200 acres of pasture, Angmering was the largest with 500 acres, followed by Singleton and Up Marden with 400 acres each;[100] while North Stoke, which was able to produce large amounts of hay, also had among the largest acreages of meadow at 44 acres, the largest being at Lyminster with 60 acres.[101] One point they all had in common was that each year the wool would be transported to Stansted in Sussex for weighing, which would take place under the vigilant eye of Arundel's council.[102]

Since Sussex was characterised by mixed sheep-corn farming it is important to realise that another significant source of manorial income came from the production of cereals and legumes. At Angmering, throughout Earl Richard II's tenure, the acreage remained stable at around 180 acres, but by 1379-80 it had declined to 165 acres, and by the following decade to just 106 acres, although by 1394-95 it was up again to 163 acres. Thus acreage certainly made way for sheep which were less labour intensive and thus more profitable, although, the progressive decline in wool prices may suggest the reasons behind the renewed increase in arable. Nevertheless, from the mid-1350s to the mid-1360s production seems to have been successful with wheat and barley as the two most important cereals. The large production of legumes and oats could be used to sustain the manorial tenants as well as pigs and horses. Large quantities of corn produced on Angmering were also sold, and made up to 35%-44% of the manor's revenue from the second half of the 1350s to the first half of the 1360s, when sales from the stables of animals and meat became more important, rising from only 6% in 1356-57 to 28% in 1394-95. This trend clearly shows how the manor changed its production methods, progressively moving from the labour-intensive agricultural exploitation of its lands to the less labour-intensive rearing of animals such as sheep and pigs. Gradually, also, a higher proportion of Angmering's income came from rents, from 17 % in 1356-57 to 31% in 1394-95, which again indicates a progressive withdrawal from the direct exploitation of the demesne. Although Angmering is but one example it does illustrate the general trend that has been seen many a time on other magnates' estates.[103]

The example of Dorking in Surrey again suggests that most of the income came from rents and farms, followed by perquisites of courts. The farms there were mostly made up of the mills, which were worth £18 yearly.[104] Dorking also had a warren, as is suggested by deliveries of rabbits made in August and September 1381 to the Fitzalans gathered at Reigate Castle: Earl Richard III received 132 rabbits and 34 hares; his sister, Countess Joan of Hereford received 24 rabbits; while Bishop Thomas Arundel received four.[105] The following year, when Arundel and his household gathered again at Reigate, he received 603 rabbits and 34 hares.[106] The number of rabbits is suggestive of the household's size and its level of consumption. Unfortunately no household accounts have survived to give an indication of the family's living patterns, but it is interesting to note that rabbit fur could be used to line clothing and formed, therefore, part of the livery given to retainers and members of the household.

The analysis of the Fitzalans' manorial revenues has brought the crucial conclusion that direct sheep farming, although very lucrative, did not form a tremendously significant part of their income. In 1376, John Philpot, Arundel's agent, sold the earl's wool in London for £2,041, from which he had already withheld his commission of 25%: thus the fleeces were sold for approximately £2,722, although it is not clear how much of this was net profit.[107] Philpot's handsome fee was in itself sufficient to sustain the rank of an earl, and many a nobleman had far less. It is nevertheless impossible that Earl Richard II could have obtained such a profit solely from his own flocks. It is not possible to know what proportion of the fleeces sold in 1376 came from Shropshire and what proportion came from Sussex, but by taking an average price of £7 per sack of 300 fleeces (£5 per sack for Sussex and 14 marks for Shropshire, based on the then prevailing prices), it is possible to evaluate the amount sold by Arundel's agent at about 389 sacks, or 116,657 fleeces. Even the Arundels, the most enterprising of Marcher lords, did not have such an enormous flock. The question this raises is: where did they get their fleeces from?

The extant evidence fails to provide any clue, but it is probable that through his network of officials and local agents, Arundel bought wool from local producers such as small farmers, ecclesiastical houses, and possibly even fellow magnates. His close association with the abbots of Haughmond and Battle, and the bishops of Chichester and Winchester, to name a few, may account for part of his acquisitions, for they were known to sell locally. The sale may have taken place on local markets or by direct agreement with the producers. Again, Arundel's case is not exceptional: the Mortimers sent and sold their Marcher wool in London and as far away as Dordrecht.[108] Earl Richard II was at the head of a highly profitable large-scale organisation, in which his sons were directly involved, and by marketing the wool directly he assumed the role of the wool-monger, the usual intermediary in the wool-market. Direct enterprise was, therefore, at the heart of the Fitzalans' financial success. The power their wealth gave them was an essential element of their political influence which in turn enabled them to influence the military fortunes and the political agenda of the realm. The use to which they put this influence depended, of course, on the individual character of each earl, as much as on the character of the kings they came to serve.

Conclusion

As members of the higher nobility the Fitzalans, earls of Arundel and Surrey, were arguably naturally predisposed to be among the ruling elite and the king's companions. Although the natural role of a magnate was to serve his king it was really personal abilities and martial skills that determined the fortunes of an individual. Personal wealth was an important factor, but this could be dramatically increased by royal grants and favours. The story of each earl of Arundel is therefore the story of each man's character as well that of his relationship with the ruler he came to serve.

The wealth and influence a family possessed came through the tenure of lands. Here the role played by Earl Edmund in securing the safety of the family's estates by settling his debts with the Crown in 1307 and 1313 was particularly significant. His favour at court and with the king enabled him to secure his family's financial future and the safety of his estates which under his father, Earl Richard I, had had little practical value since the latter was highly indebted and was never able to rise to any real prominence under Edward I. Furthermore, Earl Edmund's alliance with the Despensers after 1314, settled by the betrothal of his son Richard to Isabella Despenser, finally united in matrimony in 1321, secured Edmund a position within the most intimate of royal circles and so enabled him to increase his political and territorial influence significantly.

Following Earl Edmund's attainder in 1326, his son Richard was particularly successful in recovering the family estates and securing the new king's favour. The estates were then considerably extended in 1347 by the Warenne inheritance, thus advancing the Fitzalans to the premier ranks of the higher nobility in terms of income, since their estates had doubled in size overnight. They were now the most influential and wealthiest non-royals. Earl Richard II's new role and position had furthermore been sealed by his second marriage, in 1345, to Eleanor of Lancaster. This was an extraordinary event in itself but probably cost Arundel a place in the Order of the Garter. Arundel's life and career is also of interest because it is the only one that spanned the entirety of Edward III's reign. He fought at the side of his king and, when required, lent him the necessary funds to pursue his bellicose interests. By the time of his death, on 24 January 1376, Arundel was the wealthiest man in England and the last representative of an era. Under his tenure of the earldom a significant break with tradition occurred in that Earl Richard II chose to be buried at Lewes Priory in East Sussex rather than Haughmond Abbey in Shropshire, thus highlighting how the family's territorial and political interests had literally, physically, moved from the Marches to Sussex in the second half of the fourteenth century. This was undoubtedly accelerated by the acquisition of the Warenne inheritance with its large interest in Surrey and East Sussex, where local power was shared among a number of powerful knightly families. Arundel's son, Earl Richard III, on the other hand, later refocused his attention more on the Marches of Wales by marrying, in 1391, Philippa Mortimer and by investing in the renovation of his Marcher castles.

When King Richard II came to the throne, Earl Richard III assumed that the role his father had fulfilled in the previous reign would automatically devolve to him. However, history turned out quite differently. Arundel was certainly entrusted with a seat on the royal council and military appointments, but his favourable support of the war with France finally brought him into direct conflict with his king who favoured a peace settlement. Eventually their irreconcilable characters and ideas about how government should be carried out saw them clash in the appeal launched by the earl and his supporters in 1387-88 against the royal favourites. The decade that followed saw a considerable diminished role in politics for Arundel. However, it is clear that Earl Richard III represented a good section of the political body in his critique of the king's conduct as was shown by the widespread support Arundel's family and supporters were able to stir following his execution in 1397.

Earl Richard III's role as one of the Lords Appellant and his execution led to dramatic events that rocked the realm. Henry Bolingbroke, who had married Arundel's niece and had also been involved with the Appellants in the 1380s, returned from his exile to England in 1399 to claim his right to the Lancastrian inheritance of which he had been deprived at the death of his father. Among his supporters were Bishop Thomas Arundel and the young disinherited earl of Arundel, Thomas Fitzalan. The invasion and revolt raised such widespread support that Richard II was deposed and Henry crowned in his stead. Thomas Fitzalan was rewarded for his support and was duly restored to his estates.

The following decade formed part of Earl Thomas's military experience. The revolt in Wales of Owain Glyn Dŵr meant that for most this time Arundel was involved in suppressing the rebellions and securing Wales and its Marches. His involvement in Wales also brought him into very close contact with Prince Henry, with whom he appears to have formed a strong bond based on their shared experiences in Wales. They were young noblemen fighting to assert Lancastrian control over the realm. Once this was done they diverted their attention to the conquest of France. There was a generation gap since

Arundel's uncle, now archbishop of Canterbury, was much involved in the running of central government as chancellor and thus closer to the king. The situation was exacerbated by the fact that whilst the king was more favourable towards the Armagnacs in France, his son favoured an alliance with their enemy, the duke of Burgundy, to gain control over the French Crown. When Prince Henry finally became king in April 1413, Earl Thomas was appointed treasurer and entrusted with the conduct of war against France, while his uncle was dismissed from government. Alas, Earl Thomas died short of a personal triumph on the battlefield at the epic English victory of Agincourt.

Each of the five earls of Arundel is of particular interest because of the way they contributed to the making of England during the Hundred Years war. They always fought for their king, although some doubts may be cast on Earl Richard III's prowess as a tactician. Furthermore, all expected to be listened to by their king and his council, possibly apart from Earl Richard I, who was sidelined by the autocratic Edward I. Each contributed to the fortunes of the family either by securing more lands, more wealth, and heirs to inherit them or, as in the case of Earl Thomas, by securing a place in the annals of history through valour on the battlefield. Ultimately, however, an aristocrat is but one link in a chain of generations, and his weight is assessed in the scales of aristocracy by how strong a link he proves to be. His main priority is to pass onto the next generation at least as much as he has inherited. If he fails to do this, the chain is broken and the story of a family reaches its natural conclusion while, at the same time, the fortune of another family is made by the lands they inherit. Thus came to be the Fitzalans, earls of Arundel, and thus they passed away.

Bibliography

Abbreviations

ACA	Arundel Castle Archives, Sussex
AgHistRev	*Agricultural History Review*
BBCS	*Bulletin of the Board of Celtic Studies*
BIHR	*Bulletin of the Institute of Historical Research*
BL	The British Library
CCR	*Calendar of Close Rolls*
CChR	*Calendar of Charter Rolls*
CFR	*Calendar of Fine Rolls*
CInqPM	*Calendar of Inquisitions Post Mortem*
CPR	*Calendar of Patent Rolls*
CalScot	*Calendar of Documents Relating to Scotland*
CalPapReg	*Calendar of Papal Register relating to Great Britain and Ireland*
EHR	*The English Historical Review*
EcHR	*Economic History Review*
Foedera	T. Rymer, (ed.), *Foedera, Conventiones, Literae ...* (London, 1739)
GEC	G.E. Cokayne, *Complete Peerage of England, Scotland, Ireland, Great Britain and the United Kingdom*, (ed.) V. Gibbs, 12 vols (London, 1835-1911)
HR	*Historical Research*
HT	*History Today*
JMH	*Journal of Medieval History*
LPL	Lambeth Palace Library, London
P&P	*Past and Present*
RotParl	*Rotuli Parliamentorum ut et Petitiones et Placita in Parliamento*, 6 vols (London, 1832)
SAC	Sussex Archaeological Collections
SAS	Shropshire Archives, Shrewsbury (formerly Shropshire Record Office)
SRS	Sussex Record Society
Two Estate Surveys	*Two Estate Surveys of the Fitzalan Earls of Arundel*, (ed.) M. Clough, SRS, 67 (1969)
TNA	The National Archives, Kew
TRHS	*Transactions of the Royal Historical Society*
VCH	*Victoria County History*

Manuscript Sources

Arundel Castle Archives (ACA)

A 366-413	Manor of Bury, accounts
A 340	Hundred of Arundel. Roll of fines and receipts
A 431	Valor of the Earl of Arundel's Sussex estate
A 337	Manor of Arundel. Receiver's accounts
A 338	Manor of Arundel, account
A 420, 421	Manor of Poling, accounts
A 1775-1801	Manor of Dorking, accounts
A 1834-1840	Manor of Angmering, accounts
A 1828-1833	Manor of North Stoke, accounts
A 1872	Manor of Littlehampton, account
A 1841	Hundred of Bourne, account
A 1842-1844	Manor of Nutbourne, accounts

A 1805-1817	Manor of South Stoke, accounts
A 1863	Manor of Preston, account
A 1876	Manor of Stoke, account

Bodleian Library, Oxford
| MS Auct. D.4.4 | (one of the five Bohun Psalters) |
| MS Wood F.5 | (Genealogical history of England, dated c.1603 by Augustin Vincent, Windsor Herald. The compilation was finished by his son, John Vincent who completed the narration up to 1648. Contains lives of the Earls of Arundel. This MS might have served as a basis for Dugdale's Baronage) |

The British Library
Add. MS 24062	(1364, two letters from the Abbot of Cluny to Edward III regarding Richard II Earl of Arundel. ff. 151v-152, 187v-188)
Add. MS 6159	(1321. Letter to Pope John XXII from the Earl of Arundel. ff.102-102v)
Egerton 3003	(1345. Letter relating to the annulment of marriage, and of the remarriage of Richard II, Earl of Arundel with Lady Beaumont. f. 174)

Harleian Charter 83 C 13 (28 Feb. 1331. Edward III grants to Richard the earldom of Arundel and its lands)

| MS Egerton 3277 | (Bohun Psalter) |
| MS Harley 4840 | (18th-century transcripts of documents relating to the Earls of Arundel) |

Gloucestershire Record Office
Berkeley Castle, Select Charter 5265 (March 1350. Indenture of retinue between Richard, earl of Arundel, and Sir Gerard de Lisle)

Lambeth Palace Library, London
MS Archbishop Arundel's Register
MS Archbishop Sudbury's Register
MS Archbishop Courtenay's Register

Shropshire Archives, Shrewsbury (SAS)
Powis Collection
| 552/1/1164 | (Sept. 1350, valor of the Earl of Arundel's estates) |
| 552/1/1165 | (March 1404, valor of the Earl of Arundel's estates) |

Shrewsbury Borough Records
| 3365/67 | (The Shrewsbury Book) |

The Stobbs Collection
| 215/1 | (4 June [?] 1321 or 1326. Letter from Edmund, Earl of Arundel to Shrewsbury, concerning the money he has put into their safekeeping) |

The National Archives, Kew
C	(Chancery)
DL	(Duchy of Lancaster)
E101	(Exchequer King's Remembrancer, accounts various)

Worcestershire Record Office
Hampton (Pakington) of Westwood Park, Droitwich (Worcs)
705:349/12946/489889 (1373, grant from Richard II, earl of Arundel to John de Kingesfold of lands in cos. Buckingham and Hertford)

Primary Sources

Anglo-Norman Letters and Petitions from All Souls MS. 182, (ed.) M.D. Legge (Oxford, 1941)

AVESBURY, R. de, *De Gestis Mirabilibus Regis Edwardi Tertii*, (ed.) E. Maunde Thompson (London, 1889)

BULLOCK-DAVIES, C., *Menestrallorum Multitudo: Minstrels at a Royal Feast* (Cardiff, 1978)

Calendar of Ancient Correspondence Concerning Wales, (ed.) J.G. Edwards (Cardiff, 1935).

Calendar of Charter Rolls

Calendar of Close Rolls

Calendar of Documents Relating to Scotland

Calendar of Entries in the Papal Register relating to Great Britain and Ireland. Petitions to the Pope, vol. 1, *A.D. 1342-1419*, (ed.) W.C. Bliss (London, 1896)

Calendar of Entries in the Papal Register relating to Great Britain and Ireland. Papal Letters, vol. 4, *A.D. 1362-1404*, (eds) W.C. Bliss & J.A. Twemlow (London, 1902)

Calendar of Fine Rolls

Calendar of Inquisitions Miscellanious (Chancery)

Calendar of Inquisitions Post Mortem

Calendar of Papal Register relating to Great Britain and Ireland. Papal Letters, vol. 3, *A.D. 1342-1362*, (eds) W.C. Bliss & C. Johnson (London, 1897)

Calendar of Patent Rolls

Calendar of Pleas and Memoranda Rolls preserved among the archives of the corporation of the City of London at the Guildhall, (ed.) A.H. Thomas (Cambridge, 1926-1329)

Calendar of Wills Proved and Enrolled in the Court of Husting, London A.D. 1258-A.D. 1688, (ed.) R.R. Sharpe, 2 parts (London, 1890)

Cartulary of Haughmond Abbey, (ed.) U. Rees (Cardiff, 1985)

Cartulary of the High Church of Chichester, (ed.) W.D. Peckam, SRS, 46 (1942-3)

Chronicle of Adam of Usk 1377-1421, (ed.) C. Given-Wilson (Oxford, 1997)

Chronicon Galfridi le Baker de Swynebroke, (ed.) E. Maunde Thompson (Oxford, 1889)

Chronique de Jean le Bel, (eds) J. Viard & E. Dèprez (Paris, 1904-5)

Chroniques de London, (ed.) G.J. Augier, Camden Society, 28 (1844)

CLAY, J.W. (ed.). *Testamenta Eboracensia. A selection of wills from the registry at York*, 6 vols, 106 (Surtees Society, 1836-1902)

COKAYNE, G.E., *Complete Peerage of England, Scotland, Ireland, Great Britain and the United Kingdom*, (ed.) V. Gibbs et al., 14 vols in 15 parts (London, 1910-1998)

DEEDES, C., (ed.), *The Episcopal Register of Robert Rede, Ordinis Predicatorum, Lord Bishop of Chichester, 1397-1415*, SRS, 8-9 (1908-10)

DEVON, F., (ed.), *Issue Roll of Thomas de Brantingham, Bishop of Exeter, Lord High Treasurer of England; Containing Payments Made out of His Majesty's Revenue in the 44th Year of King Edward III. A.D. 1370* (London, 1835)

DUGDALE, W., *Monasticum Anglicanum*, 3 vols (London, 1655-73)

DUGDALE, W., *The Baronage of England*, 2 vols (London, 1675-76)

ELLIS, G., *Earldoms in Fee. A Study in Peerage Law and History* (London, 1963)

ELLIS, T.P., (ed.), *The First Extent of Bromfield and Yale A.D.1315* (London, 1924)

EMDEN, A.B. *A Biographical Register of the University of Oxford to A.D.1500* (Oxford, 1957)

FROISSART, J., *Chroniques. Livre I. Le MS d'Amiens*, (ed.) G.T. Diller, 4 vols (Geneva, 1991-93)

GALBRAITH, V.H., (ed.), *The Anonimalle Chronicle 1333 to 1381* (Manchester, 1927)

GREEN, E., (ed.), *Pedes Finium commonly called Feet of Fines for the County of Somerset*, Somerset Record Society, 17 (1902)

GRIFFITHS, R.A., *The Principality of Wales in the Later Middle Ages: The Structure and Personnel of Government*, vol. 1, South Wales 1277-1536 (Cardiff, 1972)

Heads of Religious Houses, England and Wales 1216-1377, (eds) D.M. Smith & V.C.M. London, vol. 2 (Cambridge, 2001)

HIGDEN, R., *Polychronicon*, (ed.) J. Rawson Lumby (London, 1882)

HUDSON, W., (ed.), *The Three Earliest Subsidies for the County of Sussex in the Years 1296, 1327, 1332. With Some Remarks on the Origin of Local Administration in the County Through 'Borowes' or Tithings*, SRS, 10 (1909)

JONES, G.P., *The Extent of Chirkland, 1391-1393* (London, 1933)

Knighton's Chronicle 1337-1396, (ed.) G.H. Martin (Oxford, 1995)

Le Livre de Seyntz Medicines: The Unpublished devotional treatise of Henry of Lancaster, (ed.) E.J. Arnould, Anglo-Norman Text Society (Oxford, 1940)

LEWIS, F.B., (ed.), *Pedes finium : or, Fines relating to the county of Surrey, levied in the King's court, from the seventh year of Richard I, to the end of the reign of Henry VII*, Surrey Archaeological Society, 6 vols (Guildford, 1894)

MURIMUTH, A., *Continuatio Chronicorum*, (ed.) E. Maunde Thompson (London, 1889)

NICHOLS, J., *A Collection of all the Wills, now known to be extant, of the Kings and Queens of England, ... With Explanatory Notes and a Glossary* (London, 1780)

NICOLAS, N.H., *Testamenta Vetusta*, 2 vols (London, 1826)

NICOLAS, N.H., *The Siege of Carlaverock in the 28 Edward I A.D.1300* (London, 1828)

The Oriel Record (Oxford, March 1910)

PALGRAVE, F., (ed.), *The Antient Kalendars and Inventories of the Treasury of His Majesty's Exchequer*, 3 vols (London, 1836)

PUGH, R.B., (ed.), *Abstract of Feet of Fines Relating to Wiltshire*, Wiltshire Archaeological and Natural History Society, 1 (1939) and 29 (1973)

Regesta Regum Scottorum, David II 1329-1371, (ed.) B. Webster (Edimburgh, 1982)

Register of Edward the Black Prince, (eds) A.E. Stamp & M.C.B. Davies, 4 vols (London, 1930-33)

Register of Henry Chichele Archbishop of Canterbury 1414-1443, (ed.) E.F. Jacob, 4 vols (Oxford, 1938)

Register of John of Gaunt, (ed.) S. Armitage-Smith, Camden Third Series, 20-21 (1911)

Reports from the Lords Committes Touching the Dignity of a Peer of the Realm; with Appendices, 5 vols (London, 1820-29)

Rotuli Parliamentorum ut et Petitiones et Placita in Parliamento, 6 vols (London, 1832)

RYE, W., (ed.), *A Short Calendar of the Feet of Fines for Norfolk*, 2 vols (Norwich, 1885-86)

RYMER, T., (ed.), *Foedera, Conventiones, Literae, et cujuscumque generis acta publica, inter Reges Angliae, ...*, 3 vols in 6 parts (London, 1739)

SALZMAN, L.F., (ed.), *Feet of Fines for the County of Sussex*, SRS, 23 (1916)

SHADWELL, C.L. & SALTER, H.E., (eds), *Oriel College Records*, Oxford Historical Society, 85 (1926)

SLACK, W.J., *The Lordship of Oswestry 1393-1607; a Series of Extents and Rentals Transcribed and Edited with an Introduction* (Shrewsbury, 1951)

STOW, J., *A Survey of London. Reprinted from the Text of 1603* (Oxford, 1971)

Two Estate Surveys of the Fitzalan Earls of Arundel, (ed.) M. Clough, SRS, 67 (1969)

Victoria County History

WALSINGHAM, T., *Gesta Abbatum Monasterii Sancti Albani, 1290-1349*, (ed.) H.T. Riley, vol. 2 (London, 1867)

WALSINGHAM, T., *Historia Anglicana 1271-1381*, (ed.) H.T. Riley, vol. 1 (London, 1863)

WALSINGHAM, T., *Ypodigma Neustriae*, (ed.) H.T. Riley (London, 1876)

WROTTESLEY, G., *Crécy and Calais, from the Original Records in the PRO* (London, 1898)

Secondary Sources

AILES, A., 'Heraldry in Medieval England: Symbols of Politics and Propaganda', in P. Coss & M. Keen, (eds), *Heraldry, Pageantry and Social Display in Medieval England* (Woodbridge, 2002), pp. 83-104

ALLMAND, C., *The Hundred Years War. England and France at War c.1300-c.1450* (Cambridge, 1988)

ALTSCHUL, M., *A Baronial Family in Medieval England: the Clares, 1217-1314* (Baltimore, 1965)

ARCHER, R.E., 'Piety in Question: Noblewomen and Religion in the Later Middle Ages', in D. Wood, (ed.), *Women and Religion* (Oxford, 2003), pp. 119-140

ARCHER, R.E., 'Rich Old Ladies : The Problem of Late Medieval Dowagers', in A.J. Pollard, (ed.), *Property and Politics. Essays in Later Medieval English History* (Gloucester, 1984), pp. 15-35

ARCHER, R.E., 'The Estates and Finances of Margaret of Brotherton, c.1320-1399', *HR*, 60 (1987), pp. 264-280

ASTON, M., *Thomas Arundel. A Study of Church Life in the Reign of Richard II* (Oxford, 1967)

AUTRAND, F., 'Aux origines de l'Europe moderne: l'alliance France-Ecosse au XIVe siècle', in J. Laidlaw, (ed.), *The Auld Alliance. France and Scotland over 700 years* (Edimburgh, 1999), pp. 33-46

AUTRAND, F., *Charles V le Sage*, (Paris, 1994)

AYTON, A. & PRESTON, P., *The Battle of Crécy, 1346* (Woodbridge, 2005)

AYTON, A., 'Edward III and the English Aristocracy at the beginning of the Hundred Years War', in M. Strickland, (ed.), *Armies, Chivalry and Warfare in Medieval Britain and France* (Stamford, 1998), pp. 173-206

AYTON, A., 'Knights, Esquires, and Military Service: The Evidence of the Armorial Cases before the Court of Chivalry', in A. Ayton & J.L. Price, (eds), *The Medieval Military Revolution* (London, 1995), pp. 81-103

AYTON, A., *Knights and Warhorses. Military Service and the English Aristocracy under Edward III* (Woodbridge, 1994)

BAKER, A.R.H. & BUTLIN, R.A., (eds), *Studies on Field Systems in the British Isles* (Cambridge, 1973)

BAKER, A.R.H., 'Evidence in the Nonarum Inquisitiones of Contracting Arable Lands in England during the Early Fourteenth Century', *EcHR*, 19(1966), pp. 518-32

BAKER, A.R.H., 'Some Evidence of a Reduction in the Acreage of Cultivated Lands in Sussex During the Early Fourteenth Century', *SAC*, 104 (1966), pp. 1-5

BARBER, R., *Edward, Prince of Wales and Aquitaine. A Biography of the Black Prince* (Woodbridge, 1978)

BARRELL, A.D.M.,'The Ordinance of Provisors of 1343', *HR*, 64 (1991), pp. 264-77

BARRON, C.M. & SUTTON, A.F., (eds), *Medieval London Widows, 1300-1500* (London, 1994)

BEAN, J.M.W., 'Henry IV and the Percies', *History*, 44 (1959), pp. 212-27

BEAN, J.M.W., *From Lord to Patron. Lordship in Late Medieval England* (Manchester, 1989)

BEAN, J.M.W., *The Estates of the Percy Family, 1416-1537* (Oxford, 1958)

BELLAMY, J.G. 'Appeal and impeachment in the Good Parliament', *BIHR*, 39 (1966), pp. 35-46

BELLAMY, J.G., *The Law of Treason in England in the Later Middle Ages* (Cambridge, 1970)

BENNETT, M., 'Richard II, Henry Yevele and a new Royal Mansion on the Thames', *The Antiquaries Journal*, 82 (2002), pp. 343-9

BIDDICK, K., *The Other Economy. Pastoral Husbandry on a Medieval Estate* (Berkeley, 1989)

BINGHAM, C., *The Stewart Kingdom of Scotland 1371-1603* (London, 1974)

BINSKI, P., *Medieval Death. Ritual and Representation* (London, 1996)

BIRD, R., *The Turbulent London of Richard II* (London, 1949)

BLAAUW, W.H., 'Remarks on the Nonae of 1340, as Relating to Sussex', *SAC*, 1 (1848), pp. 58-64

BLAAUW, W.H., 'The Taxpayers of the Borough of Arundel with Extracts from the Subsidy Roll of 1296 and other MSS.', *SAC*, 7 (1854), pp. 158-67

BOTHWELL, J.S., 'Edward III and the "New Nobility": Largesse and Limitation in Fourteenth-Century England', *EHR*, 112 (1997), pp. 1111-40

BOTHWELL, J.S., (ed.), *The Age of Edward III* (York, 2001)

BOTHWELL, J.S., *Edward III and the English Peerage. Royal Patronage, Social Mobility and Political Control in Fourteenth-century England* (Woodbridge, 2004)

BRANDON, P.F., 'Cereal Yields on the Sussex Estates of Battle Abbey during the Later Middle Ages', *EHR*, 25/3 (1972), pp. 403-420

BRANDON, P.F., 'Demesne Arable Farming in Coastal Sussex during the Later Middle Ages', *AgHistRev*, 19 (1971), pp. 113-134

BREEZE, A., 'A Grant of 1345 by the Earl of Arundel to the London Cell of Roncesvalles', *Nottingham Medieval Studies*, 39 (1995), pp. 106-107

BRIGHAM, T. & WOODGER, A., *Roman and Medieval Townhouses on the London Waterfront, Excavations at Governor's House, City of London*, MoLAS Monograph 9 (London, 2001)

BRITNELL, R., 'The Black Death in English Towns', *Urban History*, 21/2 (1994), pp. 195-210

BRITNELL, R.H. & POLLARD, A.J., (eds), *The McFarlane Legacy. Studies in Late Medieval Politics and Society* (Stroud, 1995)

BROWN, E.A.R., 'Ritual Brotherhood in Western Medieval Europe', *Traditio*, 52 (1997), pp. 357-381

BUCKATZSCH, E.J., 'The Geographical Distribution of Wealth in England, 1086-1843. An Experimental Study of Certain Tax Assessments', *EHR*, 3 (1950-51), pp. 180-202

BUMPUS, T.F., *London Churches Ancient & Modern. Mediæval & Early Renaissance*, First Series (London, 1908)

BURTSCHER, M., 'The Martyrdom of Edmund Fitzalan, Earl of Arundel (1285-1326)', *The Coat of Arms*, Third Series, 2 (2006), pp. 83-96, and plates 1-2

BURTSCHER, M., 'The Missing Earl: Richard Fitzalan, earl of Arundel and Surrey, and the Order of the Garter', *The Coat of Arms*, Third series, 3 (2007), pp. 93-101

CAMERON, S. & ROSS, A., 'The Treaty of Edinburgh and the Disinherited (1328-1332)', *History*, 84 (1999), pp. 237-56

CAMPBELL, B.M.S., *English Seigniorial Agriculture 1250-1450* (Cambridge, 2000)

CARRACCIOLI, C., *The Antiquities of Arundel; the Peculiar Privilege of its Castle and Lordship; with an Abstract of the Lives of the Earls of Arundell ...* (London, 1766)

CARUS-WILSON, E.M. & COLEMAN, O., *England's Export Trade, 1275-1547* (Oxford, 1963)

CARUS-WILSON, E.M., *Medieval Merchant Venturers* (London, 1954)

CATTO, J., 'Religion and the English Nobility in the Later Fourteenth Century', in H. Lloyd-Jones & V. Pearl & B. Worden, (eds), *History and Imagination. Essays in Honour of H.R. Trevor-Roper* (London, 1981), pp. 43-55

7

86

CHAPLAIS, P., *Piers Gaveston. Edward II's Adoptive Brother* (Oxford, 1994)

CHIBNALL, M., 'The Abbey of Haughmond', *VCH Shropshire* (1973), ii, pp. 62-70

CHITTY, G., *Haughmond Abbey*, English Heritage (London, 1992)

COLLINS, H.E.L., *The Order of the Garter, 1348-1461. Chivalry and Politics in Late Medieval England* (Oxford, 2000)

COOPER, W.D., 'Sussex Men at Agincourt', *SAC*, 15 (1863), pp. 123-37

COSS, P. & KEEN, M., (eds), *Heraldry, Pageantry and Social Display in Medieval England* (Woodbridge, 2002)

CRANAGE, D.H.S., *An Architectural Account of the Churches of Shropshire*, 2 vols (Wellington, 1901-3)

CROOK, D., 'Central England and the Revolt of the Earls, January 1400', *HR*, 64 (1991), pp. 403-10

CROOK, D., 'The Confession of a Spy, 1380', *HR*, 62 (1989), pp. 346-50

CROUCH, D., *The Birth of Nobility. Constructing Aristocracy in England and France, 900-1300* (Harlow, 2005)

CULLUM, P.H. & LEWIS, K.J., (eds), *Holiness and Masculinity in the Middle Ages* (Cardiff, 2004)

CURRY, A., *Agincourt. A New History* (Stroud, 2005)

DAVIES, R.R., 'Baronial Accounts, Incomes, and Arrears in the Later Middle Ages', *EHR*, 2nd ser., 21 (1968), pp. 211-229

DAVIES, R.R., *Conquest, Coexistence, and Change. Wales 1063-1415* (Oxford, 1987)

DAVIES, R.R., *Lordship and Society in the March of Wales, 1282-1400* (Oxford, 1978)

DAVIES, R.R., *The Age of Conquest. Wales 1063-1415* (Oxford, 1991)

DAVIES, R.R., *The revolt of Owain Glyn Dŵr* (Oxford, 1995)

DEMURGER, A., *Temps de crises, temps d'espoirs XIVe-XVe siècle* (Paris, 1990)

DENNISON, L., 'British Library, Egerton MS 3277: a Fourteenth-Century Psalter-Hours and the Question of Bohun Family Ownership', in R. Eales & S. Tyas, (eds), *Family and Dynasty in Late Medieval England*, Harlaxton Medieval Studies vol. 9 (Stamford, 2003), pp. 122-55

DODD, G. & BIGGS, D., (eds), *Henry IV: the Establishment of the Regime, 1399-1406* (York, 2003)

DUFFY, M., *Royal Tombs of Medieval England* (Stroud, 2003)

DUNCAN, A.A.M., (ed.), 'A Question about the Succession, 1364', *Miscellany of the Scottish History Society*, 12 (1994), pp. 1-57

EBERLE, P.J., 'Richard II and the Literary Arts', in A. Goodman & J.L. Gillespie (eds), *Richard II : the art of kingship* (Oxford 1999), pp. 231-54

ELVINS, M.T., *Arundel Priory, 1380-1980. The College of the Holy Trinity* (Chichester, 1981)

ERLER, M. & KOWALESKI, M., (eds), *Women and Power in the Middle Ages* (London, 1988)

EUSTACHE, G.W., *Arundel Borough and Castle* (London, 1922)

EVANS, K.J., 'The Maison Dieu, Arundel', *SAC*, 107 (1969), pp. 65-77

EYTON, Rev. R.W., 'The Monasteries of Shropshire: their Origin and Founders. Haughmond Abbey', *ArchJourn*, 13 (1856), pp. 145-153

FAIRBANK, F.R., 'The Last Earl of Warenne and Surrey, and the Distribution of his Possessions', *Yorkshire Archaeological Journal*, 19 (1906-7), pp. 193-264

FARRANT, J., *Sussex Depicted. Views and Descriptions, 1600-1800*, SRS, 85 (2001)

FERRIS, I., *Haughmond Abbey, Lilleshall Abbey, Moreton Corbet Castle*, English Heritage (London, 2000)

FLETCHER, C., 'Manhood and Politics in the Reign of Richard II', *P&P*, 189 (2005), pp. 1-39

FOSTER, P. & BRIGHTON, T. & GARLAND, P., *An Arundel Tomb*, Otter Memorial Paper Number 1 (Chichester, 1987)

FOWLER, K., *The King's Lieutenant. Henry of Grosmont. First Duke of Lancaster, 1310-1361* (London, 1969)

FRYDE, E.B., 'The Deposits of Hugh Despenser the Younger with Italian Bankers', in E.B. Fryde, *Studies in Medieval Trade and Finance* (London, 1982), pp. 344-362

FRYDE, E.B., *Peasants and Landlords in later medieval England, c.1380-c.1525* (Stroud, 1996)

FRYDE, E.B., *William de la Pole, Merchant and King's Banker (†1366)* (London, 1988)

FRYDE, N., 'Antonio Pessagno of Genoa, King's Merchant of Edward II of England', in *Studi in Memoria de Federigo Melis* (Naples, 1978), ii, pp. 159-78

FRYDE, N., 'Edward III's Removal of his Ministers and Judges, 1340-1', *BIHR*, 48 (1975), pp. 149-161

FRYDE, N., *The Tyranny and Fall of Edward II 1321-1326* (Cambridge, 1979)

GAUVARD, C., *La France au Moyen Age du Ve au XVe siècle* (Paris, 1997)

GEE, L.L., *Women, Art and Patronage From Henry III to Edward III* (Woodbridge, 2002)

GIVEN-WILSON, C., 'Royal Charter Witness Lists, 1327-1399', *Medieval Prosopography*, 2 (1991), pp. 35-93

GIVEN-WILSON, C., 'The Bishop of Chichester and the Second Statute of Praemunire, 1365', *HR*, 63 (1990), pp. 128-142

GIVEN-WILSON, C., 'Wealth and Credit, Public and Private : The Earls of Arundel 1306-1397', *EHR*, 106 (1991), pp. 1-26

GIVEN-WILSON, C., 'Richard II and the Higher Nobility', in A. Goodman & J.L. Gillespie (eds), *Richard II : the art of kingship* (Oxford 1999), pp. 107-28

GIVEN-WILSON, C., *The Royal Household and the King's Affinity. Service, Politics and Finance in England, 1360-1413* (London, 1986)

GLASSCOCK, R.E., 'The Distribution of Lay Wealth in Kent, Surrey, and Sussex, in the Early Fourteenth Century', *Arch. Cant.*, 80 (1965), pp. 61-68

GOODMAN, A. & GILLESPIE, J.L. (eds), *Richard II : the art of kingship* (Oxford 1999)

GOODMAN, A., *John of Gaunt. The Exercise of Princely Power in Fourteenth-Century Europe* (Harlow, 1992)

GOODMAN, A., 'Richard II's Councils', in A. Goodman & J.L. Gillespie (eds), *Richard II : the Art of Kingship* (Oxford 1999), pp. 59-82.

GOODMAN, A., 'The Countess and the Rebels: Essex and a Crisis in English Society', *Transactions of the Essex Archaeological Society*, 3rd series, 2/3 (1970), pp. 267-279

GOODMAN, A., 'John of Gaunt : paradigm of the late fourteenth-century crisis', *TRHS*, 5th Series, 37 (1987), pp. 133-48

GOODMAN, A., *The Loyal Conspiracy : The Lords Appellant under Richard II* (London, 1971)

GRANSDEN, A., 'The Legends and Traditions Concerning the Origins of the Abbey of Bury St Edmunds', *EHR*, 100 (1985), pp. 1-24

HAINES, R.M., *King Edward II. Edward of Caernarfon, His Life, His Reign, and Its Aftermath 1284-1330* (Montreal, 2003)

HARRISON, F., *Notes on Sussex Churches* (Hove, 1920)

HARRISS, G.L., *Cardinal Beaufort. A Study of Lancastrian Ascendancy and Decline* (Oxford, 1988)

HARRISS, G.L., *Shaping the Nation. England 1360-1461* (Oxford, 2005)

HARVEY, J.H., *Henry Yevele Reconsidered*, 108 (1951), pp. 100-108

HATCHER, J., *Plague, Population and the English Economy 1348-1530* (London, 1977)

HATCHER, J., *Rural Economy and Society in the Duchy of Cornwall 1300-1500* (Cambridge, 1970)

Haughmond Abbey (HMSO, 1983)

HAY, D., 'The Division of the Spoils of War, in Fourteenth-Century England', *TRHS*, 5th ser., 4 (1954), pp. 91-109

HELMHOLTZ, R.H., 'The Sons of Edward IV: a Canonical Assessment of the Claim that they were illegitimate', in P.W. Hammond (ed.), *Richard III: Loyalty, Lordship, and Law* (London, 2000), 106-120

HELMHOLTZ, R.H., *Marriage Litigation in Medieval England* (Cambridge, 1974)

HEWITT, H.J., *The Black Prince's Expedition of 1355-1357* (Manchester, 1958)

HILTON, R.H., *Bond Men Made Free : Medieval Peasant Movements and the English Rising of 1381* (London, 1973)

HOLMES, G.A., 'A Protest against the Despensers, 1326', *Speculum*, 30 (1955), pp. 207-212

HOLMES, G.A., 'Florentine Merchants in England, 1346-1436', *EcHR*, 13 (1960-1), pp. 193-208

HOLMES, G.A., *The Estates of the Higher Nobility in Fourteenth-Century England* (Cambridge, 1957)

HOLMES, G.A., *The Good Parliament* (Oxford, 1975)

HUMPHERY-SMITH, C.R., 'What became of Arundel's Tomb?', *The Coat of Arms*, 15/201 (Spring 2003), pp. 11-22

HUNTER BLAIR, C.H., 'Armorials upon English Seals from the Twelfth to the Sixteenth Centuries', *Archaeologia*, 89 (1943), pp. 1-26 and XVII plates

HUNTER BLAIR, C.H., 'Wardens and Deputy Wardens of the Marches of England towards Scotland, in Northumberland', *Archaeologia Aeliana*, 4th series, 28 (1950), pp. 18-95

JACK, R.I., 'New Light on the Early Years of Owain Glyndwr', *BBCS*, 21 (1965), pp. 162-5

JENKINSON, W., *London Churches before the Great Fire* (London, 1917)

JONES, M., *Ducal Brittany 1364-1399* (Oxford, 1970)

KEEN, M., *England in the Later Middle Ages* (London, 1973)

KEEN, M., 'Brotherhood in Arms', *History*, 47 (1962), pp. 1-17

KEEN, M., 'English Military Experience and the Court of Chivalry: the case of Grey v. Hastings', in P. Contamine, C. Giry-Deloison and M. Keen, (eds), *Guerre et société en France, en Angleterre et en Bourgogne, XIVe-Xve siècle* (Lille, 1992), pp. 123-42

KEEN, M., *Origins of the English Gentleman. Heraldry, Chivalry and Gentility in Medieval England, c.1300-c.1500* (Stroud, 2002)

KEMP, E., 'The Mediaeval Bishops of Chichester', in M.J. Kitch, (ed.), *Studies in Sussex Church History* (London, 1981), pp. 19-33

KING, A., '"They have the Hertes of People by North": Northumberland, the Percies and Henry IV, 1399-1408', in G. Dodd & D. Biggs, (eds), *Henry IV: the Establishment of the Regime, 1399-1406* (York, 2003), pp. 139-59

KING, T., *The Collegiate Church of St Mary Warwick*, A Pitkin Guide (1994)

KINGSFORD, C.L., 'Historical Notes on Mediaeval London Houses', *London Topographical Society*, vol.10 (1916), pp. 44-144 and vol.11 (1917), pp. 28-81

LAIDLAW, J., (ed.), *The Auld Alliance. France and Scotland over 700 years* (Edinburgh, 1999)

LANGDON, J., *Mills in the Medieval Economy. England 1300-1540* (Oxford, 2004)

LIGHTBOWN, R.W., *Medieval European Jewellery with a Catalogue of the Collection in the V&A* (London, 1992)

LUFFINGHAM, J.K., (ed.), *Tortington and the Black Canons* (Chichester, 2002)

MADDICOTT, J.R., *Simon de Montfort* (Cambridge, 1994)

MADDICOTT, J.R., *Thomas of Lancaster, 1307-1322. A Study in the Reign of Edward II* (Oxford, 1970)

McFARLANE, K.B., 'At the Deathbed of Cardinal Beaufort', in R.W. Hunt & W.A. Pantin & R.W. Southern, (eds), *Studies in Medieval History Presented to F.M. Powicke* (Oxford, 1948), pp. 405-428

McFARLANE, K.B., *England in the Fifteenth Century. Collected Essays* (London, 1981)

McFARLANE, K.B., *Lancastrian Kings and Lollard Knights* (Oxford, 1972)

McFARLANE, K.B., *The Nobility of Later Medieval England. The Ford Lectures for 1953 and Related Studies* (Oxford, 1973)

McKISACK, M., *The Fourteenth Century, 1307-1399* (Oxford, 1959)

MORGAN, R., 'The Barony of Powys, 1275-1360', *Welsh History Review*, 10 (1980), pp. 1-42

MORRISON, S.S., *Women Pilgrims in Late Medieval England. Private Piety as Public Performance* (London, 2000)

MORTIMER, I., *The Fears of Henry IV. The Life of England's Self-Made King* (London, 2007)

MORTIMER, I., *The Greatest Traitor. The Life of Sir Roger Mortimer, 1st Earl of March, Ruler of England 1327-1330* (London, 2003)

MORTIMER, I., *The Perfect King: the Life of Edward III, Father of the English Nation* (London, 2006)

MYERS, A.R., 'The Wealth of Richard Lyons', in T.A. Sandquist & M.R. Powicke, (eds), *Essays in Medieval History Presented to Bertie Wilkinson* (Toronto, 1969), pp. 301-329

NAPHY, W. & SPICER, A., *The Black Death and History of Plagues, 1345-1730* (Stroud, 2000)

NEVILLE, C.J., 'Scotland, the Percies and the Law in 1400', in G. Dodd & D. Biggs, (eds), *Henry IV: the Establishment of the Regime, 1399-1406* (York, 2003), pp. 73-93

NEWMAN, E.I. & HARVEY, P.D.A., 'Did Soil Fertility Decline in Medieval English Farms? Evidence from Cuxham, Oxfordshire, 1320-1340', *AgHistRev*, 45/2 (1997), pp. 119-36

NICHOLSON, R., *Edward III and the Scots. The Formative Years of a Military Career, 1327-1335* (Oxford, 1965)

ORME, N., *From Childhood to Chivalry. The Education of the English Kings and Aristocracy, 1066-1530* (London, 1984)

ORMROD, W.M., *The Reign of Edward III* (Stroud, 2000, revised ed.)

OSCHINSKY, D., *Walter of Henley and other Treatises on Estate Management and Accounting* (Oxford, 1971)

PALMER, J.J.N., 'England, France, the Papacy and the Flemish Succession, 1361-9', *JMH*, 2 (1976), pp. 339-363

PANTIN, W.A., 'Oriel College', *VCH Oxfordshire*, iii, pp. 119-131

Paris 1400: les arts sous Charles VI. Musée du Louvre 22 mars-12 juillet 2004, (Paris, 2004).

PEARSON, T., *Haughmond Abbey, Shropshire. Archaeological Investigation Report Series AI/10/2003*, English Heritage (London, 2003)

PEDERSEN, F., *Marriage Disputes in Medieval England* (London, 2000)

PELHAM, R.A., 'The Urban Population of Sussex in 1340', *SAC*, 78 (1937), pp. 211-223

PETCH, R.B.K., 'The Organisation of a College of Secular Priests as Illustrated by the Records of the College of Holy Trinity, Arundel, 1380-1544', *BIHR*, 22 (1949), pp. 54-57

PHILLIPS, J.R.S., *Aymer de Valence, Earl of Pembroke 1307-1324. Baronial Politics in the Reign of Edward II* (Oxford, 1972)

PHILLPOTTS, C., *Haughmond Abbey, Shropshire*, 2002 (unpublished English Heritage Monograph, Warwickshire County Council)

PIDGEON, H., *A Descriptive Account of Haughmond Abbey, Salop* (Shrewsbury, 1867)

PLÖGER, K., *England and the Avignon Popes. The Practice of Diplomacy in Late Medieval England* (London, 2005)

POST, J.B., 'The Obsequies of John of Gaunt', *Guildhall Studies in London History*, 5 (1981), pp. 1-12

POSTLES, D., 'The Demesne Sheep Flock at Hartington: a Note', *Derbyshire Archaeological Journal*, 94 (1974), pp. 24-5

PRATT, D., 'A Chirk Charter, 1334', *Transactions of the Denbighshire Historical Society*, 43 (1994), pp. 109-115

PRESTWICH, M., *Edward I* (London, 1988)

PRESTWICH, M., *The Three Edwards. War and State in England, 1272-1377* (London, 1980)

PRESTWICH, M., *War, Politics, and Finance under Edward I* (London, 1972)

PUGH, T.B., *The Marcher Lordships of South Wales, 1415-1536* (Cardiff, 1963)

RAWCLIFFE, C., 'Margaret Stodeye, Lady Philipot (d.1431)', in Barron, C.M. & Sutton, A.F., (eds), *Medieval London Widows, 1300-1500* (London, 1994), pp. 85-98

RAWCLIFFE, C., *The Staffords, Earls of Stafford and Dukes of Buckingham 1394-1521* (Cambridge, 1978)

RICHARDSON, H.G. & SAYLES, G.O., *The English Parliament in the Middle Ages* (London, 1981)

ROBINSON, J.M., *Arundel Castle* (Chichester, 1994)

ROBINSON, J.M., *The Dukes of Norfolk* (Chichester, 1995)

ROGERS, A., 'Henry IV and the revolt of the Earls', *HT*, 16 (1968), pp. 277-83

ROGERS, C.J., *War Cruel and Sharp. English Strategy under Edward III, 1327-1360* (Woodbridge, 2000)

ROSE, A., *Kings in the North. The House of Percy in British History* (London, 2002)

ROSENTHAL, J.T., *The Purchase of Paradise. The Social Function of Aristocratic Benevolence, 1307-1485* (London, 1972)

ROSKELL, J.S., *The Impeachment of Michael de la Pole Earl of Suffolk in 1386 in the Context of the Reign of Richard II* (Manchester, 1984)

ROUND, J.H., 'A Butler's Serjeanty', *EHR*, 36 (1921), pp. 46-50

SAALER, M., 'The Manor of Tillingdown: the Changing Economy of the Demesne 1325-71', *Surrey Archaeological Collections*, 81 (1991-2), pp. 19-40

SALTER, M., *The Old Parish Churches of Shropshire* (Malvern, 2001)

SALZMAN, L.F., 'The Property of the Earl of Arundel, 1397', *SAC*, 91 (1953), pp. 32-52

SALZMAN, L.F., *English Trade in the Middle Ages* (Oxford, 1931)

SAUL, N., *Richard II* (Yale, 1997)

SAUL, N., 'The Despensers and the Downfall of Edward II', *EHR*, 190 (1984), pp. 1-33

SAUL, N., *Scenes from Provincial Life. Knightly Families in Sussex 1280-1400* (Oxford, 1986)

SCATTERGOOD, V.J. & SHERBORNE, J.W., (eds), *English Court Culture in the Later Middle Ages* (London, 1983)

SCHEIFELE, E., 'Richard II and the Visual Arts', in A. Goodman & J.L. Gillespie (eds), *Richard II : the Art of Kingship* (Oxford 1999), pp. 255-72

SCHOFIELD, R.S., 'The Geographical Distribution of Wealth in England, 1334-1649', *EcHR*, 18 (1965), pp. 483-510

SMITH, L.B., 'Seignorial Income in the Fourteenth Century: The Arundels in Chirk', *BBCS*, 28/3 (1979), pp. 443-457

SMITH, L.B., 'The Arundel Charters to the Lordship of Chirk in the Fourteenth Century', *BBCS*, 23 (1969), pp. 153-166

SOMERVILLE, R., *History of the Duchy of Lancaster*, vol.1, 1265-1603 (London, 1953)

ST JOHN HOPE, W.H. & BRAKSPEAR, H., 'Haughmond Abbey, Shropshire', *ArchJourn*, 66 (1909), pp. 281-310

ST JOHN HOPE, W.H., 'On an Inventory of the Goods of the Collegiate Church of the Holy Trinity, Arundel, taken 1 October 1517', *Archaeologia*, 61/1 (1908), pp. 61-96

St Nicholas 1380-1480, Arundel Parish Church, Community Programmes Team St Nicholas Parish Church Arundel (1986)

St Nicholas: Font, Pulpit & Corbel Heads, St Nicholas Parish Church Arundel (1987)

St Nicholas: Wall Paintings, Arundel Parish Church, Community Programmes Team St Nicholas Parish Church Arundel (undated)

STEER, F.W., *The Fitzalan Chapel* (Arundel, 1959)

STEWART-BROWN, R., 'The Scrope and Grosvenor Controversy, 1385-1391', *Transactions of the Historic Society of Lancashire and Cheshire*, 89 (1938 for 1937), pp. 1-22

STOUCK, M.-A., 'Saints and Rebels: Hagiography and Opposition to the King in late Fourteenth-Century England', *Medievalia et Humanistica*, 24 (1997), pp. 75-94

SUMPTION, J., *The Hundred Years War*, 2 vols (London, 1990-99): vol. 1, *Trial by Battle*; vol. 2, *Trial by Fire*

Sussex Churches and Their Treasures, Sussex Historical Churches Trust (Chichester, 1957)

SUTTON, A.F. & HAMMOND, P.W., *The Coronation of Richard III, the Extant Documents* (Gloucester, 1983)

THRUPP, S.L., *The Merchant Class of Medieval London* (Michigan, 1989; 1st ed. 1948)

TIERNEY, M.A., *The History and Antiquities of the Castle and Town of Arundel; including the Biography of its Earls from the Conquest to the Present Time*, 2 vols (London, 1834)

TOUT, T.F. & BROOME, D.M., 'A National Balance Sheet for 1362-3, with Documents Subsidiary Thereto', *EHR*, 39 (1924), pp. 404-19

157

TOUT, T.F., *Chapters in the Administrative History of Medieval England*, 6 vols, Manchester, 1967 reprint of 1920-33 ed.

TUCK, A., *Crown and Nobility, 1272-1461. Political Conflict in Late Medieval England* (Totowa, 1985)

TUMMERS, H., 'The Medieval Effigial Tombs in Chichester Cathedral', *Church Monuments*, 3 (1988), pp. 3-41

TYSON, D.B., 'The Epitaph of Edward the Black Prince', *Medium Aevum*, 46 (1977), pp. 98-104

UNDERHILL, F.A., *For Her Good Estate. The Life of Elizabeth de Burgh* (London, 1999)

VALE, J., *Edward III and Chivalry. Chivalric Society and its Context, 1270-1350* (Woodbridge, 1982)

VALE, M., *The Princely Court. Medieval Courts and Culture in North-West Europe* (Oxford, 2001)

VERNON-HARCOURT, L.W., *His Grace the Steward and Trials of Peers* (London, 1907)

WALCOTT, M.E.C., *The Austin Canons' Abbey of St John the Evangelist, Haughmond* (Shrewsbury, 1900)

WALKER, D.M., *A Legal History of Scotland* (2 vols, Edinburgh, 1988-1990)

WALKER, S., 'Political Saints in Later Medieval England', in R.H. Britnell & A.J. Pollard, (eds), *The McFarlane Legacy. Studies in Late Medieval Politics and Society* (Stroud, 1995), pp. 77-106

WALKER, S., 'The Yorkshire Risings of 1405: Texts and Contexts', in G. Dodd & D. Biggs, (eds), *Henry IV: the Establishment of the Regime, 1399-1406* (York, 2003), pp. 161-84

WALKER, S., *The Lancastrian Affinity 1361-1399* (Oxford, 1990)

WARD, J.C., 'Elizabeth de Burgh, Lady of Clare (d. 1360)', in C.M. Barron & A.F. Sutton, (eds), *Medieval London Widows, 1300-1500* (London, 1994), pp. 29-45

WARD, J.C., 'Joan de Bohun, Countess of Hereford, Essex and Northampton, *c*.1370-1419: Family, Land and Social Networks', *Essex Archaeology and History*, 32 (2001), pp. 146-153

WEBB, D., 'Women Pilgrims of the Middle Ages', *History Today*, 48/7 (1998), pp. 20-26

WEBB, D., *Medieval European Pilgrimage* (New York, 2002)

WEEVER, J., *Antient Funeral Monuments of Great Britain, Ireland, and the Islands adjacent* (London, 1767, first published 1631)

WENTERSDORF, K.P., 'The Clandestine Marriages of the Fair Maid of Kent', *Journal of Medieval History*, 5 (1979), pp. 203-31

WILKINSON, B., 'The Protest of the Earls of Arundel and Surrey in the Crisis of 1341', *EHR*, 182 (1931), pp. 177-193

WILKS, M., 'Thomas Arundel: the Appellant Archbishop', in D. Wood, (ed.), *Life and Thought in the Northern Church, c.1100-c.1700: Essays in Honour of Claire Cross*, Studies in Church History, Subsidia 12, (Woodbridge, 1999), pp. 57-86

WILLIAMS, G.A., *Medieval London. From Commune to Capital* (London, 1963)

WOOD, A., (auth.) & GUTCH, J., (ed.), *The History and Antiquities of the Colleges and Halls in the University of Oxford; with a Continuation to the Present Time* (Oxford 1786)

WOOLGAR, C., *The Great Household in Late Medieval England* (London, 1999)

WRIGHT, C.E., *English Heraldic Manuscripts in the British Museum* (1973)

YEATMAN, J.P., *The Early Genealogical History of the House of Arundel* (London, 1882)

Unpublished Theses

BELL, A.R., 'Anatomy of an Army: the Campaigns of 1387-1388', (2 vols, University of Reading Ph.D., 2002)

DUNN, A.J., 'The Endowment and Disendowment of Lay Magnates in England and the Welsh Marches, 1396-1408', (University of Oxford D.Phil., 1999)

HARDING, D.A., 'The Regime of Isabella and Mortimer, 1326-1330', (University of Durham M.Phil., 1985)

McNIVEN, P., 'Political Developments in the Second Half of the Reign of Henry IV, 1405-13', (University of Manchester Ph.D., 1977)

MELVILLE, A.M.M., 'The Pastoral Custom and Local Wool Trade of Medieval Sussex, 1085-1485', (University of London M.A., 1931)

MILESON, S.A., 'Landscape, Power and Politics: the Place of the Park in Medieval English Society, *c*.1100-*c*.1535', (University of Oxford D.Phil., 2005)

OSOWIECKI, M., 'Government and Political Society in Sussex, *c*.1413-1461', (University of Cambridge Ph.D., 2004)

ROGERS, A., 'The Parliamentary Representation of Surrey and Sussex, 1377-1422', (University of Notthingham M.A., 1957)

ROGERS, M., 'The Welsh Marcher Lordship of Bromfield and Yale, 1282-1485', (University of Wales (Aberystwyth) Ph.D., 1992)

SMITH, L.O.W., 'The Lordships of Chirk and Oswestry 1282-1415', (University of London Ph.D. (Institute of Historical Research) 1970)

References

Chapter 1

1. *CCR 1279-1288*, pp. 497, 499; Davies, *Age of Conquest*, pp. 380-3.
2. Dugdale, *Baronage*, vol. 1, p. 315; Tierney, *History*, vol. 1, pp. 193-4; Robinson, *Arundel Castle*, p. 1.
3. The ten hundreds are Poling, Easewrithe, Avisford, Rotherbridge, Eastbourne, Box, Stockbridge, Bourne, Singleton, and Bury: *Two Estate Surveys*, ed. M. Clough, pp. 102-5.
4. Maddicott, *Montfort*, pp. 14, 21, 137-50.
5. Maddicott, *Montfort*, pp. 157-8, 340-2; Davies, *Age of Conquest*, pp. 310-4.
6. *CCR 1268-1272*, p. 505; Smith, unpublished thesis, 'Chirk and Oswestry', pp. 20-1. John III Fitzalan (d.1272) and his wife Isabella Mortimer were buried in Haughmond Abbey, and their gravestones are preserved in their original location at the east side of the church: Ferris, *Haughmond Abbey*, pp. 10-1. Just over a century ago on the two slabs could still be distinguished two inscriptions that read 'Vous Ki Par Ici Passez Priez Pur l'Alme Johan Fitz Aleine Ki Git Ici. Deu De Sa Alme Eit Merci. Amen', and 'Isabel De Mortimer Sa Femme Acost De Li. Deu De Lur Alme Eit Merci. Amen': M.E.C. Walcott, *The Austin Canons' Abbey*, p. 6.
7. In 1283 Maud de Verdun had married Richard de Amundeville: *CPR 1281-1292*, p. 113. Her dower consisted of the manor of Keevil (Wilts.), the manors of Acton Round, Conede, Upton, and Wroxeter (Salop); while in Sussex she held the hundreds of Bury (with the tithings of Bignor and Eringham) and Eastbourne (with the tithings of Stedham, Cocking, Graffham, Heyshott, Bekinton, Linch, Hipping, Woolbeding, Buddington, and Selham), and the manors of Easewrithe, North Stoke, Dunhurst and East Dean: *CInqPM*, vol. 2, pp. 325-6. Maud also held 100s. rent in the manor of Chipping Norton (Oxon.), and 1 knight's fee in the town of Jaye (Salop): *CCR 1279-1288*, pp. 213, 217.
8. GEC, vol. 1, pp. 240-1; Tierney, *History*, vol. 1, p. 212. Ascension that year fell on 3 May which could be a reason for the stay in a royal residence during this festival; although there is no indication that the royal couple also stayed there during those days.
9. Davies, *Age of Conquest*, pp. 380-3.
10. For Earl Richard I's estates: *Two Estate Surveys*, pp. 1-90; *CInqPM*, vol. 4, pp. 50-4.
11. *CCR 1268-1272*, pp. 82-3, 89. 499, 502, 505-517, 580-1; *CPR 1266-1272*, p. 653.
12. Ibid., pp. 46, 204, 496, 626; *CInqPM*, vol. 2, pp. 64-5, 126.
13. *CPR 1272-1281*, p. 169; *GEC*, vol. 1, p. 240; *CCR 1272-1279*, p. 350; *CCR 1279-1288*, pp. 93, 170-1.
14. *GEC*, vol. 1, p. 240; *CCR 1279-1288*, pp. 227, 260-2, 323, 451.
15. *CCR 1288-1296*, pp. 248-9; *CPR 1281-1292*, p. 465. Bishop Burnell had already lent Arundel sums of money in 1287, 1288, and 1289: *CCR 1279-1288*, pp. 487, 536; *CCR 1288-1296*, p. 56.
16. CPR 1281-1292, p. 66; *CCR 1279-1288*, pp. 235, 237.
17. *CCR 1313-1318*, p. 223. As is shown by the Falkirk Roll of 1298, Henry Percy changed his arms and used the Arundel arms as the model for the new Percy arms, with a change of tinctures. There are various families that changed their arms after an illustrious marriage, adopting a new coat of arms: Keen, *Origins of the English Gentleman*, pp. 151-2. See also Bean, *Estates of the Percy Family*, pp. 5-11.
18. See below, chapter 3, notes 10-12.
19. Wrottesley, *Crécy and Calais*, p. 96; *Testamenta Eboracensia*, ed. Clay, Surtees Society, 4 (1836), part 1, pp. 58-9; Tierney, *History*, vol. 1, p. 54.
20. Prestwich, *Edward I* (London, 1988), pp. 348-52, 419; Davies, Lordship and Society, p. 261; Prestwich, *War, Politics* (London, 1972), p. 73; Davies, *Age of Conquest*, pp. 383-5.
21. *CCR 1296-1302*, pp. 28, 70-1; Prestwich, *Edward I*, pp. 432-5.
22. *CPR 1292-1301*, pp. 86, 289; *CInqPM*, vol. 4, p. 51; Davies, *Lordship and Society*, p. 261.
23. Prestwich, *Edward I*, p. 355
24. *CPR 1272-1281*, pp. 96, 331; *CPR 1281-1292*, p. 421.
25. Peckam, *Chartulary of the High Church*, vol. 46, pp. 220, 282; *CChR 1257-1300*, pp. 187-8; Mileson, unpublished thesis, 'Landscape, Power and Politics', pp. 201-2.

26. Prestwich, *War, Politics*, pp. 76, 236-7; id., *Edward I*, p. 384, 407. According to the Fitzalans' records a sum of £4,675 0s. 2d was owed to the king since the time of John Fitzalan which remained unpaid in 1301: *Two Estate Surveys*, p. 90. In 1293, for instance, Arundel and Edmund Mortimer had been accused of refusing royal tax-collectors access to their lands: Davies, *Lordship and Society*, p. 261 n. 55.

27. 'Richard le conte de Aroundel / Beau chivaler et bien ame / I vi je richement arme / En rouge au lyon rampant de or': Nicolas, *Siege of Carlaverock*, pp. 50, 283-5.

28. *CCR 1296-1302*, p. 513.

29. *Cartulary of Haughmond Abbey*, ed. U. Rees, p. 227. Alisona (d.1292) had originally been buried at Todingham Priory and may, therefore, have later been moved; possibly after her husband's death in 1302. This was not an unusual practice and, in 1393, Earl Richard III asked for the body of his first wife to be removed from her own tomb to be reburied with him at the time of his death: Nichols, *Collection of Wills*, p. 120.

Chapter 2

1. *CCR 1296-1302*, pp. 539-40; *CPR 1301-1307*, pp. 308, 375, 377, 521, 545.

2. Tierney, *History*, vol. 1, p. 212. John certainly died before 1375; Tierney confuses him with the other Sir John (d.1379), son of Earl Richard II and Eleanor of Lancaster.

3. Prestwich, *Edward I*, pp. 121-2; Bullock-Davies, *Menestrallorum Multitudo*, pp. xxvii-xxxviii. *CPR 1301-1307*, pp. 521, 545-6. 'of £4,234 3s. 4¾d. remainder of £5,266 7s. 0¾d., debts of himself or his ancestors'. In 1302 Edmund was said to owe £1,000 for his father to the Crown: *CCR 1296-1302*, p. 513. It is possible that this sum was the relief owed for the earldom.

4. *CPR 1307-1313*, pp. 52-3. Vernon-Harcourt, *His Grace the Steward*, p. 42 n. 2. The office of chief butler was quite distinct from that of the butler, a member of the royal household: Round, 'A Butler's Serjeanty', pp. 46-50. For Earl Hugh: *RotParl*, vol. 1, p. 154b; for Earl Richard III: *CCR 1377-1381*, p. 3; in Richard II's reign Sir John de Clifton challenged Arundel's right to the office of chief butler claiming that it was attached to the manors of Rokingham (Northants.) and Wymondham (Norf.): *RotParl.*, vol. 3, p. 131b; Earl Thomas officiated at the coronation of Elizabeth Woodville and Henry VII as well as, probably, that of Richard III: Sutton & Hammond, *Coronation of Richard III*, pp. 27, 44-5, 247, 250. See also Tierney, *History*, vol. 1, p. 279 n. b. *RotParl.*, vol. 2, p. 96a; *CCR 1377-1381*, p. 4.

5. Haines, *King Edward II*, p. 74; Chaplais, *Piers Gaveston*, p. 69. The exact barb of these insults has been lost in time, but it seems likely that 'Arden' was a reference to the Forest of Arden in Warwickshire north-west of the Avon; 'Joseph the Jew' may have been a reference to Pembroke's role as a feoffee for some properties in Ironmonger Lane, London, which had formerly belonged to Hagin, son of Master Moses, a notable Jew of London and archpresbyter of the English Jews. As for 'ceorl' this was a churl, a member of the Anglo-Saxon lower social classes which then also came to indicate a person of ill manners.

6. *CCR 1313-1318*, 79.

7. *CCR 1313-1318*, pp. 407, 467, 493, 563; *CPR 1313-1317*, p. 645.

8. *CCR 1318-1323*, p. 227.

9. *CalPapReg Petitions*, vol. 1, p. 81; BL, Add. MS 9951. The following day Arundel settled some manors on the newly-weds by enfeoffing John de Coumbe parson of the church of Stoke by Arundel, of the manors of Wenge, Blackwell and Keevil, with the advowson of the priory of Wenge to be re-granted to the earl with remainder to 'Richard, son of the said earl, and to Isabella, daughter of Hugh le Despenser, the younger, his wife': *CPR 1317-1321*, p. 562.

10. The earls of Arundel, Pembroke, Warenne, and Richmond were approached, on 27 July, by the other magnates and presumably forced to join them against the Despensers. Given the ultimatum that either they were exiled or the king deposed, it is clear that, under the circumstances, Arundel had but little choice but to join Lancaster's course of action: Maddicott, *Thomas of Lancaster*, p. 280; Phillips, *Aymer de Valence*, pp. 209-10.

11. *CCR 1318-1323*, pp. 510-1; *CCR 1318-1323*, pp. 510-1, 541-6; Fryde, *Tyranny and Fall*, pp. 58-61; Haines, *King Edward II*, pp. 132-41; Phillips, *Aymer de Valence*, pp. 209-10.

12. *CCR 1318-1323*, p. 437; *CCR 1318-1323*, pp. 3, 19, 127; *CPR 1321-1324*, pp. 98, 215, 268, 274 302-3.

13. TNA, E 163/2/22.

14. The names given are John Fitz Owyny of Brompton, bailiff of the manor of Lydley; Richard Child of 'Dedelebury', receiver of the manor of Oswestry; John de la Halle of Cudlow, baillif of the manor of

Shrawardine; and Richard de Bradbury parson of Rodington, receiver of the manor of Chirk: TNA, E 163/2/22.

15. Ibid.

16. Fryde, *Tyranny and Fall*, pp. 108-9, 194; Haines, *King Edward II*, pp. 144, 157-60. Although Caerphilly Castle may have had in its treasury as much as £13,295: Given-Wilson, 'Wealth and Credit', p. 3.

17. For Badlesmere: *CPR 1321-1324*; 145-6; for Wauton: *CPR 1321-1324*, 177; for Cheney: *CPR 1321-1324*, 196, and Cheney's recognisances of debt: TNA, E 163/2/22.

18. Given-Wilson, 'Wealth and Credit', p. 2.

19. Fryde, *Tyranny and Fall*, p. 75. A letter, dating from the 1320s, which Arundel addressed to the citizens of Shrewsbury is a further example of the way in which financial blackmail was used to secure the town's allegiance to the king as well as the safety of the money itself deposited there: SAS, Stobbs Collection 215/1.

20. *CPR 1321-1324*, p. 239; TNA, E 163/2/22; *CPR 1324-1327*, pp. 274, 297.

21. Fryde, *Tyranny and Fall*, p. 3.

22. Dugdale, *Baronage*, vol. 1, p. 316a; Maddicott, *Thomas of Lancaster*, p. 319.

23. *CCR 1323-1327*, p. 163; *CPR 1324-1327*, p. 281.

24. Weever, *Antient Funeral Monuments of Great Britain*, p. 310.

25. *GEC*, vol. 12, pp. 372-4.

26. *CPR 1324-1327*, p. 288.

27. TNA, C 47/3/53/7. Fryde, 'Deposits of Hugh Despenser the Younger', p. 358, n. 10; Given-Wilson, 'Wealth and Credit', pp. 2-3.

28. TNA, C 47/3/53/7; E 142/56/13 and E 101/383/8, f. 5.

29. Oliver Ingham, a supporter of Mortimer, was among the twelve lords constituting the council of the young King Edward in 1327: Haines, *King Edward II*, pp. 185, 195-6. See also Williams, *Medieval London*, p. 292. TNA, E 163/3/6.

30. The fines and other debts owed to Arundel were annulled in 1327, but the sentence was reversed on 14 January 1331: *CPR 1330-1334*, p. 41; *CCR 1330-1333*, p. 276.

31. *CCR 1313-1318*, p. 615; *CCR 1318-1323*, pp. 236, 360; TNA, E 163/3/6. Robert atte Cirn owed £40. In his case it could be a debt of £40 contracted on 8 March 1324 by a certain Robert atte Gerne (*sic*) and Ralph atte Halle of Gerne: *CCR 1323-1327*, p. 163; *CCR 1330-1333*, p. 303; TNA, E 163/3/6. Oliver de Ingham owed 500 marks, which he might have contracted on 10 March 1321/2 with two other associates, Henry Nasard and Hugh Matefray: *CCR 1318-1323*, p. 360; *CCR 1330-1333*, p. 319; TNA, E 163/3/6. Henry Nasard and Hugh Madefray had already borrowed sums of money from Earl Edmund on other occasions. For Henry Nasard: *CCR 1313-1318*, p. 615; *CCR 1318-1323*, p. 236; *CCR 1327-1330*, pp. 47, 50; TNA, E 163/3/6. For Hugh Matefray: *CCR 1318-1323*, p. 372; TNA, E 163/3/6. Sir John Pecche owed £126 13s 4d, which he had contracted on 13/14 February 1325: *CCR 1323-1327*, p. 348; *CCR 1330-1333*, p. 330; TNA, E 163/3/6.

32. Williams, *Medieval London*, pp. 129-30.

33. *CCR 1318-1323*, p. 356.

34. Fryde, 'Antonio Pessagno of Genoa', vol. 2, pp. 159-78.

35. Fryde, *Tyranny and Fall*, pp. 204-5.

36. According to R. Morgan, Charlton captured Arundel as early as 13 April, but this does not seem to be possible as Arundel stayed with the king until they weighed anchor off the Glamorgan coast in October. Apparently Arundel was trying to capture Shrewsbury with the aid of his Welsh tenants of Oswestry: 'The Barony of Powys, 1275-1360', p. 28 n. 180.

37. See below chapter 3, Life of Earl Richard II and chapter 6, Fitzalan Estates.

38. Quoting the thirteenth-century English law book *Bracton*: Fryde, *Tyranny and Fall*, p. 78.

39. BL, Cotton MS Nero A. iv, f. 57ᵛ.

40. As early as 1 March 1325/6 it was arranged with the abbey that six candles should burn around Earl Edmund's body: *Cartulary of Haughmond Abbey*, p. 227. This may suggest that, in view of Queen Isabella's invasion, Earl Edmund made arrangements in case he were to die.

41. *VCH Shropshire*, vol. 2, p. 64. The representation of Earl Edmund's effigy in BL, MS Egerton 3277, f. 142 may be based on his tomb at Haughmond: Burtscher, 'Martyrdom of Edmund Fitzalan', pp. 87-96.

42. *CPR 1340-1343*, p. 389.

43. *CPR 1343-1345*, p. 56.

44. Given-Wilson, 'Wealth and Credit', p. 4; *CCR 1323-1327*, p. 625.

45. *CPR 1327-1330*, pp. 153, 328-9, 554; *CPR 1330-1334*, pp. 2, 7; *CCR 1327-1330*, pp. 101-2

46. *CCR 1327-1330*, pp. 47, 50.
47. Tout, *Chapters*, pp. 39-40. For an analysis of the parallel between Earl Edmund's martyrdom and the cult of Earl Richard III, see below chapter 4 life of Earl Richard III
48. *CPR 1327-1330*, p. 153; *CCR 1327-1330*, pp. 101-2; 511, 515, 560.
49. Haines, *King Edward II*, p. 200.
50. *CFR 1327-1337*, p. 181; *CPR 1327-1330*, p. 574.

Chapter 3
1. *CPR 1327-1330*, p. 562; *CFR 1330-1334*, p. 20.
2. BL, Harleian Charter 83 C 13; *RotParl*, vol. 2, p. 56a.
3. *CPR 1330-1334*, pp. 41, 194; *CCR 1330-1333*, p. 381.
4. *CCR 1330-1333*, p. 280.
5. Bothwell, *Age of Edward III*, pp. 35-52.
6. Nicholson, *Edward III and the Scots*, pp. 108-110, 128, 177, 201; *CCR 1330-1333*, p. 487; *CCR 1333-1337*, pp. 26-7.
7. *CCR 1333-1337*, pp. 591, 679; *CCR 1337-1339*, pp. 184, 564; *CCR 1339-1341*, p. 59; *CCR 1341-1343*, 72, pp. 178-9; *CCR 1346-1349*, p. 31; *CPR 1354-1358*, p. 629; *CCR 1354-1360*, p. 378; *CCR 1360-1364*, p. 181; *CPR 1358-1361*, p. 539.
8. *CCR 1333-1337*, p. 701.
9. *CCR 1337-1339*, pp. 40, 448.
10. *CPR 1334-1338*, p. 342; *Cal Scot 1307-1357*, vol. 3, nos. 1218, 1219, 1300. On 24 June 1158 King Malcolm IV the Maiden confirmed the grant to Walter Fitzalan: Vernon-Harcourt, *His Grace the Steward*, pp. 61-3.
11. Walker, *Legal History*, vol. 1, pp.. 77, 146; Bingham, *Stewart Kingdom of Scotland*, pp. 21-2.
12. Walker, *Legal History*, vol. 2, pp. 155-7.
13. Duncan, ed., 'Question about the Succession, 1364', p. 6. See also Cameron & Ross, 'Treaty of Edinburgh and the Disinherited (1328-1332)', pp. 237-56.
14. Given-Wilson, 'Wealth and Credit, p. 17; *Calendar of Ancient Correspondence Concerning Wales*, ed. J.G. Edwards, pp. 244-5, 248.
15. *CCR 1337-1339*, pp. 204, 209-210, 216; *CalScot 1307-1357*, vol. 3, no. 1298.
16. *CCR 1341-1343*, pp. 535, 542-3. For the indentures of Arundel and Salisbury: TNA, E 101/20/33 and C 47/2/31/7; Norfolk Record Office, Hare 6227.228x6.
17. Tout, *Chapters*, vol. 3, pp. 39-40; vol. 6, p. 60.
18. *RotParl*, vol. 2, p. 348. The petitioners accused Arundel of having enriched himself at the expense of the Crown and the sheriffs. The petition was presented so as to give the impression that Arundel was encroaching on the royal prerogative which, technically, he was not. It was indeed the king who had granted such extensive powers and privileges.
19. Tout, *Chapters*, vol. 3, p. 39.
20. *Knighton's Chronicle 1337-1396*, p. 5. Dunbar was again besieged from 1 March to 6 June 1339. It is possible that Arundel took also part in this second siege: *CCR 1339-1341*, pp. 271, 382, 388.
21. Nicholson, *Scotland*, pp. 136-7; Sumption, *Trial by Battle*, vol. 1, pp. 234-7.
22. *CCR 1337-1339*, p. 396. This grant was confirmed on 6 February 1340: *CPR 1338-1340*, p. 417.
23. *CalScot 1307-1357*, vol. 3, no. 1267; Tout, *Chapters*, vol. 3, p. 84.
24. *CCR 1337-1339*, pp. 454, 527. Because the borough was thus unable to pay the fifteenth, Arundel offered to give sixty sacks of wool to the king in compensation for that loss of revenue: *CCR 1337-1339*, p. 464; *Foedera, ed. Rymer*, vol. 2/2, p. 1059.
25. *CPR 1338-1340*, p. 112; Barber, *Prince of Wales*, p. 29. When the Duke of Cornwall was reappointed Keeper of the Realm, in May 1340, Arundel would seem to have still been a member of his council, and he was provided with summer clothes by the prince's household: Tout, *Chapters*, vol. 5, pp. 318, 322.
26. *CCR 1337-1339*, p. 542. For the appointment to justice see: *CCR 1333-1337*, p. 352; *CPR 1334-1338*, p. 406.
27. *CFR 1337-1347*, p. 140; Tout, *Chapters*, vol. 3, p. 40.
28. *RotParl*, vol. 2, p. 118; Tout, *Chapters*, vol. 3, p. 113.
29. *CPR 1338-1340*, p. 112; Ormrod, *Edward III*, p. 13.
30. Fryde, 'Edward III's Removal of his Ministers and Judges, 1340-1', p. 152; Allmand, *Hundred Years War*, pp. 12-3; *CCR 1339-1341*, pp. 467, 482, 621.

31. *CCR 1339-1341*, p. 488; *CPR 1340-1343*, pp. 238, 313; Fryde, *William de la Pole, Merchant and King's Banker (†1366)*.

32. *Chroniques de London*, p. 90; Wilkinson, 'Protest of the Earls of Arundel and Surrey', pp. 179-81, 188.

33. Walsingham, *Gesta Abbatum Monasterii Sancti Albani*, vol. 2, p. 366.

34. *CCR 1341-1343*, pp. 3, 9, 111, 248, 256.

35. *CCR 1341-1343*, p. 256.

36. *CPR 1340-1343*, pp. 313, 336; Tuck, *Crown and Nobility*, p. 126.

37. Jones, *Ducal Brittany*, pp. 1-21.

38. Tuck, *Crown and Nobility*, p. 128; TNA, E 101/68/3/57: indenture made on 18 May, to serve from 15 July for a quarter of a year. On 31 May 1342 they received £1,823 11s. and £3,647 2s. to cover the expenses of their expedition: *CCR 1341-1343*, pp. 535, 542-3.

39. Froissart, *Chroniques. Livre I. Le MS d'Amiens*, vol. 2, pp. 286, 289; Hunter Blair, 'Wardens and Deputy Wardens', p. 42.

40. Sumption, *Trial by Fire*, vol. 1, p. 406.

41. Keen, *England in the Later Middle Ages*, pp. 132-4; Autrand, *Charles V le Sage*, pp. 153-4.

42. See below chapter 4 life of Earl Richard III.

43. GEC, vol. 1, p. 243; *CalPapReg Petitions*, vol. 1, p. 81.

44. *CPR 1343-1345*, pp. 45, 150, 183, 224; *CPR 1348-1350*, pp. 272-3, 483; *CPR 1330-1334*, p. 275; Morrison, *Women Pilgrims*, pp. 47, 158. Note that Morrison incorrectly identifies Eleanor of Lancaster as Edward III's sister.

45. Sybil's sisters had also been provided with first class husbands: Philippa married Roger Mortimer, earl of March; Elizabeth married firstly Giles, Lord Badlesmere, secondly Hugh Despenser and, thirdly, Sir Guy Brian; while Agnes married John, lord Grey of Ruthin: *GEC*, vol. 11, p. 388 n. (b).

46. TNA, DL 10/299.

47. Breeze, 'Grant of 1345', p. 106. Possibly in view of his imminent departure Arundel had granted, on 16 September 1343, 30 acres of land in Arundel to the priory of St Nicholas there to fund a chaplain to celebrated a daily service in honour of Christ and St Mary: *CPR 1343-1345*, pp. 120-1. A number of English ladies from the aristocracy travelled to Santiago de Compostela during the fourteenth century, notably Alice Bigod, countess of Norfolk and Elizabeth Luttrell: Morrison, *Women Pilgrims*, pp. 45, 47. See also Webb, 'Women Pilgrims of the Middle Ages', pp. 20-26; ead., *Medieval European Pilgrimage*, pp. 89-98, 103-8.

48. *CalPapReg, Letters*, vol. 3, p. 188.

49. *CalPapReg, Petitions*, vol. 1, p. 75.

50. *CalPapReg, Petitions*, vol. 1, p. 81; Pedersen, *Marriage Disputes in Medieval England*, pp. 139-52.

51. *CalPapReg, Petitions*, vol. 1, pp. 75, 99. Both Isabella and Eleanor descended from William Beauchamp, earl of Warwick, through his daughter Isabel, their grandmother who married twice: firstly Payn Chaworth with whom she had Maud who married Henry, earl of Lancaster, and secondly with the elder Hugh Despenser with whom she had the younger Hugh who then married Eleanor de Clare.

52. *CalPapReg, Letters*, vol. 3, pp. 176, 188, 254. She was also know as Lady Beaumont: BL, MS Egerton 303 (f. 174).

53. *GEC*, vol. 1, p. 244 n. (b). Edmund certainly still had powerful family connections on which he could rely for his own career. His mother Isabella was still alive in 1351-52 when she sent a gift of fish to her wealthy and influential aunt, Elizabeth de Burgh: Underhill, *Elizabeth de Burgh*, p. 90; *CPR 1358-1361*, pp. 393, 395, 505; *CPR 1361-1364*, p. 451; *CalPapReg, Letters*, vol. 4, pp. 27, 47.

54. LPL, MS Archbishop Sudbury's Register, f. 94.

55. BL, Harleian Charter 53.E.II.

56. BL, Add. MS 45133, f. 55. See also Wright, *English Heraldic Manuscripts in the British Museum*, p. 6.

57. Hunter Blair, 'Armorials upon English Seals', plate XVI seal (aa).

58. Wood & Gutch, eds, *History and Antiquities of the Colleges and Halls*, p. 134.

59. Ayton, 'Knights, Esquires, and Military Service', pp. 81-103. Stewart-Brown, 'Scrope and Grosvenor Controversy', pp. 1-22; Keen, 'English Military Experience and the Court of Chivalry', pp. 123-42.

60. Ailes, 'Heraldry in Medieval England', pp. 87-8.

61. *Reports from the Lords Committees touching the Dignity of a Peer*, vol. 167/2, p. 672; *CCR 1374-1377*, pp. 413-4, 511.

62. *CPR 1374-1377*, pp. 492-3, 551; *CPR 1377-1381*, p. 92.

63. Edmund was buried there next to his wife: Stow, *Survey of London*, vol. 1, p. 178; Weever, *Antient Funeral Monuments*, p. 203.

64. Wrottesley, *Crécy and Calais*, p. 193; Ayton & Preston, *Battle of Crécy, 1346*, pp. 143, 149, 163. 315-7, and Table 2.
65. Wrottesley, *Crécy*, pp. 89, 107; *CPR 1348-1350*, p. 19; *CCR 1346-1349*, pp. 290-1; TNA, E 43/129.
66. *Chronicon Galfridi le Baker*, pp. 109, 280; Barber, *Prince of Wales*, p. 99.
67. 'Sed dolo et fraude Gallorum, quibus jugiter adhaerebant, una cum conniventia Domini Papae, a concordia est discessum. Rex vero Edwardus, ex hoc non modicum est exasperatus': Walsingham, *Historia Anglicana 1271-1381*, vol. 1, p. 278. The French received a preferential treatment from the pope as they were also given extra gifts such as pears, apples, chestnuts, and cheese: Plöger, *Diplomacy*, p. 203 n. 862, pp.281, 286. The gargantuan amounts of provisions required to sustain the French and English embassies, described by Plöger, were certainly the main cause that made Ranulph Higden remark that that year one could not get hold of anything, from metal to spices: 'quo anno etiam coepit magna caristia rerum videlicet, bladi, plumbi, ferri, stagni, aeris, lignorum, canabi, et specierum': Higden, *Polychronicon*, p. 356.
68. Hewitt, *Black Prince's Expedition*, p. 20; Fowler, *King's Lieutenant*, p. 155.
69. *CPR 1358-1361*, p. 47.
70. Autrand, *Charles V*, pp. 221-356.
71. Fowler, *King's Lieutenant*, pp. 197, 202.
72. *CPR 1360-1364*, p. 52; *CCR 1360-1364*, pp. 96-7.
73. Fowler, *King's Lieutenant*, p. 210; Sumption, *Trial by Fire*, Vol. 2, p. 454.
74. TNA, E 101/314/4; E 403/401, m. 26.
75. TNA, E 27/8.
76. Lancaster made his will on 15 March, and the following day he made Arundel one of his feoffees: *CPR 1358-1361*, pp. 575-6, 580.
77. TNA, E 27/8.
78. *CCR 1364-1368*, p. 123.
79. *Cal Scot 1357-1509*, vol. 4, nos. 127, 128; *Regesta Regnum Scottorum, David II 1329-1371*, vol. 6, pp. 396-7. Duncan, 'Question about the Succession', pp. 13-20.
80. Given-Wilson, 'Bishop of Chichester', pp. 128-34.
81. *CCR 1364-1368*, pp. 83-4, 371.
82. LPL, MS Archbishop Sudbury's Register, f. 94ᵛ. The bond of brotherhood was a relationship based on the reciprocal oath to aid and succour one another in every situation and was, hence, also enforce-able in a court of law; a brother-in-arms was, in idea at least, one of one's blood and kin: Keen, 'Brotherhood in Arms', p. 5; Brown, 'Ritual Brotherhood in Western Medieval Europe', pp. 357-81.
83. Tout, *Chapters*, vol. 3, pp. 267, 276-278.
84. *Calendar of Pleas and Memoranda Rolls Preserved among the Archives of the Corporation of the City of London*, pp. 7-8, 149. *Calendar of Wills Proved and Enrolled in the Court of Husting*, p. 385.
85. Tout, *Chapters*, vol. 3, pp. 278, 288-9, 301; Holmes, *Good Parliament*, pp. 64-8, 101-11; Bellamy, 'Appeal and Impeachment in the Good Parliament', pp. 35-46.
86. Tyson, 'The Epitaph of Edward the Black Prince', pp. 98-104. Post, 'The Obsequies of John of Gaunt', pp. 2-3; Nichols, *Collection of Wills*, pp. 66-77, 84.
87. Nichols, *Collection of Wills*, p. 120; Catto, 'Religion and the English Nobility', pp. 50-1; McFarlane, *Lancastrian Kings*, pp. 207-20.
88. The slab measures 109.5cm x 205.5cm. Arundel's effigy is 190cm in length while that of Eleanor is 176cm. As the slabs were, allegedly, moved from Lewes Priory to Chichester Cathedral during the Dissolution there are no skeletal remains that could have been used to establish whether the effi-gies were lifesize. See also Foster & Brighton & Garland, *An Arundel Tomb*, pp.6-7, 19; Tummers, 'Medieval Effigial Tombs', pp.31-6.
89. LPL, MS Archbishop Sudbury's Register, f. 92ᵛ.
90. Foster, *Arundel Tomb*, plate p. 20.
91. King, *Collegiate Church of St Mary Warwick*, pp. 2, 7.
92. Duffy, *Royal Tombs of Medieval England*, pp. 229-33.
93. *CCR 1374-1377*, p. 59.
94. 'pur le grant noun qil a destre riches': BL, Add. MS 24062, f. 151ᵛ.
95. BL, MS Harleian 4840, f. 393.
96. Fryde, *Tyranny and Fall*, pp. 87, 94.
97. LPL, MS Archbishop Sudbury's Register, f. 94; McFarlane, *Nobility*, p. 90.
98. LPL, MS Archbishop Sudbury's Register, ff. 92ᵛ-94ᵛ; BL, MS Harley 4048, f. 393. Actual sums bequeathed are: 17,000 marks to his children and grandchildren, 7,100 marks to his nephews and

nieces, 5,000 marks to fight Sir Edmund Arundel's claim to the inheritance, 700 marks to people of his entourage, 8,992 marks to religious houses and other charitable causes, and 2,000 marks for his burial and the execution of his will.

99. *Register of John of Gaunt*, pp. 420-36; Nichols, *Collection of Wills*, 145-75.

100. LPL, MS Archbishop Sudbury's Register, ff. 94^v-95^v.

101. ACA, SX Box 3/6, item 1.

102. 'walplates de camera domini in cervis 8d. ... Memorandum quod expendat in vadijs carpent' circa cameram Novam de festo Sancti Michaelis Archangel anno .xvij. ... Item in .ij. querc' et .C. tabul emp' per eundem temp' .xxxvij.s .ij.d ... Item in bordnayl et spykyng emp' pro nova camera et pro fenestre et hostijs nove aule et celar novo .xxvij.s': SAS, 6000/5924.

103. Shadwell & Salter, *Oriel College Records*, 85 (1926), pp. 29-36; Wood & Gutch, *History and Antiquities* pp. 133-5; *The Oriel Record* (Oxford, March 1910), pp. 95-6; *VCH Oxford*, vol. 3, pp. 119-31; Aston, *Thomas Arundel*, p. 13.

104. Saul, *Scenes from Provincial Life*, pp. 149-52.

105. *CCR 1389-1392*, pp. 413-5; Cranage, *Architectural Account of the Churches of Shropshire*, vol. 1, pp. 399-400; Salter, *Old Parish Churches of Shropshire*, p. 54; Davies, *Owain Glyn Dŵr*, pp. 38-9.

106. *CalPapReg, Letters*, vol. 4, p. 129.

107. *CalPapReg, Petitions*, vol. 1, p. 281.

108. *CPR 1348-1350*, p. 89; Emden, *Biographical Register*, vol. 1, p. 48. Note that Emden incorrectly identifies Edmund Arundel as the son of Earl Richard II thus confusing him with Sir Edmund Arundel.

109. *CalPapReg, Petitions*, vol. 1, p. 8; *CPR 1338-1340*, p. 311. In 1340, Edmund Arundel was presented to three prebends in the diocese of York: Hotham (co. S.R. Yorks) and Nunnington, in the collegiate church of Ripon, and Husthwaite, in the church of St. Peter (all in co. N. Yorks). It was also ordered that in Husthwaite he should be assigned a stall in the choir and a place in the chapter: *CPR 1340-1343*, pp. 24, 37, 58.

110. *CalPapReg, Petitions*, vol. 1, pp. 8, 128, 186, 194.

111. *CalPapReg, Petitions*, vol. 1, p. 102.

112. Holmes, 'Florentine Merchants in England', pp. 193-208; Myers, 'Wealth of Richard Lyons', pp. 301-29; Fryde, *William de la Pole*.

113. Princess Joan had probably been able to repay her debt by borrowing the money from the king. In his will, Edward III bequeathed her the jewels she had pledged to him for a prest of 1,000 marks: BL, MS Harleian 4840, f. 393; Nichols, *Collection of Wills*, p. 61.

114. BL, MS Harleian 4048, f. 393.

115. If this debt dates only from October 1371 it may explain why it is not included in the list of creditors for Michaelmas 1371: SAS, MS 6000/5923, in Given-Wilson, 'Wealth and Credit', Appendix I.

116. For Suffolk there were two distinct sums of 1,250 marks and 3,000 marks: *CCR 1369-1374*, p. 339. For Warwick: *CCR 1369-1374*, p. 441.

117. LPL, MS Archbishop Sudbury's Register, f. 94.

118. 'povres marchantz qe pur cheantz sount anientiz': Nichols, *Collection of Wills*, p. 41.

119. Thrupp, *Merchant Class*, pp. 30-1, 36.

120. *CCR 1349-1354*, pp. 205-6.

121. He could be the same Thomas de Batesford who, as representative of Bury St Edmunds (co. Suffolk), made an oath of allegiance to Queen Isabella and Mortimer on 13 January 1327: *Calendar of Pleas and Memoranda Rolls*, p. 14; *CCR 1341-1343*, pp. 387, 537; *CCR 1343-1346*, p. 79; TNA, E 199/10/13; E 199/29/29. For further loans and land transactions in Suffolk: *CCR 1339-1341*, pp. 480-2; *CCR 1341-1343*, p. 480; *CCR 1346-1349*, p. 171.

122. Thrupp, *Merchant Class*, p. 360; Bird, *Turbulent London of Richard II*, pp. 44-62; Rawcliffe, 'Margaret Stodeye, Lady Philipot (d. 1431)', pp. 85-98.

123. BL, MS Harleian 4048, ff. 393^{r-v}.

124. *Register of John of Gaunt*, vol. 20, p. 79; vol. 21, p. 36.

125. Given-Wilson, *Royal Household*, pp. 123-4.

126. Aston, *Thomas Arundel*, pp. 195-6.

127. *Calendar of Wills Proved and Enrolled in the Court of Husting*, p. 275.

128. An itinerary of the earl of Pembroke, attributed to Edward III's reign, shows that it was possible to travel quite easily from Windsor to Arundel in two days: the first day from Windsor to Guildford (Surrey), and the following day from there to Arundel, with a break at Midhurst (Sussex) for lunch. On the return journey they stopped at Petworth (Sussex) to feed the horses, and then again at Chiddingfold

(Surrey) for lunch. They then travelled the same day to Guildford, where they stopped: TNA, E 101/317/35.

129. LPL, MS Archbishop Sudbury's Register, f. 93ᵛ; Stow, *Survey of London*, vol. 2, p. 12; Kingsford, 'Mediaeval London Houses', 10 (1916), pp. 64-66.
130. LPL, MS Archbishop Sudbury's Register, ff. 102-102ᵛ; MS Archbishop Arundel's Register, ff. 221ᵛ-222ᵛ.
131. Stow, *Survey of London*, vol. 2, pp. 358-9.
132. Dugdale, *Baronage of England*, vol. 1, p. 320b; *GEC*, vol. 11, pp. 390-1.
133. TNA, E 210/805; E 210/5888; *Register of Henry Chichele, Archbishop of Canterbury*, vol. 2, p. 72; Kingsford, 'Mediaeval London Houses', 11 (1917), pp. 74-8.
134. Brigham & Woodger, *Roman and Medieval Townhouses*, pp. 50-52, 59-64; Kingsford, 'Mediaeval London Houses', 11 (1917), p. 75; Stow, *Survey of London*, vol. 2, pp. 237-238, 322.

Chapter 4
1. Goodman, *Loyal Conspiracy* p. 105; Given-Wilson, 'Wealth and Credit', p. 19.
2. Goodman, *Loyal Conspiracy*, p. 14.
3. Holmes, *Estates*, pp. 24-5; Ward, 'Joan de Bohun, Countess of Hereford, Essex and Northampton, *c.*1370-1419', p. 147; Goodman, 'The Countess and the Rebels', p. 268.
4. Saul, *Richard II*, p. 18.
5. Aston, *Thomas Arundel*, pp. 134-6.
6. *CalPapReg Letters*, vol. 4, p. 129.
7. Aston, *Thomas Arundel*; Wilks, 'Thomas Arundel', pp. 57-86.
8. Bothwell, 'Edward III and the "New Nobility"', pp. 1111-3.
9. Given-Wilson, 'Richard II and the Higher Nobility', pp. 108-9.
10. Barber, *Prince of Wales*, p. 238. For a discussion of his literary and artistic patronage refer to: Eberle, 'Richard II and the Literary Arts', pp. 231-53; Scheifele, 'Richard II and the Visual Arts', pp. 256-71.
11. Fletcher, 'Manhood and Politics', p. 7.
12. *CCR 1377-1381*, p. 3.
13. Goodman, *John of Gaunt*, pp. 64-5, 70-1.
14. Goodman, 'John of Gaunt: Paradigm', pp. 134-5; Goodman, 'Richard II's Councils', pp. 65-7; Saul, *Richard II*, p. 28.
15. *CCR 1374-1377*, p. 487.
16. Goodman, *Loyal Conspiracy*, p. 6; Walsingham, *Historia Anglicana*, vol. 1, p. 439.
17. On 27 February 1377, possibly to finance the siege of Harfleur, Arundel lent 2,000 marks to Salisbury: *CCR 1377-1381*, p. 119.
18. Goodman, *Loyal Conspiracy*, p. 7; Crook, 'The Confession of a Spy, 1380', pp. 346-7.
19. *CCR 1377-1381*, p. 63.
20. Goodman, *Loyal Conspiracy*, p. 4; Given-Wilson, 'Wealth and Credit', pp. 14-5.
21. Crook, 'Confession of a Spy', p. 347.
22. Hilton, *Bond Men Made Free*, pp. 158-64; Fryde, *Peasants and Landlords*, pp. 8-53.
23. Fowler, *King's Lieutenant*, p. 214.
24. Saul, *Richard II*, pp. 56-82; McKisack, *Fourteenth Century*, pp. 411-2; McFarlane, *Lancastrian Kings*, p. 18.
25. McFarlane, *Lancastrian Kings*, p. 19.
26. Goodman, *Loyal Conspiracy*, p. 8; *CCR 1381-1385*, pp. 84-5.
27. Roskell, *Impeachment of Michael de la Pole, Earl of Suffolk*, p. 131.
28. *CCR 1381-1385*, pp. 14, 42, 182-3, 255; Goodman, *Loyal Conspiracy*, p. 9.
29. *Westminster Chronicle 1381-1394*, p. 69.
30. Ibid., p. 69.
31. Roskell, *Michael de la Pole*, p. 33; Saul, *Richard II*, pp. 117-8; Holmes, *Estates*, pp. 42-3.
32. Roskell, *Michael de la Pole*, pp. 49-54; Goodman, *Loyal Conspiracy*, pp. 12-3.
33. McFarlane, *Lancastrian Kings*, pp. 26-7; Aston, *Thomas Arundel*, pp. 336-8; McNiven, unpublished thesis, 'Political Developments', pp. 280-1.
34. McFarlane, *Lancastrian Kings*, p. 27.
35. *CCR 1385-1389*, p. 195; Walsingham, *Historia Anglicana*, vol. 2, p. 153; Saul, *Richard II*, pp. 166-8. Arundel's own retinue seems to have been totalled 600 men, in 10 ships: *CCR 1385-1389*, pp. 208-9, 308; TNA, E 364/21/6v; E 101/40/34-35.

36. Walsingham, *Historia Anglicana*, vol. 2, pp. 154-5.
37. *Westminster Chronicle*, pp. 196-203; Goodman, *Loyal Conspiracy*, p. 20.
38. Walsingham, *Historia Anglicana*, vol. 2, pp. 163-4; Saul, *Richard II*, pp. 176-7, 182; Goodman, *Loyal Conspiracy*, pp. 74, 135-9.
39. Goodman, *Loyal Conspiracy*, pp. 156-64; Holmes, *Estates*, pp. 38-9; Archer, 'Estates and Finances of Margaret of Brotherton', pp. 264-280.
40. Walker, *Lancastrian Affinity*, pp. 167-8.
41. *Westminster Chronicle*, pp. 206-9.
42. Ibid., pp. 212-5.
43. Ibid., pp. 218-23, 224-9; Saul, *Richard II*, pp. 187-90.
44. *Westminster Chronicle*, pp. 228-33.
45. Ibid., pp. 234-319; Saul, *Richard II*, p. 191.
46. Ibid., pp. 194-5.
47. *Westminster Chronicle*, pp. 374-7.
48. Ibid., pp. 390-3; Goodman, *Loyal Conspiracy*, pp. 52-3.
49. *Westminster Chronicle*, pp. 392-3; Goodman, *Loyal Conspiracy*, pp. 53-4.
50. Ibid., pp. 55-6; id., *John of Gaunt*, pp. 144-6.
51. *Westminster Chronicle*, pp. 440-1.
52. Arundel and Philippa married without royal licence. Arundel was forced to pay a fine of undetermined amount and was then pardoned on 20 November 1391: *CCR 1389-1392*, p. 413.
53. Davies, *Owain Glyn Dŵr*, pp. 38-9.
54. *CCR 1392-1396*, pp. 317-8, 320, 323.
55. Goodman, *Loyal Conspiracy*, p. 58.
56. *Westminster Chronicle*, pp. 490-1.
57. Goodman, *Loyal Conspiracy*, p. 60.
58. Saul, *Richard II*, pp. 219-22; Goodman, *Loyal Conspiracy*, pp. 60-1.
59. Ibid., p. 61.
60. Walsingham, *Historia Anglicana*, p. 215.
61. *CCR 1392-1396*, pp. 307, 368.
62. Walsingham, *Historia Anglicana*, p. 223; Saul, *Richard II*, p. 366; Goodman, *Loyal Conspiracy*, p. 66.
63. Saul, *Richard II*, pp. 366-8.
64. *The Chronicle of Adam of Usk*, pp. 27-31.
65. Ibid., p. 35.
66. Walsingham, *Historia Anglicana*, p. 225.
67. *CPR 1396-1399*, pp. 200-10, 213-6, 220, 280-1; Saul, *Richard II*, pp. 381-2.
68. *Chronicle of Adam of Usk*, p. 31. Adam of Usk had direct patronage from Archbishop Thomas Arundel: Wilks, 'Thomas Arundel', p. 58.
69. Stow, *Survey of London*, vol. 1, p. 178; Weever, *Antient Funeral Monuments*, p. 203; Jenkinson, *London Churches before the Great Fire*, p. 132.
70. Walsingham, *Historia Anglicana*, pp. 225-6.
71. Tierney, *History*, vol. 1, 264.
72. Nichols, *Collection of Wills*, p. 120; LPL, MS Archbishop Sudbury's Register, ff. 102-102v.
73. Stow, *Survey of London*, vol. 1, p. 178; Bumpus, *London Churches*, pp. 126-30; Jenkinson, *London Churches*, pp. 131-2.
74. Goodman, *Loyal Conspiracy*, p. 69.
75. Stouck, 'Saints and Rebels', p. 79; Walker, 'Political Saints', p. 81.
76. Burtscher, 'Martyrdom of Edmund Fitzalan', pp. 83-96.
77. *CalPapReg Petitions*, vol. 1, pp. 75, 99; *CalPapReg Letters*, vol. 3, pp. 176, 188.
78. Ibid., vol. 3, p. 573; *CalPapReg Petitions*, vol. 1, pp. 269, 278-9.
79. Eustache, *Arundel Borough and Castle*, p. 72.
80. LPL, MS Archbishop Sudbury's Register, f. 93. Licence for this foundation of a yearly rent had been granted on 20 July 1375: *CPR 1370-1374*, p. 129.
81. *VCH Sussex*, vol. 5/1, pp. 214-24.
82. *CPR 1377-1381*, p. 402.
83. LPL, MS Archbishop Sudbury's Register, ff. 92v - 93v.
84. Nichols, *Collection of Wills*, pp. 122-6; Elvins, *Arundel Priory*, Appendix 1, pp. 74-8.
85. *CPR 1377-1381*, p. 494; TNA, E 135/15/3; Elvins, *Arundel Priory*, p. 4.

86. *VCH Sussex*, vol. 2, pp. 108-9.

87. ACA, FA 86. In 1385, Bishop William Read of Chichester left thirteen books to the College with a sum of 20 marks to be expended in chaining them in the library: St John Hope, 'On an Inventory of the Goods of the Collegiate Church', p. 79; Aston, *Thomas Arundel*, p. 12.

88. Elvins, *Arundel Priory*, p. xv; Robinson, *Dukes of Norfolk*, pp. 225-6; id., *Arundel Castle*, pp. 45-6.

89. Evans, 'The Maison Dieu, Arundel', pp. 65-77; *VCH Sussex*, vol. 2, p. 97.

90. *Sussex Churches and Their Treasures*, p. 19.

91. Tierney, *History*, vol. 1, p. 241.

Chapter 5

1. McFarlane, *Lancastrian Kings*, p. 65.

2. Tierney, *History and Antiquities*, vol. 1, p. 277.

3. Aston, *Thomas Arundel*, pp. 372-3.

4. *Chronicle of Adam of Usk*, p. 51.

5. McFarlane, *Lancastrian Kings*, p. 47; Saul, Richard II, pp. 405-6; Demurger, *Temps de crises*, pp. 80-7.

6. Saul, *Richard II*, pp. 406-7.

7. Walsingham, *Historia Anglicana*, p. 232; *Chronicle of Adam of Usk*, p. 52; Saul, Richard II, p. 407; Bennett, 'Henry of Bolingbroke and the Revolution of 1399', p. 12.

8. Rose, *Kings in the North*, pp. 344-7; Saul, *Richard II*, pp. 408-9.

9. Ibid., pp. 409-12.

10. Ibid., pp. 414-7.

11. M.A. Tierney suggests that King Richard remained in Arundel's custody also once he was later removed to Pontefract: *History and Antiquities*, vol. 1, pp. 278-9.

12. *Chronicle of Adam of Usk*, p. 65-7; Saul, *Richard II*, pp. 417-9.

13. *Chronicle of Adam of Usk*, p. 69; Saul, *Richard II*, p. 423; Wilks, 'Thomas Arundel', p. 85.

14. 'Et si estoit grant bouteillier / Un, qui fu Counte darondel, / Qui est assez jeune et ysnel.': Tierney, *History and Antiquities*, vol. 1, p. 279 n. (b); *Chronicle of Adam of Usk*, pp. 71-3.

15. *CPR 1399-1401*, p. 134; *RotParl*, vol. 3, pp. 435a-436b.

16. Saul, *Richard II*, pp. 423-4.

17. *Chronicle of Adam of Usk*, pp. 87-9; McFarlane, *Lancastrian Kings*, pp. 67-9. See also Rogers, 'Henry IV and the revolt of the Earls', pp. 277-83; Crook, 'Central England and the Revolt of the Earls, January 1400', pp. 403-10.

18. *Chronicle of Adam of Usk*, p. 89.

19. Tierney, *History and Antiquities*, vol. 1, pp. 279-80; Harriss, *Shaping the Nation,* p. 494.

20. Collins, *Order of the Garter*, pp. 110-1, 292.

21. Thomas Beaufort was the son of John Beaufort, earl of Somerset, and Henry IV's half-brother and chamberlain from November 1399: Harriss, *Cardinal Beaufort*, pp. 11-3; McFarlane, *Lancastrian Kings*, pp. 67-8; Collins, *Order of the Garter*, pp. 110-1.

22. *Chronicle of Adam of Usk*, p. 89.

23. Saul, *Richard II*, pp. 424-6.

24. Davies, *Age of Conquest*, p. 442.

25. Jack, 'New Light on the Early Years of Owain Glyndwr', pp. 162-6; Davies, *Owain Glyn Dŵr*, p. 137.

26. Davies, *Owain Glyn Dŵr*, pp. 129-8.

27. Rogers, unpublished thesis, 'Bromfield and Yale', p. 75.

28. Harriss, *Cardinal Beaufort*, p. 13; Davies, *Owain Glyn Dŵr*, pp. 102-3.

29. Davies, *Age of Conquest*, p. 443.

30. *Chronicle of Adam of Usk*, p. 129.

31. Davies, *Owain Glyn Dŵr*, pp. 103-4; Davies, *Age of Conquest*, p. 443.

32. Rogers, 'Bromfield and Yale', p. 76; Pugh, unpublished thesis, 'Marcher Lordships of South Wales'. For the pardon granted, in March 1401, to those rebels of the Arundel lordships see *CPR 1399-1401*, p. 451.

33. Smith, 'Chirk and Oswestry', pp. 385-6; Davies, *Owain Glyn Dŵr*, p. 215.

34. *CPR 1401-1405*, pp. 138-9.

35. Allmand, *Henry V*, p. 22; Bean, 'Henry IV and the Percies', p. 224.

36. Neville, 'Scotland, the Percies and the Law in 1400', p. 85; King, '"They have the Hertes of People by North"', pp. 139-59.

37. Rose, *Kings in the North*, pp. 359-60; Harriss, *Shaping the Nation*, pp. 496-7, 521-2; Allmand, *Henry V*, p. 26.

38. Bean, 'Henry IV and the Percies', pp. 226-7; McNiven, unpublished thesis, 'Political Developments in the Second Half of the Reign of Henry IV, 1405-13', p. 8.
39. Walker, 'The Yorkshire Risings of 1405: Texts and Contexts', pp. 161-84; Rose, *Kings in the North*, p. 361.
40. *CPR 1401-1405*, pp. 294, 438.
41. Harriss, *Shaping the Nation*, p. 522.
42. Ibid., p. 522; Allmand, *Henry V*, p. 27.
43. *CPR 1405-1408*, p. 65. On 11 June, Arundel was granted the forfeited manors of Pumpton and Berkomp to the value of £100 yearly, which had belonged to another rebel, lord Bardolf: *CPR 1405-1408*, p. 25.
44. *Chronicle of Adam of Usk*, p. 203; McNiven, unpublished thesis, 'Political Developments', pp. 12-4.
45. Harriss, *Shaping the Nation*, p. 498; McFarlane, *Lancastrian Kings*, p. 74; Bean, 'Henry IV and the Percies', pp. 222-3.
46. McFarlane, *Lancastrian Kings*, p. 75; Harriss, *Shaping the Nation*, p. 497.
47. *CPR 1405-1408*, p. 80. In July 1407 and November 1409, Arundel was appointed to a commission to audit the accounts of Shrewsbury to ensure that the monies for the town's defence were appropriately invested: Ibid., p. 341; *CCR 1408-1413*, p. 146.
48. Walsingham, *Historia Anglicana*, p. 272. Already in July 1403 the king had granted to Arundel to marry whom he pleased: *CPR 1401-1405*, p. 242.
49. Tierney, *History and Antiquities*, vol. 1, p. 283 n. (a); *CPR 1409-1413*, p. 301.
50. *CPR 1405-1409*, p. 525; *CPR 1409-1413*, pp. 59, 183-5.
51. Allmand, *Henry V*, p. 40. For Henry IV's illness see McFarlane, *Lancastrian Kings*, p. 103. Thus in May and again in November 1409 the royal council ordered Arundel and other marcher lords to return to Wales.
52. Harriss, *Cardinal Beaufort*, pp. 44-6.
53. Allmand, *Henry V*, p. 42.
54. *CPR 1409-1413*, p. 204.
55. *CPR 1409-1413*, p. 315.
56. Gauvard, *La France au Moyen Age*, pp. 453-4; Demurger, *Temps de crises*, pp. 88-90.
57. Allmand, *Henry V*, pp. 47-9.
58. Davies, *Owain Glyn Dŵr*, p. 293. Sir Rees Davies saw, as the final act of the rebellion, the acceptance by Maredudd an Owain, Glyn Dŵr's surviving son, of a pardon by the king of England on 8 April 1421: Ibid., p. 293.
59. Allmand, *Henry V*, pp. 48-9.
60. TNA, C54/266, m. 23; *CCR 1413-1419*, p. 304.
61. Allmand, *Henry V*, p. 49.
62. Harriss, *Shaping the Nation*, p. 504.
63. For Bishop Beaufort's career see: Harriss, 'Cardinal Beaufort', pp. 129-48; Id., *Cardinal Beaufort*.
64. Humphery-Smith, 'What became of Arundel's Tomb?', pp. 11-22.
65. *Chronicle of Adam of Usk*, p. 247.
66. *CPR 1413-1416*, p. 1.
67. *CPR 1413-1416*, p. 1. That same day he was also ordered to make all necessary repairs to the buildings within Dover Castle, its walls, towers, the church, etc.: Ibid., p. 38. Allmand, *Henry V*, p. 48. Following Arundel's death, the constableship and wardenship were granted, on 23 June 1416, to the king's brother Humphrey, duke of Gloucester: *CPR 1416-1422*, p. 34.
68. *CPR 1413-1416*, pp. 105, 155.
69. Given-Wilson, 'Wealth and Credit', p. 17; Harriss, 'Cardinal Beaufort', p. 134.
70. Allmand, *Henry V*, pp. 313, 316-7.
71. Demurger, *Temps de crises*, p. 98.
72. *CPR 1413-1416*, p. 329; Curry, *Agincourt*, p. 57.
73. Harriss, *Shaping the Nation*, p. 542.
74. Cooper, 'Sussex Men at Agincourt', p. 124. The roll of wages listing the men who served in Arundel's retinue has been published: Ibid., pp. 128-33. Curry, *Agincourt*, pp. 58, 85.
75. *CInqPM 1413-1418*, pp. 207-11.
76. Walsingham, *Historia Anglicana*, p. 309. According to Adam of Usk the earl simply died of dysentery: *Chronicle of Adam of Usk*, p. 257.
77. Cooper, 'Sussex Men at Agincourt', pp. 127-8.

78. Harriss, *Shaping the Nation*, pp. 542-3.
79. For the most detailed account see Curry, *Agincourt*, pp. 170-224. See also Allmand, *Henry V*, pp. 90-6; Harriss, *Shaping the Nation*, pp 542-4.
80. Demurger, *Temps de crises*, pp. 101-2.
81. *Register of Henry Chichele,* vol. 2, pp. 71-8.
82. Ibid., vol. 2, pp. 75-6.
83. *CCR 1413-1419*, p. 290.
84. Ibid., p. 413. These documents were certainly used to then compile the earl's inquisition post mortem: *CInqPM 1413-1418*, pp. 207-11.
85. TNA, C54/266, m. 23; *CCR 1413-1419*, p. 304.
86. *CPR 1413-1416*, p. 344.
87. The accounts for Arundel's troops were, nonetheless, rendered by Countess Beatrice and two of the earl's executors, Sir William Wiltshire and John Bartelot, clerk: Cooper, 'Sussex Men at Agincourt', p. 127. A list of the men who fought at Agincourt is published in Curry, *Agincourt*, Appendix E.
88. *CPR 1416-1422*, p. 39; *CFR 1413-1422*, pp. 162-7.
89. *Register of Henry Chichele*, vol. 2, pp. 71-3, 77.
90. *CCR 1435-1441*, p. 17.
91. *CPR 1416-1422*, p. 172; *CPR 1429-1436*, p. 269; *CPR 1436-1441*, pp. 30, 148, 276; Smith, unpublished thesis, 'Chirk and Oswestry', p. 44.
92. *RotParl*, vol. 4, pp. 442-3.
93. Ellis, *Earldoms in Fee*, p. 98; Rogers, 'Bromfield and Yale', pp. 79-89. A licence for the enfeoffment of the lordships of Lewes and Reigate had been granted on 29 May 1415: *CPR 1413-1416*, p. 336
94. Robinson, *Dukes of Norfolk*, p. 12.
95. *CPR 1413-1416*, p. 400; see also *CCR 1413-1419*, pp. 267, 313, 407.
96. Ibid., p. 265.
97. Ibid., p. 466.
98. *RotParl*, vol. 4, p. 130b; *CPR 1416-1422*, p. 325; *CCR 1419-1422*, pp. 172-3.
99. *CPR 1429-1436*, p. 250.
100. Tierney, *History and Antiquities*, vol. 1, p. 283 n. (a).
101. *CPR 1436-1441*, pp. 483-4, 562; *CPR 1441-1446*, p. 351; *CInqPM*, vol. 4, p. 239.
102. Only three such hearses survive in England. The other two are the hearse of Sir Hugh Calverley in Bunbury Church (Cheshire) and that of Lord Marmion in West Tanfield Church (Yorkshire).

Chapter 6
1. Davies, *Lordship and Society*, pp. 188-9, 196; Rogers, 'Bromfield and Yale', p. 175.
2. Davies, *Lordship and Society*, pp. 176-96; Smith, 'Arundel Charters to the Lordship of Chirk in the Fourteenth Century', pp. 153-60; ead., 'Seignorial Income in the Fourteenth Century: The Arundels in Chirk', pp. 447-8; *CCR 1333-1337*, p. 352; *CPR 1334-1338*, p. 45; *CPR 1334-1338*, pp. 406, 415.
3. *CPR 1324-1327*, pp. 271-2.
4. Somerville, *Duchy of Lancaster*, vol. 1, p. 33.
5. Fairbank, 'The Last Earl of Warenne and Surrey', pp. 249-50; Rogers, unpublished thesis, 'Bromfield and Yale', pp. 58-68; Maddicott, *Thomas of Lancaster*, pp. 197-8, 234-7; Phillips, *Aymer de Valence*, pp. 114-5, 195.
6. *CPR 1345-1348*, p. 480.
7. Ibid., pp. 16, 51.
8. Fowler, *King's Lieutenant*, pp. 172-3; Holmes, *Estates*, p. 38.
9. *Register of Edward the Black Prince*, vol. 1, pp. 96, 111-2, 114; *CPR 1345-1348*, pp. 434, 437; Rogers, unpublished thesis, 'Bromfield and Yale', pp. 167, 417.
10. *CPR 1358-1361*, pp. 455, 458-9.
11. *CPR 1321-1324*, p. 49; *CChR*, vol. 3, p. 442; *CPR 1327-1330*, pp. 141, 328.
12. Holmes, *Estates*, pp. 14-5; TNA, E 40/4882.
13. *CCR 1354-1360*, p. 93; Tout & Broome, 'A National Balance Sheet for 1362-3', p. 418.
14. Bellamy, *Law of Treason*, pp. 59-61.
15. BL, Harleian Charter 83 C 13; *RotParl*, vol. 2, p. 56a.
16. *RotParl*, vol. 2, pp. 224, 226-7b. An interesting parallel, on which Arundel may have hoped to capitalize, was Henry of Lancaster's petition of 1327 for annulment of judgement against Thomas Lancaster: Somerville, *Duchy of Lancaster*, vol. 1, p. 32.

17. *CPR 1350-1354*, p. 499; *CCR 1349-1354*, p. 562.
18. McKisack, *Fourteenth Century*, p. 257.
19. *RotParl*, vol. 2, pp. 256b-257.
20. *Feet of Fines for the County of Sussex*, ed. L.F. Salzman, pp. 89, 91, 93, 95, 98, 99, 109, 121, 123, 124, 128, 129, 137, 143-4, 147-9, 153, 157, 158, 163-4, 165, 175; *A Short Calendar of the Feet of Fines for Norfolk*, ed. W. Rye, vol. 2, pp. 224, 227, 342, 381, 382; *Abstract of Feet of Fines Relating to Wiltshire*, ed. R.B. Pugh, vol. 1,p. 130; vol. 29, pp. 120-1; *Feet of Fines for the County of Somerset*, ed. E. Green, vol. 17, pp. 36, 84-5, 88, 188; *CCR 1349-1341*, p. 548; *CCR 1369-1374*, pp. 576, 581, 589; *Pedes Finium: Fines relating to Surrey*, ed. F.B. Lewis, vol. 1, pp. 119, 131, 134, 136, 143.
21. *Sussex Fines*, pp. 177, 180-3, 185, 199, 202.
22. Britnell, 'The Black Death in English Towns', pp. 195-210. The average human loss throughout Europe was estimate by Pope Clement to be around 31% this, contemporary, estimate supports the more recent evidence suggesting that although Venice may have lost as much as 60% of it population, cities such as Antwerp (20-25%) and London (25-50%) lost fewer lives. The population in England was further decimated during later recurrences of the pestilence, notably in 1361 (20%) and 1369-71 (10%-15%): Hatcher, *Plague, Population and the English Economy*, p. 25; Naphy & Spicer, *Black Death and History of Plagues*, pp. 34-6.
23. Baker, 'Evidence in the Nonarum Inquisitiones', p. 518.
24. Baker, 'Some Evidence of a Reduction in the Acreage of Cultivated Lands in Sussex', pp. 1-5; Pelham, 'The Urban Population of Sussex in 1340', pp. 211-23.
25. *Sussex Fines*, pp. 93, 144, 158, 165, 185.
26. Brandon, 'Demesne Arable Farming in Coastal Sussex', p. 113 n. 3. Although Canterbury may only have held about 3,000 acres in Sussex, the complexity of its estate comprised an estimated 8,400 acres under cultivation, while Westminster Abbey and the Bishop of Winchester cultivated about 4,800 and 7,000 acres, respectively: Biddick, *Other Economy*, p. 62.
27. ACA, MD 487.
28. *CInqPM*, vol. 6, pp. 474-5.
29. On 20 December 1343, certainly as part of the annulment settlement Arundel granted Isabella Despenser the Essex manors of Wolhampton, High Roding, Ovesham, and Margaretting held in chief: *CPR 1345-1348*, p. 18.
30. *CPR 1343-1345*, pp. 487-8. John de Alresford could be a John Aldersfold who had a cottage in Wonneworthe (Sussex) in the 1380s; *Two Estate Surveys*, pp. 48, 141.
31. *Sussex Fines*, pp. 123-4. This entail was of particular significance when, after 1415, the heirs claimed the earldom: Ellis, *Earldoms in Fee*, pp. 98-9; *CPR 1345-8*, pp. 328-9.
32. *Sussex Fines*, p. 137.
33. *Sussex Fines*, pp. 163-4; *Surrey Fines*, vol. 1, p. 221, no. 663. On 7 June 1373, John de Kyngesfold was, furthermore, entrusted by Earl Richard II with lands in Buckinghamshire and Hertfordshire: Worcestershire Record Office, Hampton (Pakington) of Westwood Park, Droitwich (Worcs), Collection, 705:349/12946/489889.
34. *Sussex Fines*, pp. 163-4; *Surrey Fines*, vol. 1, p. 221, no. 664.
35. *CPR 1374-1377*, p. 243. Earl Richard III's aunt Katherine and her husband Andrew Peverell were then also feoffees: *Sussex Fines*, p. 177; *Surrey Fines*, vol. 1, p. 222, no. 740.
36. *CPR 1374-1377*, p. 243.
37. *CCR 1396-1399*, pp. 72, 84.
38. Goodman, *Loyal Conspiracy*, p. 71; Dunn, unpublished thesis, 'Endowment and Disendowment of Lay Magnates', pp. 86-7.
39. Holmes, *Estates*, p. 51.
40. Ellis, *Earldoms in Fee*, p. 98.
41. Earl Thomas did have an illegitimate son, John, for whom he had made provision to inherit the lordship of Chirk and a number of manors, through an enfeoffment drawn up on 10 August 1415. It is possible that John died a minor in Countess Beatrice's ward, as no reference to him appears after 1415: *Register of Henry Chichele*, vol. 2, pp. 73, 77.
42. *First Extent of Bromfield and Yale, 1315*, ed. Ellis; BL, Add. MS 10,013 is the survey for 1391; *Extent of Chirkland, 1391-3*, ed. Jones, while for a rental of Clun and Oswestry for 1301 there is *Two Estate Surveys*, esp. pp. 51-90. The data from these surveys should, however, be handled with circumspection as they are not based on the same comparable figures.

43. Smith, 'Chirk and Oswestry', pp. 158 n. 1, 166 n. 2, 183; Rogers, unpublished thesis, 'Bromfield and Yale', pp. 47-8; Davies, *Lordship and Society*, p. 196, where he also gives valuations for all the other Marcher lordships.
44. SAS, MS 6000/5923, in Given-Wilson, 'Wealth and Credit', Appendix I. BL, Harleian 4840, f. 393. When, in September 1370, Arundel lent 10,000 marks to the king these had to be brought from Shrewsbury to London at the Crown's expense: Devon, *Issue Roll of Thomas de Brantingham*, p. 228.
45. Rogers, unpublished thesis, 'Bromfield and Yale', pp. 174-5.
46. Davies, *Lordship and Society*, pp. 193-4; id., *Owain Glyn Dŵr*, pp.38-9; Rogers, 'Bromfield and Yale', p. 382; Smith, unpublished thesis, 'Chirk and Oswestry', pp. 223, 422.
47. ACA, A 431; *Two Estate Surveys*.
48. Davies, *Lordship and Society*, p. 120. A compelling and intimate account of the different perception of Wales as seen through the eyes of two very different travellers, one a Welsh poet the other an English official, is given in Davies, *Owain Glyn Dŵr*, chapter 1, and map 1, p. 7 for the two circuits.
49. Davies, *Owain Glyn Dŵr*, pp. 6-8.
50. Ibid., pp. 38-9.
51. *CCR 1392-1396*, pp. 317-8, 320, 323.
52. Davies, 'Baronial Accounts', pp. 214-5; Campbell, *English Seigniorial Agriculture*, pp. 26-41.
53. Rogers, 'Bromfield and Yale', pp. 105-6.
54. Rawcliffe, *Staffords*, pp. 54-5.
55. ACA, A 1841.
56. Smith, unpublished thesis, 'Chirk and Oswestry', pp. 52-3.
57. Ibid., p. 214.
58. Ibid., pp. 56 n.1, 61-3.
59. LPL, MS Archbishop Arundel's Register, ff. 183v-186v. See also Davies, *Owain Glyn Dŵr*, pp. 38-9.
60. Smith, 'Chirk and Oswestry', pp. 66-71.
61. Davies, *Lordship and Society*, p. 115.
62. Smith, 'Chirk and Oswestry', pp. 72-3, 86; Davies, *Lordship and Society*, pp. 206-8; Davies, *Owain Glyn Dŵr*, p. 42
63. Rogers, 'Bromfield and Yale', pp. 90-2.
64. Ibid., pp. 102, 116-7; ACA, A 1838, m. 2.
65. In one instance there is a mention of a seneschal on the Sussex estates, but this may simply be because the survey was compiled mainly for the Marcher estates and thus by officials accustomed with their own titulatures: SAS, 1093/Box 1, m. 3v. It is possible, therefore, that the receiver of Arundel held an office similar in scope to that of the Marcher seneschal. It must be pointed out that many magnates had their estates administered very similarly as, for instance, the case of the duchy of Cornwall shows: Hatcher, *Rural Economy and Society*, pp. 37-44.
66. Rogers, 'Bromfield and Yale', p. 104; Smith, 'Chirk and Oswestry', pp. 442-3.
67. Oschinsky, *Walter of Henley*, pp. 93, 264.
68. ACA, A 1807. In previous years William Beche had been collector of the rents in Southstoke, thus indicating a flexibility and movement within the households and the official structure of the lordship's administration.
69. BL, Harleian 4840, f. 393.
70. Given-Wilson, 'Bishop of Chichester', p. 134 n.
71. BL, MS Harleian 4048, f. 393; LPL, MS Archbishop Sudbury's Register, f. 94v.
72. BL, MS Harleian 4048, f. 393; ACA, A 1777.
73. Smith, 'Chirk and Oswestry', pp. 73-6 nn. 1-2.
74. LPL, MS Archbishop Sudbury's Register, ff. 94v, 95v.
75. Smith, 'Chirk and Oswestry', pp. 78-9; Davies, *Lordship and Society*, p. 205.
76. Rogers, 'Bromfield and Yale', p. 121.
77. The best, and possibly only example, of such a career is that of William de Wolverton who was receiver of Oswestry in 1345-46 and of Chirk in 1353-57; then steward of both in 1335, 1364, 1367, 1369. There are, however, doubts as to whether the William steward in 1335 was the same as the other: Smith, 'Chirk and Oswestry', Appendices 4-5.
78. Smith, 'Chirk and Oswestry', pp. 81-3.
79. ACA, A 337.
80. Davies, 'Baronial Accounts', pp. 211-29.

81. 'idem Johanes incarceratus fuit et liberatus extra carcerem ex precepto domini comitis eo quod testatus fuit quod dominum Johanes nul h ... bonis ... dev... Rec' dicto': ACA, A 1838, m. 2.

82. Ibid., m. 2.

83. BL, Harleian MS 4840, f. 393.

84. Salzman, *English Trade*, pp. 285-296; Carus-Wilson, *Medieval Merchant Venturers*, pp. 239-62; Carus-Wilson & Coleman, *England's Export Trade*, pp. 40-55, 124.

85. There were a further 964 sheep in Chipping Norton (Oxon.), Tyke, Keevil and Knighton (Wilts.); 452 at Oswestry; and 422 at Ruyton: SAS, 1093/Box 1. In 1301 there had been a comparatively smaller flock in Clun with only 300 sheep, at Oswestry there had been 160, and a further 900 in the Shropshire demesne: *VCH Shropshire*, vol. 3, p. 94. It must also be pointed out that by the following year, 1350-51, there were only 2,304 ewes left at Clun: SAS, 552/1/1164, m. 1. The figures given in the 1349 valor are consistent with another valor for 1349-50 drawn up the same year for the Sussex estates, where a total of 6,899 sheep is given, of which 661 were actually on manors that had been farmed out. A further 390 sheep were kept in Wiltshire and 577 in Surrey. Excluding the number of sheep in the Marches, which the valor does not give, this came to a total of 7,866 sheep in England alone: ACA, A 431.

86. Melville, unpublished thesis, 'Pastoral Custom', p. 21; Newman & Harvey, 'Did Soil Fertility Decline in Medieval English Farms?', pp. 121-2.

87. *Two Estate Surveys*.

88. Postles, 'Sheep Flock at Hartington', pp. 24-5; Altschul, *Baronial Family*, pp. 215-7; Biddick, *Other Economy*, p. 62.

89. Good examples are the Lancastrian manor of Hartington and the Clare manor of Tillingdown. Particularly on the latter, after the Black Death, officials widely experimented to initiate an economic recovery, however, after the second outbreak of plague, in 1361-62, direct exploitation of the demesne was completely abandoned: Postles, 'Sheep Flock at Hartington', pp. 24-5; Saaler, 'The Manor of Tillingdown', p. 38. Further examples are given in: Davies, *Lordship and Society*, pp. 126-20.

90. Smith, 'Chirk and Oswestry', pp. 144-5, and Appendix 17.

91. *VCH Shropshire*, vol. 3, pp. 94-5.

92. Ibid., vol. 3, pp. 94-5.

93. ACA, A 431.

94. ACA, A 1834.

95. ACA, A 1838.

96. ACA, A 1839.

97. In 1381-82, there were 578 wethers, to which came 93 before sheering (24 from Bourne), 12 ewes, and 90 hoggets; and 90 lambs from Singleton. After shearing 25 wethers were returned to Singleton: ACA, A 1863.

98. In 1357-58 there were 333 wethers, to which came 50 from Charlton after shearing; of the 297 lambs, 200 were sent to Singleton, 50 to Merton and 47 to Charlton all before shearing; then there were 120 lambs received from Poling and 182 from Lyminster before shearing: ACA, A 1828. In 1364-65 there were 284 wethers to which came 45 before shearing brought by the shepherd Walter Shephinde; of the 191 hoggets one was given to Walter Shepirde *sic*! and 190 were sent to Storrington; as for the lambs 126 were received from Charlton before shearing, 106 from Poling before shearing and 60 from Shopwyke; after shearing 297 lambs were sent to Storrington: ACA, A 1829. In 1365-66, there were 293 wethers to which came 38 brought by Walter Sheperd; 150 lambs were received form Charlton, 155 from Poling, 2 from Offham, 2 from South Stoke before shearing, and after 100 were sent to Shopwyke: ACA, A 1830. In 1374, 169 lambs came from Lyminstre, 111 from Poling, 90 from Cudlow, and after shearing 200 were sent to Heen and 127 to Feld: ACA, A 1831. A similar pattern appears the following year, 1376-77, when 185 lambs were received from Lyminster, 113 from Poling, and after shearing 200 were sent to Heene and 67 to Field: ACA, A 1832.

99. ACA, A 1828. A number of carts were also sold.

100. *Two Estate Surveys*, pp. 95, 100. These large lands may also account for the large herds of pigs varying in size from 140 to 180: ACA, A 1834-1840. Although in 1349-50 there had been only 51 pigs on this manor: ACA, A 431.

101. *Two Estate Surveys*, p. 95.

102. 'consilij domini ... apud Stansted tempore ponderacionis lanarum': ACA, A 1841, m. 2.

103. ACA, A 1834-1840.

104. ACA, A 1775-1779.

105. ACA, A 1777. The delivery also included 311 fells. It is possible that some liveries were given at the end of September once accounts had been rendered, thus rewarding some of the officials. The rabbits and hares for Countess Joan had been ordered directly through her own household and tallied separately.
106. ACA, A 1778. This delivery also included 270 fells, less than the previous year.
107. BL, Harleian MS 4840, f. 393v.
108. Davies, *Lordship and Society*, pp. 118-9.

Index